The SOUTH of FRANCE for Art Lovers

ERIC RINCKHOUT

INTRODUCTION

When we think of the South of France, it conjures up images of the sea, the sun, beaches, palm trees, tasty food and joie de vivre. But there is so much more to take in: the South of France is an art lover's paradise, giving Paris a real run for its money when it comes to art and culture.

This guide doesn't list everything there is to see. Instead it mainly focusses on modern times and in particular on artists and their homes, studios, museums, galleries and festivals, from Collioure to Menton and from Toulouse to Grasse. And also: which paintings, films, books and songs were inspired by the South?

Since 1880, countless artists have been drawn to the South of France. Painters such as Van Gogh, Cézanne, Matisse and Picasso sought inspiration in the dazzling light and vivid colours of the South. They captured their experiences in groundbreaking works, turning the South of France into the cradle of modernism. The South continues to attract artists: some have founded their own museum, such as Bernar Venet and Pierre Soulages, or have transformed vacant churches, like Louise Bourgeois and Jean-Michel Folon. Sculpture parks are popping up everywhere, while city palaces and old chapels are converted into superb arts centres.

Seminal filmmakers, writers, singers, architects and theatre makers were and are inspired by the scents, colours and landscapes of the South: they are a motley crew, including Le Corbusier and Brigitte Bardot, Peter Mayle and Aldous Huxley, Tadao Ando and Katherine Mansfield, Grace Kelly and The Rolling Stones. The list of artists who have left a trace in the South of France seems to go on and on.

I was guided by my curiosity and my passion for all things art while writing this book. And in so doing, I made many surprising and fun discoveries. I didn't think I could love the South of France any more than I already do, but there you have it. *Suivez le guide!*

Eric Rinckhout

HOW TO USE THIS BOOK

This guide lists over 380 things you need to know if you're visiting the South of France and are specifically interested in modern and contemporary art and culture. The author wanted to share as many stories as possible about the many generations of artists who have been drawn to the South of France. All these stories combine to form a comprehensive biography of the South.
Most of the selected items are places to visit: museums, artist's studios, galleries, repurposed chapels, churches and mansions, sculpture gardens, new builds, neighbourhoods, street art, music festivals and so on. But the guide also discusses paintings, films and songs that were inspired by certain places. You get the story behind them and practical information to help you find your way.
You can follow in the footsteps of artists and find out more about their life and work. But the guide also features stories about the houses where artists and writers lived, some of which are not open to the public or only under certain conditions. Where applicable this is mentioned.

This guide was written during a difficult period, i.e., the worldwide coronavirus pandemic. The information was checked right up until publication but it is always possible that a museum remains closed or that a shop, cafe or restaurant does not reopen.

Please bear in mind that the selection of addresses presented in this guide is highly personal. You might not always agree with it, or you might find that a certain place is missing. If you want to leave a comment, recommend a spot or share your favourite art spot, please follow *@500hiddensecrets* on Instagram or Facebook and get in touch with the publisher. And of course it's always a good idea to visit our website *www.the500hiddensecrets.com*, where you'll find lots of new content, constantly updated info and travel inspiration about many other destinations.

ABOUT THE AUTHOR

ERIC RINCKHOUT lives in Antwerp, Belgium, at the crossroads of Europe. He is a journalist and art critic, for such publications as *Knack* and *Collect Magazine*. For more than 40 years Eric has travelled widely through the South of France, mainly in the footsteps of the amazing artists who lived and worked there.

In 2017, he wrote *Magritte Unveiled. A biography in 50 pictures* about Belgium's most famous surrealist painter René Magritte. He shares his passion for art with others, in books, articles and talks about old masters and contemporary artists. He has published a selection of his art columns under the title *Ontrafeld (Unravelled*, 2014, only available in Dutch) and written contributions for Luc Tuymans's exhibition 'Glasses' (MAS Antwerp and National Portrait Gallery London, 2016-17) and for Art Autun 2020, in addition to publishing articles on Louise Bourgeois, Henri Matisse, Pablo Picasso, Vincent van Gogh, Pierre Bonnard, Nicolas De Staël, Camille Claudel and Tracey Emin.

Eric wants to thank his many *compagnons de route*. Starting with Winny De Vriendt who had the idea of combining all these wonderful art destinations in the South of France in one guide. Thank you for all your patience, all these years. The artist Sofie Muller, who pointed him in the right direction. Many thanks to Sandy Logan, who has translated this guide into English and enriched it with some recommendations of her own. Thanks to Arnaud Moro for bringing this book to life with his photographs, and to Sarah Schrauwen for the graphic design. Eric also wants to thank the following Francophiles for the many tips, good advice and help: Eric Min, Bart Van Loo, Luc De Vries, Dirk Leyman, Rolly Smeets, Marie-Paule De Vil and Yasmine Geukens, Jan Vanriet, Ronny and Jessy Van de Velde, and Véronique Van Passel. And last but not least, Eric wants to thank Dettie Luyten, Marc Verhagen, Hadewijch Ceulemans and Hilde Seys at Luster for the hard work and the inspiring collaboration.

THE SOUTH OF FRANCE

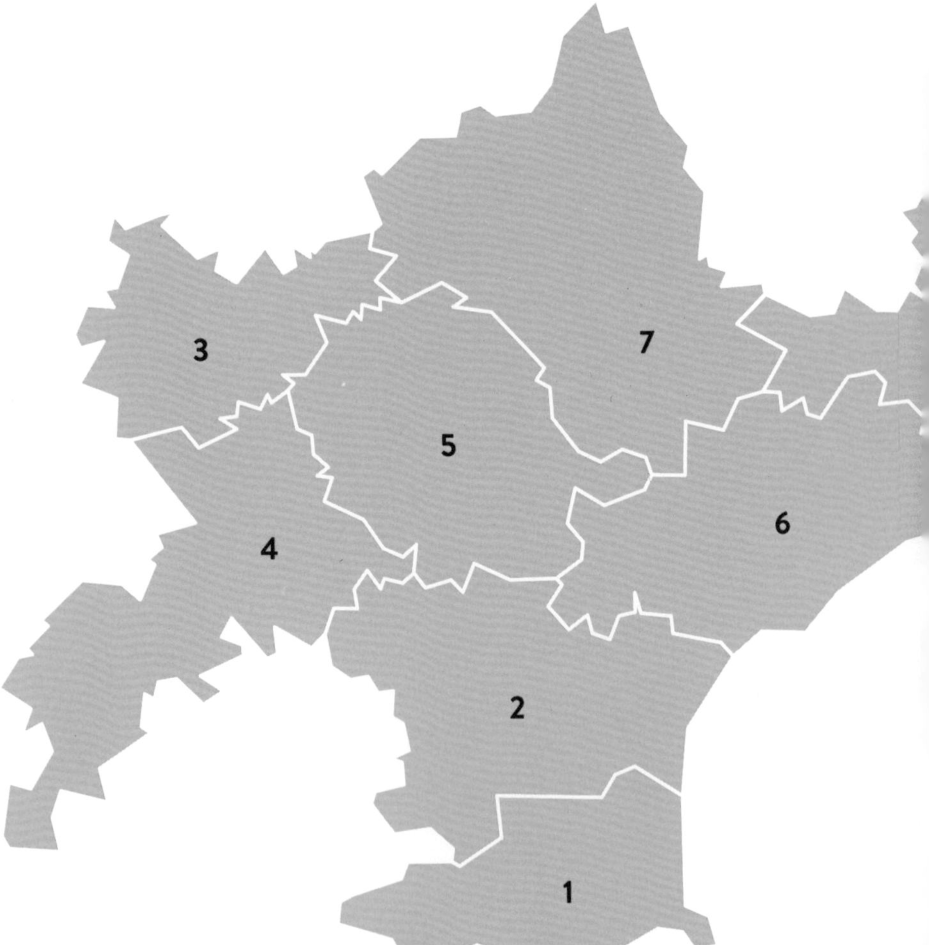

1	PYRÉNÉES-ORIENTALES	8	GARD
2	AUDE	9	BOUCHES-DU-RHÔNE
3	TARN-ET-GARONNE	10	VAUCLUSE
4	HAUTE-GARONNE	11	VAR
5	TARN	12	ALPES-DE-HAUTE-PROVENCE
6	HÉRAULT	13	ALPES-MARITIMES
7	AVEYRON	14	MONACO

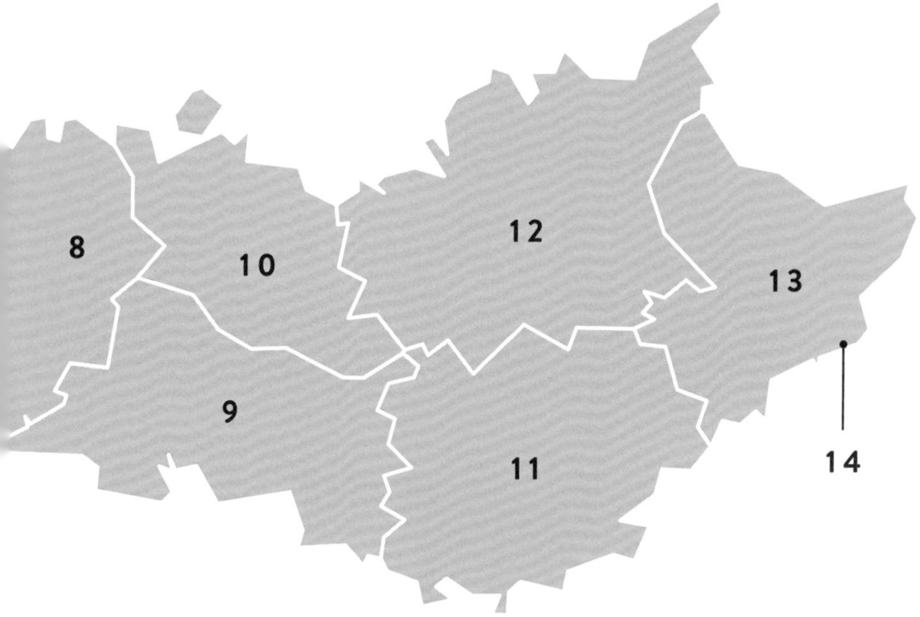

1 PYRÉNÉES-ORIENTALES + 2 AUDE

PYRÉNÉES-ORIENTALES

#	BANYULS-SUR-MER
237	Musée Maillol
242	Aristide Maillol

	CÉRET
58	Musée d'art moderne de Céret
260	Fontaine Picasso
261	Fontaine des Neuf Jets

	COLLIOURE
62	Musée d'art moderne de Collioure
245	Le Chemin du Fauvisme
316	Anchois Roque
357	Balco del Mar/ La voile
366	Hôtel des Templiers

	PERPIGNAN
13	Musée d'Art Hyacinthe Rigaud
102	Gare de Perpignan

AUDE

	BAGES
329	Latuvu Art Contemporain

	CARCASSONNE
28	Musée des Beaux-Arts de Carcassonne
225	Maison Joë Bousquet

	GRUISSAN
210	Gruissan Plage – Les Chalets sur Pilotis

	LAGRASSE
123	Abbaye de Lagrasse
173	Pont Vieux
342	La Petite Maison

	MONTOLIEU
317	Bookshops and art galleries

	NARBONNE
43	Jazz à L'Hospitalet
45	Festival Musique et Histoire
293	Maison Natale de Charles Trenet

3 TARN-ET-GARONNE
+ 4 HAUTE-GARONNE + 5 TARN

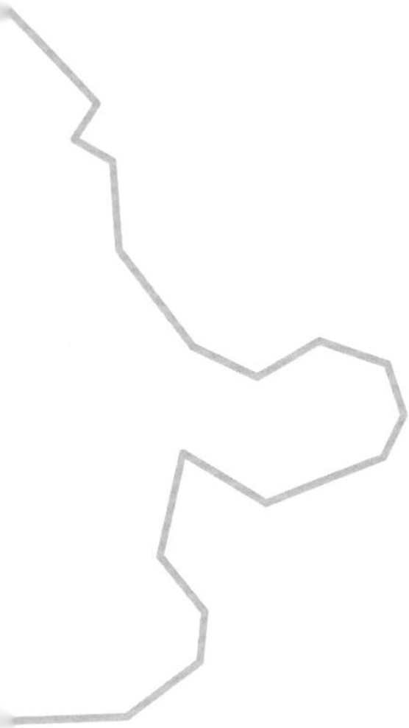

6 HÉRAULT + 7 AVEYRON + 8 GARD

9 BOUCHES-DU-RHÔNE

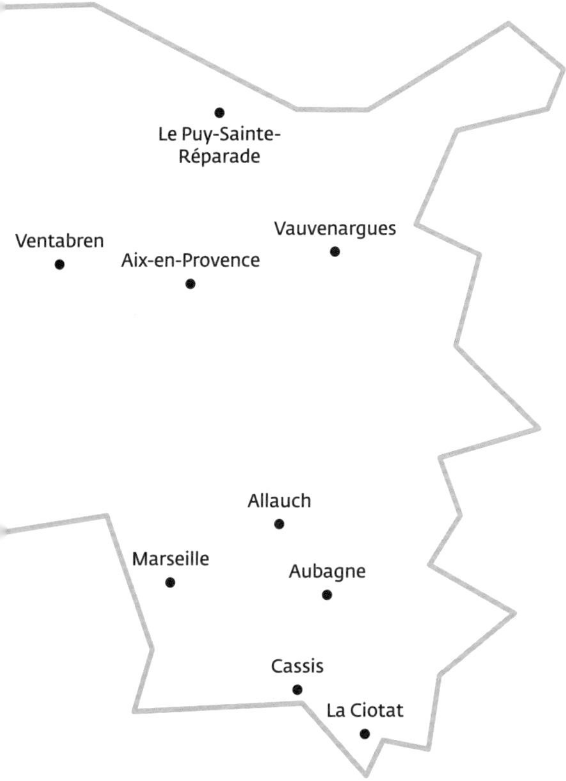
Le Puy-Sainte-Réparade
Ventabren
Aix-en-Provence
Vauvenargues
Allauch
Marseille
Aubagne
Cassis
La Ciotat

10 VAUCLUSE

Vaison-la-Romaine
Piolenc
Sault
Carpentras
Monieux
Avignon
L'Isle-sur-la-Sorgue
Le Thor
Fontaine-de-Vaucluse
Roussillon
Apt
Coustellet/Cabrières-d'Avignon
Ménerbes
Oppède-le-Vieux
Bonnieux
Vaugines
Lourmarin
Cucuron

11 VAR

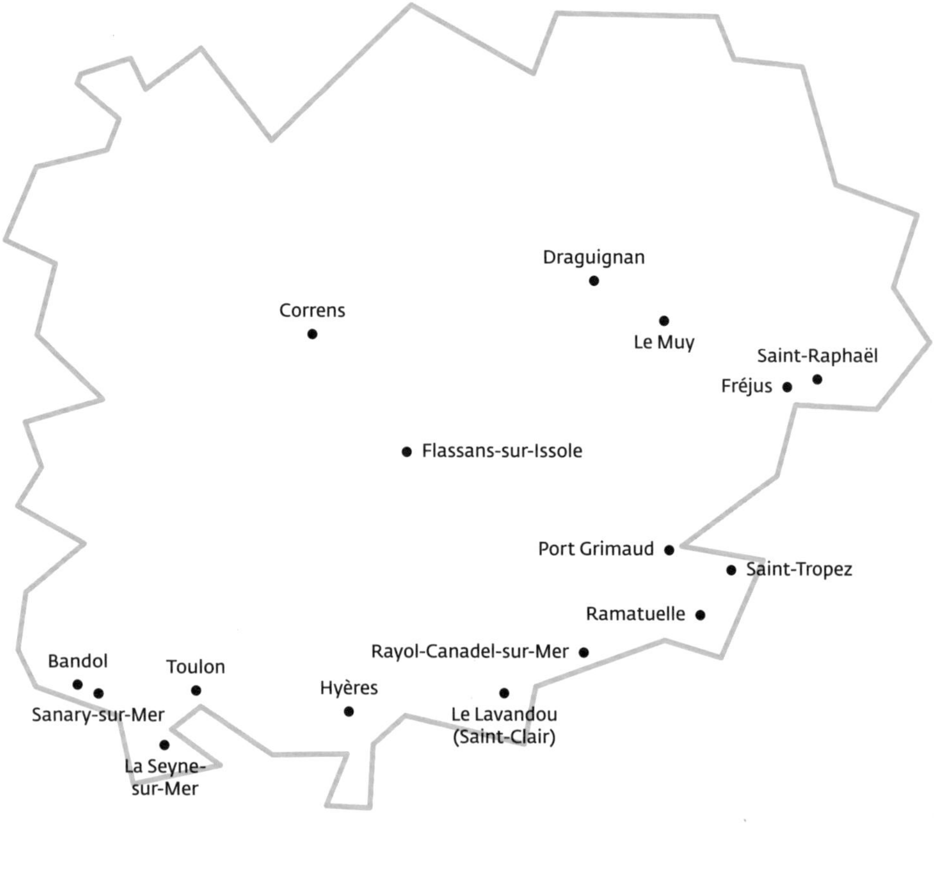
Draguignan
Correns
Le Muy
Saint-Raphaël
Fréjus
Flassans-sur-Issole
Port Grimaud
Saint-Tropez
Ramatuelle
Rayol-Canadel-sur-Mer
Bandol
Toulon
Hyères
Sanary-sur-Mer
Le Lavandou
(Saint-Clair)
La Seyne-
sur-Mer

12 ALPES-DE-HAUTE-PROVENCE

13 ALPES-MARITIMES + 14 MONACO

ALPES-MARITIMES

MUSÉE DES BEAUX-ARTS DE MARSEILLE

ART & CULTURE

1 SKY MIRROR

Impressive
PUBLIC ART

1 SKY MIRROR

BY: ANISH KAPOOR
IN FRONT OF:
Monte-Carlo Casino
Place du Casino
98000 Monaco

Anish Kapoor's majestic mirror sculpture sits in the square in front of Monte-Carlo's casino. The polished disc of concave steel, measuring 2,5 metres across, is an installation by British-Indian artist Anish Kapoor and was created in 1999. On the one hand, the simple sculpture contrasts strongly with the Casino's belle époque splendour; on the other hand, *Sky Mirror* turns the world upside down, giving the illusion of bringing the sky down to street level. Perhaps Kapoor wanted to add a playful albeit critical element to the chic elegance of Monaco and its casino?

2 PABLO

BY: GABRIËL STERK
Place des Patriotes
06250 Mougins
Alpes-Maritimes

This oversized bronze statue of Pablo Picasso's head was carved in 2008 by the Dutch artist Gabriël Sterk. You can find his statues of Paul Cézanne and Vincent van Gogh in La Rotonde in Aix-en-Provence and in front of the asylum in Saint-Paul-de-Mausole, respectively. This one stands on a terrace with a panoramic view overlooking the countryside around the hilltop town of Mougins. The statue is hard to miss as it is 2,4 metres tall and weighs 500 kilos. The work is a tribute to Pablo Picasso, who lived and worked in Mougins from 1961 until 1973, the year he died. The famous artist's studio used to be housed in the building where the town's tourist office is now located. He and his wife Jacqueline Roque lived in Mas de Notre Dame de Vie, next to the eponymous chapel.

3 CONVERSATION À NICE

BY: JAUME PLENSA
Place Masséna
06000 Nice
Alpes-Maritimes

Place Masséna is a striking central (and car-free) square in Nice. Look up and you will spot seven figures, each sitting on an aluminium pole, high above people's heads and the tram lines. The city of Nice commissioned this installation from the Catalan artist Jaume Plensa in 2007. Perhaps they are chess pieces on the square's chequerboard paving? Or maybe they represent the seven continents. They are different but similar. Either way, these statues look very peaceful, elevated above the crowds. At night, they light up, in all the colours of the rainbow.

4 RAYONNANT (RADIANT COLUMNS)

BY: DANIEL BUREN
AT: LA CIGALIÈRE
Parc de la Cigalière (D19)
34410 Sérignan
Hérault
+33 (0)4 67 32 33 05
beziers-in-mediterranee.com

Not one work, but an entire installation in public space. The French artist Daniel Buren installed an incredible 170 columns around La Cigalière, Sérignan's theatre and concert hall. The openwork metal towers of this remarkable work of art fan out into the adjoining streets, squares and car parks. At night they light up in an infinite array of colours, creating a playful and magical effect. It took him two years, from 2000 until 2002, to install this artistic intervention, which is titled *Rayonnant*, with the help of the architect Nicolas Guillot. Daniel Buren also created an in-situ work for the nearby Musée Regional d'Art Contemporain in Sérignan.

5 STATUE OF CLAUDE NOUGARO

BY: SÉBASTIEN LANGLOŸS
Square Charles de Gaulle
31000 Toulouse
Haute-Garonne

Singer and songwriter Claude Nougaro (1929-2004) is one of Toulouse's icons. This life-size statue was unveiled on 9 September 2014, 85 years after his birthdate and ten years after his death. The popular artist often sang the praises of his hometown in his chansons. That's why his statue, which was created by Sébastien Langloÿs, was given a place of honour in a small park behind the city hall.

6 **L'HOMME AU MOUTON (MAN WITH RAM)**

BY: PABLO PICASSO

Place de l'Homme au Mouton
06220 Vallauris
Alpes-Maritimes
vallauris-golfe-juan.fr/l-homme-au-mouton.html

Picasso's monument to peace. The artist donated this larger than life-sized bronze statue of a man carrying a ram in his arms to the city of Vallauris. At his request, it was installed in its current location in 1950. It was Picasso's first sculpture in public space. He regarded it as a seminal work in his oeuvre. He made the first sketches for the statue in 1942 after visiting an exhibition in Paris of the monumental sculptures of Hitler's favourite artist Arno Breker. The exhibition was organised by the German occupying forces. *L'Homme au mouton* is Picasso's artistic response to Breker's work and exudes sensitivity and humanity. In 1950, shortly after the start of the Korean War, the statue was installed as a symbol of peace in Vallauris, where Picasso lived and worked from 1948 until 1955. Here he discovered ceramics, a medium that was new to him, and the art of pottery. The Musée National Picasso, home to Picasso's vibrant *Guerre et Paix (War and Peace)* murals, is nearby.

7 **BUST OF FERNANDEL**

BY: JACQUES CHOQUIN

Corner of Boulevard Chave and Boulevard Eugène Pierre
13005 Marseille
Bouches-du-Rhône
tourisme-marseille.com/fiche/statue-de-fernandel-marseille

The famous French comic Fernandel – France's answer to Charlie Chaplin – was born in 1903 in Marseille as Fernand-Joseph-Désiré Contandin. In 2008, this bronze bust by the artist Jacques Choquin was installed around the corner from Fernandel's birthplace at 72 boulevard Chave. Fernandel was a famous film star in France in the years before and after World War II. Although he worked as a comedian, a singer and a film director, he achieved his greatest success as an actor in, among others, an enormously popular French-Italian series of comedies, in which he played a pugnacious village priest called Don Camillo who locked horns with the communist Mayor Peppone time and again. He also starred in serious films such as *La Vache et le Prisonnier (The Cow and I)* and *Heureux qui comme Ulysse*. His 'horse-like' teeth, as he liked to call them, became his trademark. He died in 1971 in Paris.

8 STATUE OF CARLOS GARDEL

BY: SÉBASTIEN LANGLOŸS
AT: JARDINS COMPANS CAFFARELLI
1 allée Francisco Ponzan Vidal
31000 Toulouse
Haute-Garonne

You may be surprised to learn that Carlos Gardel, Argentina's legendary grandmaster of tango, was born in Toulouse on 11 December 1890 as Charles Gardès. His mother was a French laundrywoman, his father unknown. Charles Gardès was just two years old when he emigrated to Buenos Aires with his mum. From there he would go on to conquer the world as the world-famous 'king of tango', from New York and Rio de Janeiro to Paris. On 24 June 1935, Gardel and his band died when his airplane crashed near Medellín in Colombia. This bronze statue of the singer, composer and film star was unveiled in June 2018 in the Jardins Compans Caffarelli, around the corner from the house where he grew up, at 4 rue du Canon d'Arcole. Note the miniature couple dancing a tango in his left hand.

9 COARAZE SUNDIALS

06390 Coaraze
Alpes-Maritimes
villagesetpatrimoine.fr/coaraze

The streets of one of France's sunniest villages, Coaraze, are decorated with eleven remarkable sundials, which were all made by modern and contemporary artists such as Jean Cocteau, Henri Bernard Goetz and Angel Ponce de Léon. The latter also painted the town's La Chapelle Bleue. Jean Cocteau created the first sundial in 1961 at the request of the then mayor. It features a lizard, the symbol of Coaraze. Legend has it that the devil disguised himself as a lizard to destroy the village church. He was discovered by a farmer who grabbed him by the tail, but the lizard was able to get away. Since then, a lizard sans tail has graced Coaraze's coat of arms. Besides Cocteau, five other artists contributed designs for the first series of sundials in 1961. In 2008, five new ones were added by Ben (Vautier) and Sacha Sosno, among others.

8 STATUE OF CARLOS GARDEL

10 BUST OF YVES MONTAND

BY: BRUNO CATALANO

Place Jean Jaurès
13001 Marseille
Bouches-du-Rhône
tourisme-marseille.com/fiche/statue-yves-montand-place-jean-jaures-marseille

The French actor and singer Yves Montand grew up in Marseille and made his debut just before the start of World War II in the local cabarets and music halls, including the famous L'Alcazar. His real name was Ivo Livi and he was born in 1921 near Florence, Italy. Given their communist leanings, the family was forced to flee in 1923 when Mussolini and his fascist allies came to power. The family settled in a working-class neighbourhood in Marseille, where Ivo's father established a broom factory. Ivo's childhood was marked by poverty and cruelty: he was bullied and called a 'spaghetti eater'. But Ivo overcame the hardship and developed a passion for American dance films starring his idol, Fred Astaire. After earning a living as a hairdresser, a dock worker and a pasta factory worker, he made his stage debut. His breakthrough as an actor in the USA and Europe came after World War II, in such films as *Let's Make Love* (1960), *Vivre pour vivre (Live for Life)* (1967), *Z* (1969), *L'Aveu (The Confession)* (1970) and *État de siège (State of Siege)* (1972). In the eighties Montand starred in one of his more memorable roles as the cunning farmer Le Papet in the films *Jean de Florette* (1986) and *Manon des Sources* (1986), based on Marcel Pagnol's novels. So how did he come up with his stage name? Ivo was gallicised as Yves, and he thought of 'Montand' because he remembered how his mother used to call to him in Italian: *"Ivo, monta!"* – "Ivo, come up!".

SINGLE-ARTIST

museums

11 **MUSÉE FRAGONARD**
AT: HÔTEL DE VILLENEUVE
14 rue Jean Ossola
06130 Grasse
Alpes-Maritimes
+33 (0)4 93 36 02 07
fragonard.com

Frivolous art in the perfume capital of the world. Jean-Honoré Fragonard (1732-1806) is a French painter with a predilection for piquant and even erotic but always light-hearted scenes of temptation and deception. Born in Grasse but working in Paris, he embodied the – sexual – liberties of the Enlightenment in addition to being one of the principal painters of French rococo. Hélène and Jean-François Costa were great collectors of 18th-century paintings. Over the years, they acquired fifteen canvases by Fragonard in addition to works by two lesser-known painters from Grasse. In 2011, they opened their museum in the magnificent 18th-century Hôtel de Villeneuve. The museum has the second largest collection of works by Fragonard in France, after the Louvre.

12 **MUSÉE SOULAGES**
AT: JARDIN DU FOIRAIL
Avenue Victor Hugo
12000 Rodez
Aveyron
+33 (0)5 65 73 82 60
musee-soulages-rodez.fr

This striking building in raw corten steel and glass in the centre of Rodez, which dates from 2014, looks like an impregnable fortress. However, it is home to the museum dedicated to the French abstract artist Pierre Soulages, who was born around the corner in 1919. Soulages is a jack-of-all-trades as you can tell from the museum's collection, which includes paintings on canvas and paper as well as drawings, etchings, sculptures and designs for stained-glass windows. The building – a design of the Catalan architects RCR – has different types of rooms: from a chapel-like space for the stained-glass windows to more intimate galleries for the delicate works on paper. A monument to one of France's most important contemporary artists.

13 MUSÉE D'ART HYACINTHE RIGAUD

21 rue Mailly
66000 Perpignan
Pyrénées-Orientales
+33 (0)4 68 66 19 83
www.musee-rigaud.fr

This spacious and pleasant new build, which dates from 2017, is home to the museum's collection of old masters. From the 13th to the 16th century, Perpignan was a prosperous centre of cloth manufacture and a hub for trade with Flanders and the Middle East. The collection's highlights include the paintings of the baroque artist Hyacinthe Rigaud, who was born in 1659 in Perpignan and served as court painter to the French king Louis XIV. The emphasis is mainly on his intimate portraits and self-portraits. But there's more to the museum than this. The historic wing in the 18th-century Hôtel de Lazerme showcases the Musée Rigaud's modern art collection. Between 1953 and 1956, art patrons Jacques and Paule de Lazerme received artists such as Marc Chagall, Raoul Dufy, Jean Cocteau and Pablo Picasso here. The latter became a good friend of the Lazermes, which explains why one of the rooms in the museum is dedicated to Picasso. Also worth seeing, the excellent ensembles by the sculptor Aristide Maillol and the painter Raoul Dufy, who had a studio in Perpignan in the forties. Alfons Mucha and Jules Chéret have their own room. In the late 19th century, they designed the advertising posters for the legendary JOB rolling papers and Byrrh, a wine aperitif, both of which were produced in Perpignan.

14 MUSÉE YVES BRAYER

Place François de Herain
13520 Les Baux-de-Provence
Bouches-du-Rhône
+33 (0)4 90 54 36 99
www.yvesbrayer.com

A tranquil haven in the busy and touristy mountain village of Les Baux. Yves Brayer (1907-1990) is a lesser-known painter but the modest museum dedicated to his work, which is located on one of Les Baux's narrow streets, provides a fascinating overview of his neorealistic oeuvre. Brayer travelled far and wide. In 1927 and 1928, he committed his impressions of Spain, Italy and Morocco to canvas: scenes from daily life with colourful, sometimes bold contrasts in a somewhat naïve style. His Provençal paintings are his best work, however, featuring often desolate landscapes in nice light. Brayer loved Les Baux so much that he started to spend a few months of the year here from 1945 onwards. He also decorated the Chapelle des Pénitents Blancs, near the museum, with pastoral scenes from Provence. You can find his grave in the cemetery of Les Baux.

13 MUSÉE D'ART HYACINTHE RIGAUD

15 FONDATION VASARELY

1 avenue Marcel Pagnol
13090 Aix-en-Provence
Bouches-du-Rhône
+33 (0)4 42 20 01 09
fondationvasarely.org

You may be forgiven for thinking that this is an office building or an industrial property at first glance, because of the gigantic black and white circles and squares on the façades. But it is actually a museum, located on a bizarre site in between two motorways to the south-west of Aix-en-Provence. This monumental edifice is dedicated to the Hungarian-French artist Victor Vasarely (1906-1997), the father of the optical art or 'Op Art' movement: abstract art, with strong contrasts between light and dark, trompe l'oeil, vibrant colours and geometrical patterns that appear to be moving. The building, which was inaugurated in 1976, was designed and financed by Vasarely himself, who conceived it as a massive 'lumino-kinetic' work of art. You can see 44 large works by Vasarely on the inside and outside of the 5000-square-metre museum. It's a great place to immerse yourself in his fascinating op art. The museum also hosts multiple simultaneous temporary exhibitions about Vasarely, who also designed, among other things, the famous logo of the Renault car brand.

16 MUSÉE MATISSE

164 avenue des Arènes de Cimiez
06000 Nice
Alpes-Maritimes
+33 (0)4 93 81 08 08
www.musee-matisse-nice.org

Along with Pablo Picasso, Henri Matisse (1869-1954) is one of the 20th century's greatest and most versatile artists. So it's only fitting that his life and work is remembered in not one, but two museums: one in his hometown of Le Cateau-Cambrésis, near the Belgian border, and one in Nice, the city where the artist spent a lot of time from 1917 onwards and where he eventually settled in 1925. The Musée Matisse is close to the Hôtel Régina where Matisse lived and worked during the last sixteen years of his life. He donated thirty canvases and various objects to the museum but died before it opened in 1963. The Musée Matisse offers an excellent survey of Matisse's early career, with his dark colour palette when he was heavily influenced by the painters of the north, followed by the storm of colour that exploded in his Collioure period and the birth of fauvism, right up to the preparatory sketches for his chapel in Vence. The museum pays a lot of attention to Matisse's connection with Nice. *La Piscine*, the monumental ensemble of ceramic murals (measuring 2 × 8 metres) and based on gouaches by the artist, is one of the museum's highlights.

17 MUSÉE ZIEM

11 boulevard du 14 juillet
13500 Martigues
Bouches-du-Rhône
+33 (0)4 42 41 39 60
ville-martigues.fr

The small town of Martigues likes to style itself as the 'Venise Provençal' – the Venice of Provence. The town does indeed have a few canals, picturesque houses and a fine church (Sainte-Madeleine), the façade of which is beautifully reflected in the water. These days, however, you can't help but notice the stark contrast with the petrochemical industry around the Étang de Berre. When the *plein air* painter Félix Ziem arrived in Martigues in 1860, it was just a fishing village. The artist was drawn to this location by the bright light and the region's unspoilt nature. The Musée Ziem's collection features several of Ziem's light-impressionist works, supplemented with marine art and urban scenes by, among others, Othon Friesz, Francis Picabia and André Derain, who all worked in or around Martigues at some point.

15 FONDATION VASARELY

18 MUSÉE BONNARD

16 boulevard
Sadi Carnot
06110 Le Cannet
Alpes-Maritimes
+33 (0)4 93 94 06 06
museebonnard.fr

In 1926, Pierre Bonnard, one of the 20th century's most important post-impressionist painters, bought a modest cottage called Le Bosquet in the hills above Cannes. The famous designer of art nouveau posters and painter of urban scenes in Paris increasingly withdrew here with his wife Marthe. It was here, near the Mediterranean Sea, that he would paint what is widely considered his best work: lush, vividly coloured landscapes or his representation of his own earthly paradise, the recurring daily rituals of ordinary but also enchanting life. And dozens of strange, claustrophobic portraits of his wife Marthe as she reclined in the bath. Bonnard died in 1947, at the age of 79, at Le Cannet and was buried there. In 2011, the excellent Musée Bonnard opened in the former Hôtel Saint-Vianney, a typical belle époque building in Le Cannet. For the record, Bonnard never lived here. The museum is a lovely, intimate place. Drenched in the light of the sun-soaked Mediterranean, it has a nice collection of Bonnard's works, which is continually expanded with donations and temporary exhibitions about Bonnard, his era and his friends/colleagues such as Vuillard and Matisse.

18 MUSÉE BONNARD

19 MUSÉE NATIONAL MARC CHAGALL

36 avenue Docteur Ménard
06000 Nice
Alpes-Maritimes
+33 (0)4 93 53 87 20
en.musees-nationaux-alpesmaritimes.fr/chagall

The oeuvre of Marc Chagall (1887-1985) is imbued with magical realism fused with imagined, dreamlike scenes. In a sense, the Franco-Russian painter symbolises the fate of the 'wandering Jew': on the one hand, he was always on the move, on the other he never forgot his native Russia and Russian-Jewish traditions. Chagall, born Movsja Zacharovitsj Sjagal in the *shtetl* of Liozna, near the city of Vitebsk in tsarist Russia (Belarus), travelled between Russia, Paris and the United States. He ended up settling in Vence in 1950. The Musée Chagall in Nice was inaugurated in 1973 and was laid out as a 'house', in line with the artist's wishes. The austere and stark architecture lacks intimacy, however. Chagall donated seventeen large paintings of his *Message Biblique* cycle, in addition to designing a mosaic and creating three huge stained-glass windows that depict the *Creation of the World* for the auditorium. The museum organises occasional concerts there. Chagall was a real music lover. He designed, among other things, the costumes for the 1949 performance of Igor Stravinsky's *Firebird* ballet by the New York City Ballet.

20 MUSÉE DE RÉGION AUGUSTE CHABAUD

41 cours National
13690 Graveson
Bouches-du-Rhône
+33 (0)4 90 90 53 02
museechabaud.com

Auguste Chabaud (1882-1955) is an unjustly forgotten painter, a contemporary of Matisse and Derain. He met them both while training as a painter in Paris. Chabaud was born in Nîmes, led an adventurous life as a harbour pilot in West Africa, and completed his military service in Tunisia (1903-1906), before returning to Paris where he discovered the city's nightlife. His paintings combine vivid fauvist colours with dynamic brushwork although the angular shapes are more reminiscent of the German expressionists. Between 1906 and 1914 he exhibited his work in Paris, Marseille and Berlin, along with other avant-garde artists. Following the death of his brother, Chabaud returned to Graveson to assist his mother with the management of the family's estate.
It forced him to take another, closer look at his native region, which compelled him to start painting scenes of daily life in Provence. Most of the paintings in the collection of the small Musée de Région Auguste Chabaud in Graveson date from this later period. Definitely an interesting introduction. Follow in Chabaud's footsteps and take a walk through the old, picturesque town after your museum visit.

21 MUSÉE TOULOUSE-LAUTREC

AT: PALAIS DE LA BERBIE
Place Sainte-Cécile
81003 Albi
Tarn
+33 (0)5 63 49 48 70
musee-toulouse-lautrec.com

This museum in Albi has the world's largest collection of art by the French painter, draughtsman, graphic artist and poster designer Henri de Toulouse-Lautrec (1864-1901). He captures the hedonistic vibrancy of Parisian nightlife and the cafes, cabarets and brothels of Montmartre. His stylised posters for shows at the Moulin Rouge are world-famous, as are his remarkably empathic, non-moralising paintings of the *maisons closes*, where he was given the opportunity to observe the city's prostitutes as they went about their daily business. Henri de Toulouse-Lautrec was born in Albi into one of France's oldest aristocratic families. They lived in the Hôtel du Bosc at 14 rue Toulouse-Lautrec. Henri's mother founded the museum in 1922 in the former bishop's palace in Albi. In it, visitors can trace the evolution of this unusual artist's oeuvre, from the first sketches and portraits he made in his childhood years to the last paintings he worked on before he died at the young age of 36, from alcoholism and syphilis. What's more, Toulouse-Lautrec suffered from poor health and brittle bones. After fracturing both of his femurs as a child, he never fully recovered. He suffered from short stature for the rest of his life. His illness may also have been the result of inbreeding, given that his parents were first cousins.

21 MUSÉE TOULOUSE-LAUTREC

23 MUSÉE PICASSO, ANTIBES – NICOLAS DE STAËL 'LE CONCERT'

22 MUSÉE DES BEAUX-ARTS – HÔTEL FAYET

9 rue du Capus
34500 Béziers
Hérault
+33 (0)4 67 49 04 66
beziers-in-mediterranee.com

Tucked away in an alley in the historic town centre of Béziers, this somewhat dusty but charming little museum is a pleasant surprise. It is housed in a small 17th-century city palace, which belonged to the artist, collector and art patron Gustave Fayet (1865-1925). The museum is entirely dedicated to the sculptor Jean-Antoine Injalbert, who was born in Béziers in 1845. His name probably doesn't ring a bell, but he is known for the monumental allegorical statues that he sculpted for the pont Mirabeau, the pont Bir-Hakeim and the Petit Palais, all in Paris. He also created the statues in front of the opera house in Montpellier and the theatre of Sète. Besides finished smaller sculptures, the musée Fayet mainly exhibits sketches, preliminary studies and plaster models of the monumental and recently restored Titan fountain, among others, which Injalbert designed for Le Plateau des Poètes, Béziers' municipal park.

23 MUSÉE PICASSO, ANTIBES

AT: CHÂTEAU GRIMALDI
Place Mariejol
06600 Antibes
Alpes-Maritimes
+33 (0)4 92 90 54 28
www.antibes-juanlespins.com

This former 16th-century fortress in Antibes is one of several museums around the world dedicated to Picasso. But this one stands out. In 1946, the director of the then Musée Grimaldi offered Pablo Picasso the opportunity to use part of the building as his studio. At the time, the artist was looking for a place to create monumental works of art, which is why he leaped at the chance. Supposedly Picasso said: "I won't only paint for myself here; I will create a museum." He produced the majority of the works on display in just one season: 23 paintings and 44 sketches, inspired by the Mediterranean Sea and its mythical creatures. True to his promise, Picasso donated all of the works to the museum. The collection was significantly enriched later on, following donations by Picasso's second wife Jacqueline Roque and the acquisition of a large number of ceramic pieces that Picasso made between 1948 and 1949 in the nearby village of Vallauris. The museum offers a dazzling introduction to this versatile artist. Don't forget to visit the room devoted to Nicolas de Staël, where you can admire his monumental painting, *Le Concert*, the last piece that he finished before committing suicide on 16 March 1955 in Antibes. The museum also has a fine collection of abstract paintings donated by the artists Hans Hartung and Anna-Eva Bergman. To top it all off, the terrace also offers a stupendous panoramic view of the endless azure waters of the Med in addition to a series of sculptures by the likes of Joan Miró, Germaine Richier and Daniel Spoerri.

OLD MASTERS
to admire

24 **MUSÉE CALVET**
65 rue Joseph Vernet
84000 Avignon
Vaucluse
+33 (0)4 90 86 33 84
musee-calvet.org

A museum with an impressive and diverse collection, in a majestic 18th-century city palace. Here you can see prehistoric objects, sculptures, Egyptian and Islamic art, goldwork, porcelain, and much more. Plenty of fascinating discoveries await in the old masters galleries, including works by some lesser-known artists. Keep an eye out for the pipe smoker by Cornelis Dusart (c. 1690), an almost surrealistic Calvary scene by Jan van Noordt (c. 1650) and a striking nude titled *La Mort de Joseph Bara*, a martyr of the French Revolution, by Jacques-Louis David (1793). The museum also has a handful of magnificent works from the 1920s by Chaïm Soutine – landscapes and his signature twisting, distorted portraits – as well as a few good paintings by the Provence expressionist Auguste Chabaud.

25 **MUSÉE DES BEAUX-ARTS DE MARSEILLE**
AT: PALAIS LONGCHAMP, LEFT WING
13004 Marseille
Bouches-du-Rhône
+33 (0)4 91 14 59 24/35
musees.marseille.fr/musee-des-beaux-arts-mba

The impressive Palais Longchamp in Marseille is a work of art in itself. It was built in the 1850s and is a perfect example of the ornate yet festive Beaux Arts style: it looks like a giant wedding cake. Two majestic staircases enclose a huge fountain, leading to a massive, curved colonnade. The right wing houses the Musée de l'Histoire Naturelle, the left wing is home to the Musée des Beaux-Arts. Some of the collection's highlights include Peter Paul Rubens's *La Chasse au sanglier (Boar Hunt)* (1616), a well-executed copy by Louis Finson of Caravaggio's *Mary Magdalen in Ecstasy* (c. 1613) and Gustave Courbet's *Le Cerf à l'eau (The Stag Taking to the Water)* (1861). The museum combines lesser-known 19th-century landscape painters from Marseille with leading French artists such as Corot, Millet and Puvis de Chavannes.

25 MUSÉE DES BEAUX-ARTS DE MARSEILLE

26 MUSÉE FABRE

39 boulevard
Bonne Nouvelle
34000 Montpellier
Hérault
+33 (0)4 67 14 83 00
museefabre.
montpellier3m.fr

The Musée Fabre in Montpellier is one of the biggest and most important fine arts museums in France outside Paris. It was founded in 1824 when the painter and art collector, Baron François-Xavier Fabre, donated his collection to the city. From 1828, it was displayed in the Hôtel de Massilian, an 18th-century city palace. Beginning in 2003, the museum underwent a thorough renovation, which was completed in 2007 and which significantly expanded the galleries. One of the architectural highlights is the building's impressive colonnade. The Musée Fabre has an excellent collection of European paintings from the 14th century to the present day and all the major names are represented. There are a few paintings and ensembles in particular that merit your attention, including a gruesomely realistic *Étude de pieds et de main* from 1818-1819 by Théodore Géricault, the famous painter of *The Raft of the Medusa* which you can see in the Louvre. The museum also has sixteen paintings by Gustave Courbet, the once controversial 'father of European realism', including a captivating self-portrait, a portrait of the poet Charles Baudelaire and the famous *Bonjour, Monsieur Courbet* (1854), the scene in which Courbet runs into his patron Alfred Bruyas somewhere outside Montpellier, dressed and equipped to go paint in the open air. Courbet's no-nonsense realism is offset by eleven works by Alexandre Cabanel, a well-known painter in the academic style. After the museum's renovation was completed, the abstract painter Pierre Soulages (b. 1919) donated twenty works, spanning his career from 1950 to the present.

27 MUSÉE D'ART CLASSIQUE DE MOUGINS

32 rue Commandeur
06250 Mougins
Alpes-Maritimes
+33 (0)4 93 75 18 22
mouginsmusee.com

The Musée d'Art Classique de Mougins, which opened in 2011, is another pleasant surprise. It has a large collection of Egyptian sarcophagi, Greek and Roman sculptures, vases and jewellery, as well as one of the world's largest private collections of ancient arms and armour. This may not sound that special but the museum's founder, the retired British hedge fund manager Christian Levett, had the brilliant idea to show visitors how the antique world has influenced modern and contemporary art. Works by Marc Chagall, Alexander Calder and Jean Cocteau are displayed alongside Egyptian artefacts. The art of Damien Hirst and Pablo Picasso contrasts with the ancient Roman busts. Greek and Roman gods find themselves in the good company of Andy Warhol, Yves Klein and Georges Braque. As you can tell, there's a lot to see in a relatively small space. Unfortunately, many of the museum's treasures are kept behind glass, and for good reason. Nonetheless, the museum offers a fascinating foray through history.

28 MUSÉE DES BEAUX-ARTS DE CARCASSONNE

15 boulevard Camille Pelletan
11000 Carcassonne
Aude
+33 (0)4 68 77 73 70
carcassonne.org

Carcassonne's main attraction is its historic fortified city, which is the third most popular tourist destination in France, after Paris and the Mont Saint-Michel. The small but nice Musée des Beaux-Arts is located in downtown Carcassonne. As you would expect from a provincial museum, the collection features a number of second-rate pieces as well as some nice surprises. Besides some fine landscapes by Gustave Courbet and Jean-Baptiste-Camille Corot, an interesting still-life by Jean-Baptiste Siméon Chardin, an excellent urban scene by Albert Marquet and an abstract piece by the underestimated Serge Poliakoff, the museum also has a few paintings that represent Carcassonne in different ways. The 18th-century painter Jacques Gamelin, who was born in the city, mainly specialised in historical paintings and intimate portraits, the 19th-century history painter Jean-Paul Laurens studied the medieval fortified city, while Henry Valensi created a cubist version of Carcassonne in 1934.

28 **MUSÉE DES BEAUX-ARTS DE CARCASSONNE**

29 **FONDATION VINCENT VAN GOGH ARLES**

35ter rue du Docteur Fanton
13200 Arles
Bouches-du-Rhône
+33 (0)4 90 93 08 08
fondation-vincent vangogh-arles.org

The Fondation Vincent van Gogh Arles was founded in 1983 to pay tribute to the legendary painter who lived and worked in Arles from February 1888 until May 1889. The museum highlights how Van Gogh inspired and influenced later generations and continues to do so to this day. In 1985, the Fondation acquired art works by Francis Bacon, Roy Lichtenstein and David Hockney paving the way for the museum's creation. The actual museum was inaugurated in 2014. Here the Fondation hosts temporary exhibitions with work by contemporary artists, always in relation to Van Gogh. The 15th-century building became a Banque de France in 1924. In 2014, it was renovated from top to bottom by the architects of FLUOR, who chose to give free rein to the sparkling natural daylight of Provence, which plays such a prominent role in Van Gogh's work. The artist Bertrand Lavier painted the foundation's gates whereas the colourful glass sculpture on the roof of the bookshop is the work of Raphael Hefti.

30 COLLECTION LAMBERT

5 rue Violette
84000 Avignon
Vaucluse
+33 (0)4 90 16 56 20
collectionlambert.com

The Collection Lambert in Avignon is the brainchild of the Parisian gallerist and art collector Yvon Lambert. The collection comprises approximately 2000 artworks, giving it all the allure of a museum, all the more so after the exhibition space was expanded in 2015. Two 18th-century mansions – the Hôtel de Montfaucon and the Hôtel de Caumont – were renovated by the architects Berger&Berger, who added a minimalistic but monumental staircase and a striking skylight. The Lambert Collection, which celebrated its twentieth anniversary in Avignon in 2020, offers an impressive survey of the various aspects of international contemporary art from 1960 to the present day, including minimal, conceptual and land art, in addition to photography, video art, and the revival of figurative painting. You can find all this and more here, including large ensembles by Sol LeWitt, Lawrence Weiner, Nan Goldin, Andres Serrano, Christian Boltanski, Daniel Buren, Anselm Kiefer and Cy Twombly. Take your time to explore this extensive, surprising collection in spacious galleries.

30 COLLECTION LAMBERT

31 NOUVEAU MUSÉE NATIONAL DE MONACO

AT: VILLA SAUBER

17 avenue Princesse Grace
98000 Monaco
+377 98 98 91 26
nmnm.mc

In anticipation of a new home, the New National Museum of Monaco currently has two villas at its disposal for exhibitions: Villa Paloma (temporarily closed) and Villa Sauber, one of the Principality's last belle époque villas. The theme of the exhibitions is 'Training for a Museum': each exhibition is set up as a research project, exploring the role of a contemporary museum in Monaco and what it should show. The exhibitions are therefore quite varied: from a retrospective of the work of painter Kees van Dongen and contemporary ceramics to urban planning developments and the possible plans for the Principality's future.

32 MAMAC NICE

32 MAMAC NICE

1 place Yves Klein
06364 Nice
Alpes-Maritimes
+33 (0)4 97 13 42 01
mamac-nice.org

The Musée d'Art Moderne et d'Art Contemporain or MAMAC looks like an impregnable fortress in the centre of the city. It was designed in 1990 by the architects Yves Bayard and Henri Vidal and combines large volumes, with white façades and curved glass windows. The MAMAC is a big museum. It will take you at least two hours just to see the highlights. It offers an interesting dialogue between artists from Nice and their foreign counterparts or, to be more precise, between French new realism and American pop art with artists such as Andy Warhol, Claes Oldenburg and Robert Rauschenberg. In the sixties, the Côte d'Azur was an important place for artistic experiments. Many artists like Arman (who assembled giant sculptures using cars), César (who crushed and compressed cars into sculptures) and Christo & Jeanne-Claude (who wrapped all kinds of objects) criticised consumer society. The museum focusses specifically on two artists: Yves Klein (born in Nice in 1928), who explored new themes with his performances and monochrome works in bright 'Yves Klein' blue, and Niki de Saint Phalle – she of the colourful, monumental outdoor sculptures and paintings riddled with bullets. Outside the building you can find installations by, among others, Alexander Calder and Niki de Saint Phalle. On the rooftop terrace you can see Yves Klein's *Le Mur de Feu (The Wall of Fire)* and enjoy a marvellous view across the city.

33 **MUSÉE RÉGIONAL D'ART CONTEMPORAIN OCCITANIE/PYRÉNÉES-MÉDITERRANÉE**

33 MUSÉE RÉGIONAL D'ART CONTEMPORAIN OCCITANIE/ PYRÉNÉES-MÉDITERRANÉE

146 avenue de la Plage
34410 Sérignan
Hérault
+33 (0)4 67 17 88 95
mrac.laregion.fr

The small town of Sérignan, between the coast and Béziers, has a surprisingly good contemporary art collection, with several works by the artist Daniel Buren. You can find his *Rayonnant* – an installation comprising 170 metal openwork columns – on the city's fringe. For his in-situ work *Rotation*, he wrapped the Musée Régional MRAC, covering the windows with colourful planes. They create all kinds of visual effects inside and outside of the building, like contemporary stained-glass windows. His equally colourful *Cabane éclatée* (1999-2000), a giant, 'exploded' cube, also has a prominent place in the museum's collection. But the MRAC has much more to offer: the fascinating and surprising survey of all aspects of contemporary art since 1960, with works by famous and lesser-known names such as Bertrand Lavier, Mimosa Echard and Robert Crumb. The museum also hosts relevant exhibitions, like *La mesure du monde*, about landscape and climate. Quite a discovery.

34 MUSÉE D'ART DE TOULON (MAT)

113 boulevard
Général Leclerc
83000 Toulon
Var
+33 (0)4 94 36 81 01
toulon.fr

This imposing neorenaissance building from 1888 closed in February 2020 for the second and last phase of its renovation. At the time of publication it was unclear when the Musée d'Art de Toulon will reopen. The collection focusses on major contemporary art movements: conceptual art, French *nouveau réalisme* (Arman, Christo, Yves Klein and Martial Raysse), minimalism (Donald Judd and Sol LeWitt) and Supports/ Surfaces (Claude Viallat). The museum also owns an extensive photo collection with works by Henri Cartier-Bresson, Edward Steichen, Willy Ronis and Robert Doisneau.

35 ESPACE DE L'ART CONCRET

AT: CHÂTEAU DE MOUANS

Rue du Château
06370 Mouans-Sartoux
Alpes-Maritimes
+33 (0)4 93 75 71 50
espacedelartconcret.fr

An exceptional abstract art collection is displayed in the 16th-century castle of Mouans-Sartoux as well as in the austere, functional and eye-catching yellow-green museum building in the castle garden. The latter was built in 2004 by the Swiss architects Mike Guyer and Annette Gigon. Gottfried Honegger (1917-2016) was a Swiss artist who created abstract-geometric art in addition to collecting it with his partner Sybil Albers. They cultivated friendships with major artists from the USA and Europe and were thus able to build an impressive collection with works by leading artists such as Daniel Buren, Richard Long, Imi Knoebel, Bernar Venet, Carl Andre, Donald Judd and Richard Serra. In 2000, they decided to donate their 'concrete art' collection, of approximately 700 pieces, to the French government. The term 'concrete art' refers to any type of non-figurative, abstract or geometric art, plus minimalism, arte povera and conceptual pieces. In recent years, the already impressive collection was expanded thanks to donations by artists and collectors, resulting in a colourful and exceptionally diverse range of art works from the early 20th century to the present day, including some very nice design and interior objects. All shown in a spacious, light and attractive museum.

36 CATHÉDRALE SAINT-SAUVEUR

ONE PAINTING
worth the visit

36 **CATHÉDRALE SAINT-SAUVEUR**
34 place des Martyrs-de-la-Résistance
13100 Aix-en-Provence
Bouches-du-Rhône
cathedrale-aix.net

Aix-en-Provence's cathedral is home to a sizeable collection of art treasures, including a 6th-century octagonal baptistery but the real eye-catcher is an intriguing monumental painting titled *Le Buisson ardent (The Burning Bush)* from 1476, by the French painter Nicolas Froment (c. 1430-1486). Only a handful of paintings are attributed to him and, what's more, the theme of this triptych is exceedingly rare in paintings. In all likelihood, the French King René d'Anjou commissioned this biblical scene for the chapel he had built for the burial of his entrails. The left wing depicts the kneeling king; the right wing a portrait of his second wife Jeanne de Laval. The middle panel represents Moses before the burning blackberry bush, who is struck with astonishment at the vision of the Virgin Mary with Jesus on her lap. The bush is burning but not consumed by the fire. According to the Bible (Exodus 3:2-4), God himself appears to Moses. In the Middle Ages, however, the burning blackberry bush was regarded as a symbol of Mary's perpetual virginity. Nicolas Froment's painting can be found in the Lazarus Chapel.

37 CATHÉDRALE SAINTE-CÉCILE

Place Sainte-Cécile
81000 Albi
Tarn
+33 (0)5 63 38 47 40
albi-tourisme.fr/en/saint-cecilias-cathedral

Below the organ in the monumental brick cathedral basilica of Albi – or 'fortress' church – you can see a gigantic fresco of *The Last Judgement*, attributed to unknown Flemish painters. It was probably painted between 1474 and 1483. Unfortunately, the central area, depicting Christ on his throne, was later removed to make way for a chapel and replaced with an impressive portal. The left section of the fresco represents the apostles with their golden halos, as well as the saints and the chosen mortals who will be admitted to heaven. On the right, dark clouds gather over the heads of the damned who are condemned to live in hell. The bottom register depicts six of the seven deadly sins, from left to right. Sloth used to be in the middle but, alas, has since disappeared.

38 CATHÉDRALE NOTRE-DAME-DU-PUY

Place du Petit Puy
06130 Grasse
Alpes-Maritimes
+33 (0)4 93 36 10 34
paysdegrassetourisme.fr/en/node/91

Rubens in Grasse? Who would have guessed! In fact, the cathedral of Grasse has not one but three paintings by Peter Paul Rubens. Admittedly, they all belong together. This was the first altarpiece that the Antwerp master painted aged 25, while living and working in Rome. These early paintings lack the characteristic panache and virtuosity of his later works. Rubens painted *Saint Helena and the Exaltation of the Holy Cross*, a commission for Santa Croce in Gerusalemme church, in 1602 as an altarpiece for the underground chapel of Saint Helena. Two smaller works flanked the central panel: *The Mocking of Christ* – the most personal and best executed work of the three – and *The Elevation of the Cross*. The original of the latter was destroyed in the 17th century but thankfully a copy exists in Grasse. In 1812, the triptych was bought by a French collector at an auction in London. He donated it to the hospital of Grasse in 1827. Since 1972, the three paintings are on display in one of the cathedral's side aisles.

39 MUSÉE ANGLADON

5 rue Laboureur
84000 Avignon
Vaucluse
+33 (0)4 90 82 29 03
angladon.com

The Musée Angladon in Avignon owns the only painting by Vincent van Gogh on display in Provence today. All the paintings that the artist created between February 1888 and May 1890 in Arles and Saint-Rémy-de-Provence now reside in leading international museums such as the Van Gogh Museum in Amsterdam. Van Gogh painted *Railway Carriages in Arles* (45 × 50 cm, oil on canvas) near the city's marshalling yard. In a letter to his brother Theo dated Sunday 12 August 1888, Vincent writes that he painted 'a study' of train carriages on the Paris-Lyon-Méditerannée line, on a day with 'glorious, powerful heat, with no wind'. That same day he also painted studies of thistles on a piece of waste ground and the caravans of some fairground people. *Railway Carriages in Arles* is a powerful work, capturing the luminous light of the Midi with faster and looser brushwork. Van Gogh even left parts of the canvas unpainted, using its brown colour for the railway embankment. The Musée Angladon, which was founded by the artists Jean Angladon and Paulette Martin, showcases the extensive and high-quality art collection of the pioneering couturier Jacques Doucet (1853-1929), which includes works by Cézanne, Modigliani, Picasso and Degas. Doucet was an avid contemporary art collector and the first owner of Pablo Picasso's mythical painting *Les demoiselles d'Avignon* (1907), which is now in the Museum of Modern Art in New York.

40 MUSÉE DU VIEIL AIX

17 rue Gaston de Saporta
13100 Aix-en-Provence
Bouches-du-Rhône
+33 (0)4 88 71 74 31
aixenprovence.fr

Originally, this *Annunciation* (c. 1442) by Barthélemy d'Eyck was painted for the cathedral of Aix-en-Provence. It was commissioned by a cloth merchant from Aix for his burial chapel. At some point, the work – originally a triptych – was sold and dispersed (one of the wings was even cut into pieces). Today the left wing can be found in the Museum Boijmans van Beuningen (Rotterdam), a fragment of the left wing representing a still-life of books is in the Rijksmuseum Amsterdam while the right wing is in the Royal Museum of Fine Art in Brussels. Only the centre panel is still in Aix. It is usually displayed in Église de la Madeleine, but this church closed in 2006 for renovation. In short: this painting has a rather turbulent history. We don't know much about its maker, Barthélemy d'Eyck, either. He was active between about 1440 to 1470, he is believed to have come from the Principality of Liège and to be related to Jan van Eyck. In any event, this painting is phenomenal: the perspective of the church and the textiles are very well executed. Do look at some of the more remarkable details like the bats in the arch above the angel and Jesus depicted as a foetus floating towards Mary in a beam of light.

41 PALAIS DES PAPES

Place du Palais
84000 Avignon
Vaucluse
+33 (0)4 32 74 32 74
palais-des-papes.com

The Palais des Papes (Popes' Palace) in Avignon is an enormous Gothic palace with two courtyards and twelve towers. It was built in the 14th century after the Papal Curia was moved to Avignon from Rome. Magnificent frescoes decorate the chapels and the popes' chambers. In 1344 and 1345, Pope Clement VI commissioned frescoes for the Saint-Martial Chapel from the Italian artist Matteo Giovannetti. Martial was the first bishop of Limoges. The dazzling colours, the realistic postures and the individual faces of the figures make these 35 lively scenes even more remarkable. The chapel is currently being restored. For the time being, you can only see a video of the frescoes.

Wonderful
MUSIC FESTIVALS

42 **JAZZ À JUAN**
AT: PINÈDE GOULD
06160 Juan-les-Pins
Alpes-Maritimes
jazzajuan.com

This jazz festival takes place every year in July. It was first organised in 1960, making it Europe's oldest jazz festival. It's also one of the best-known festivals: some of the most famous American, European and African jazz musicians have taken to the stage here, from Louis Armstrong, Count Basie, Duke Ellington and Ella Fitzgerald to Charles Mingus, Sonny Rollins, Shirley Horn and Weather Report. Since then, more than fifty musicians (including B.B. King, George Benson, Keith Jarrett and Stevie Wonder) have left their handprints in the pavement of the Boulevard Edouard Baudoin, near where the central stage is usually set up.

43 **JAZZ À L'HOSPITALET**
AT: CHÂTEAU L'HOSPITALET
Route de
Narbonne-Plage
11100 Narbonne
Aude
+33(0)4 68 45 28 50
chateau-hospitalet.com/
jazz-arts

Since 2004, the gorgeous vineyard of the Château L'Hospitalet, which is just a ten-minute drive from Narbonne, has been the setting for this annual jazz festival. Held during the last week of July, it includes open-air concerts by major as well as surprising international jazz artists, such as Melody Gardot, Gregory Porter, Jamie Cullum, Selah Sue, George Benson and Norah Jones.

44 **FESTIVAL DE NÎMES**

45 **FESTIVAL MUSIQUE ET HISTOIRE**

44 FESTIVAL DE NÎMES

Boulevard des Arènes
30000 Nîmes
Gard
festivaldenimes.com

Every summer, international rock stars flock to Nîmes for this festival. Several famous artists have performed in the city's Roman arena in the past, including Santana, Neil Young, David Bowie and Metallica. This amazing structure, which dates from the year 100, was originally used for gladiator battles and chariot races. In the olden days, the arena could accommodate a crowd of up to 24.000 spectators. Today the audiences in this beautifully preserved Roman arena may be smaller, but the acoustics remain unrivalled. The line-up of the Nîmes Festival includes stars such as Sting and the Foo Fighters as well as younger artists such as Stromae, Angèle and Gorillaz.

45 FESTIVAL MUSIQUE ET HISTOIRE

AT: L'ABBAYE DE FONTFROIDE
Chemin de Fontfroide
11100 Narbonne
Aude
+33 (0)4 68 45 11 08
www.fontfroide.com

L'Abbaye de Fontfroide is hidden among cypress groves in a charming valley in the Languedoc and is one of the region's most beautiful and magnificent abbeys. Its history is just as remarkable. In its heyday, three hundred monks lived in this 11th-century abbey. In 1901, all religious orders in France were dissolved under a new law, forcing the monks to leave their abbey. Following a public auction in 1908, the art lovers Gustave and Madeleine Fayet acquired the abbey, saving it in the process. In those days, many elements from abbeys in Catalonia and France were disassembled stone by stone and shipped to the USA. The Fayets paid for the abbey's restoration, inviting their artist friends to work there. The abbey tour includes Odilon Redon's monumental triptych *Le Jour, La Nuit et le Silence* (1910) as well as the frescoes and stained-glass windows of Richard Burgsthal (1912 and later). Every year, contemporary visual artists are invited to work in situ. Since 2005, the abbey also hosts an annual music festival in the summer, which is directed by Jordi Savall, the virtuoso Catalan viol player and conductor and early music (baroque and Renaissance) expert. A concert in the abbey's historical setting is always a wonderful, unforgettable experience.

46 FESTIVAL D'AIX-EN-PROVENCE

AT: PALAIS DE L'ANCIEN ARCHEVÊCHÉ
13100 Aix-en-Provence
Bouches-du-Rhône
+33 (0)4 34 08 02 17
festival-aix.com

The Festival d'Aix-en-Provence is an internationally renowned annual festival devoted to opera and classical music. First organised in 1948, it mainly takes place in July. Most of the concerts are still performed in open air in the beautiful courtyard of 'l'Ancien Archevêché' – the former archbishop's palace. Over the years, the festival has sought to reach a wider audience, by organising concerts and performances all over the city: in squares and courtyards, but also in the 18th-century Théâtre du Jeu de Paume and at the foot of the Mont Sainte-Victoire. In 2007, the Grand Théâtre de Provence was inaugurated with a performance of Richard Wagner's *Die Walküre*. The state-of-the-art theatre was built especially for the festival.

47 PAUSE GUITARE

AT: DIFFERENT LOCATIONS IN ALBI
2bis boulevard Montebello
81000 Albi
Tarn
+33 (0)5 63 60 55 90
pauseguitare.net

This six-day festival in Albi, which was first organised in 1996, takes place every year in early July with concerts by a wide range of French and international artist. Mano Solo, Patti Smith, Vanessa Paradis, Joe Cocker, Iggy Pop and Sting are just a few of the stars who have performed here in the past. The festival is also committed to promoting new names and upcoming talent from French-speaking Canada. The concerts take place in and around the Jardin National on the fringe of the city centre.

Important
ART FESTIVALS

48 FESTIVAL DE CANNES

AT: PALAIS DES FESTIVALS ET DES CONGRÈS
1 boulevard de la Croisette
06400 Cannes
Alpes-Maritimes
+33 (0)1 53 59 61 00
festival-cannes.com

Say 'Cannes' and most people will immediately think of the prestigious annual film festival, to which the city plays host, in the Palais des Festivals et des Congrès on La Croisette. Every year in May, film stars, directors and producers from all over the world descend on the high-end seaside resort to present their newest films – and to walk the famous red-carpet stairway of the Palais, of course. Starlets make the most of the world-wide media frenzy by getting their photo taken on the beach in varying states of undress. The most prestigious film prize is the Palme d'Or (Golden Palm) for the best film. But the festival isn't for film professionals only; every night during the festival the public flocks to Cinéma de la Plage for a series of open-air film screenings on the beach, often in the company of actors and directors.

49 LES RENCONTRES D'ARLES

34 rue du Docteur Fanton
13200 Arles
Bouches-du-Rhône
+33 (0)4 90 96 76 06
rencontres-arles.com

Les Rencontres d'Arles is the biggest and most important photography festival in the world. First held in 1970, the festival has since taken over the town of Arles every summer, with an overview of the best international contemporary photography. Different exhibitions are set up in dozens of locations in and outside Arles; 17th-century chapels and industrial buildings are exceptionally open to the public.
In 2019, the festival attracted 145.000 visitors for its 50th-anniversary edition. Besides exhibitions, you can also attend performances, talks, panel discussions and book signings. Every major name in photography, from Joel Meyerowitz, Annie Leibovitz, Andres Serrano, Martin Parr, to Nan Goldin, Harry Gruyaert and Hiroshi Sugimoto have been invited over the years.

50 **FESTIVAL D'AVIGNON**

AT: CLOÎTRE SAINT-LOUIS

20 rue du Portail Boquier
84000 Avignon
Vaucluse
+33 (0)4 90 27 66 50
+33 (0)4 90 14 14 60 (billets)
festival-avignon.com

Every year in July, Avignon becomes the theatre capital of Europe. The famous Festival d'Avignon, which was founded in 1947 by Jean Vilar as a modest 'theatre week', has since developed into one of the most important international performing arts festivals. Major theatre and dance productions are staged in the Cour d'Honneur, the vast courtyard of the Palais des Papes. At the same time, the festival fans out across the city, with performances in thirty different locations including gardens, chapels, schools and even quarries. Some of the world's most famous artists have already performed here. Between 2004 and 2013, the festival has had a different artistic director every year, including Thomas Ostermeier, Jan Fabre, Valérie Dréville, Romeo Castellucci and Wajdi Mouawad. In 1966, 'Off Avignon' was established, which has grown into an independent festival with hundreds of performances, from cabaret and circus to dance and stand-up comedy. In 2020, the Festival d'Avignon was cancelled for the first time ever because of the coronavirus pandemic.

51 **FESTIVAL MOLIÈRE**

7bis rue Henri Reboul
34120 Pézenas
Hérault
+33 (0)4 67 32 59 23
ville-pezenas.fr/theatre

Every year, the lovely market town of Pézenas pays tribute to one of its most famous residents with a festival: the playwright Jean-Baptiste Poquelin (1622-1673), better known by his *nom de plume* Molière. After his first theatre company had gone bankrupt in Paris, Molière toured the provinces with an itinerant troupe between 1645 and 1658. They mainly performed comical plays, which were influenced by the Italian Commedia dell'Arte. In 1653, they stopped in Pézenas, where Molière met the Prince of Conti, who enjoyed these comedies tremendously. Conti, who became his patron, was a connoisseur of the genre and together he and Molière analysed the company's performances and discussed the highlights of classic and modern comedy. That is how the foundation was laid for the famous plays that Molière would go on to write later in life, such as *Tartuffe*, *Dom Juan*, *L'École des femmes* and *Le malade imaginaire*. The annual Festival Molière in Pézenas stages dozens of theatre productions in the 19th-century theatre, in squares and courtyards and in the open-air theatre, in addition to talks, panel discussions and film screenings.

Interesting

STREET ART

52 **L'ARLÉSIENNE / MOLIÈRE**

Corner Allées Paul-Riquet and Rue Boïeldieu / Avenue Alphonse Mas and Rue Cordier
34500 Béziers
Hérault

Two convincing wall-sized optical illusions by A. Fresco in Béziers. *L'Arlésienne* refers to a story and a play by Alphonse Daudet, after an idea by Frédéric Mistral, and set to music by Georges Bizet in 1872. The 'Arlésienne' (or girl from Arles) is a mysterious woman whose infidelity drove her lover to suicide. The mural shows her standing on her balcony. Daudet and Mistral talking in the cafe beneath her as Bizet looks on. A few streets over you'll run into the playwright Molière sat on a balcony, writing *Le Dépit Amoureux*, a comedy that premiered in Béziers in 1656. The characters are standing at the window, one floor below.

53 **LE MUR DES AMOUREUX DE PEYNET**

2-8 jard de l'Edem
06110 Le Cannet
Alpes-Maritimes

The French illustrator Raymond Peynet became famous because of a whimsical drawing that he created in 1942 of two young lovers, which found its way onto all kinds of objects, including tie clips, calendars, cups and saucers. The instantly recognisable boy with a bowler hat and girl with a ponytail are visibly smitten with each other. In 1990, Peynet and Guy Ceppa painted a gigantic mural of the two lovers in Le Cannet: the newly-weds float up to heaven, surrounded by white doves. An ode to dreams and *joie de vivre* – the mural is located on the corner of a street called Jard de l'Edem, the 'garden of Eden', by the way. Walk down the street towards the parking garage to see another large mural: the painter Pierre Bonnard in a beach chair. The Musée Bonnard is nearby.

52 L'ARLÉSIENNE / MOLIÈRE

54 MUSÉE À CIEL OUVERT (MACO)

34200 Sète
Hérault
+33 (0)4 99 04 71 71
tourisme-sete.com

Since 2008, more than 30 street artists have left their mark in the port and seaside resort of Sète. The project was aptly named Musée à Ciel Ouvert, the open-air museum. Download the city map with the locations of the murals to start exploring the city.

55 STREET ART TOULOUSE

INFO: OFFICE DE TOURISM DE TOULOUSE AT: DONJON DU CAPITOLE
Square Charles de Gaulle
31000 Toulouse
Haute-Garonne
+33 (0)5 17 42 31 31
toulouse.streetartcities.com
toulouse-visit.com/street-art-toulouse

In the 1980s, the first graffiti and street art pioneers found their way to Toulouse. Influenced by the New York hip-hop scene, local artists like Mosquito started to cover the crumbling walls of the old city centre with their monumental urban art – graffiti was a bad word and illegal in those days. We've come a long way since then: the city centre is now a hipster hangout and has dozens of graffiti art works, all neatly listed on an official website. Toulouse also hosts an annual Street Art Festival.

56 ARTCAN GALLERY

18 rue Dragon
13006 Marseille
Bouches-du-Rhône
+33 (0)6 81 69 90 58
artcan-gallery.com

The ArtCan Gallery was founded in Montpellier in 2016 and later relocated to the centre of Marseille. It now also has a location in Paris. The gallery presents a wide range of Contemporary Urban Art, from graffiti pioneers to the most recent street artists, including well-known in-crowd names such as L'Atlas, Zest, Spyk, Toxic, Levalet and Wes21. From the streets to the gallery.

57 TRAMS IN MONTPELLIER

34000 Montpellier
Hérault

The trams of Montpellier are like moving works of art. In 2000, the Paris-based design duo Garouste & Bonetti decorated the cars of the brand new lines 1 and 2 with stylised white swallows against a blue background and some funky, psychedelic brightly coloured flowers. The French fashion designer Christian Lacroix, who was born in 1951 in Arles, designed the livery for lines 3 and 4. Line 3 features fish and starfish, drawing inspiration for its marine motifs from the illustrations of 18th-century naturalists while the design for line 4 refers to old engravings and the architectural motifs of two nearby monuments, the *Château d'eau du Peyrou* and the *Three Graces* fountain. The blazing golden backdrop is encrusted with pearls, precious stones and jewels.

57 TRAMS IN MONTPELLIER

MODERN ART

museums

58 **MUSÉE D'ART MODERNE DE CÉRET**
8 boulevard
Maréchal Joffre
66400 Céret
Pyrénées-Orientales
+33 (0)4 68 87 27 76
musee-ceret.com

Céret, a tiny village in the foothills of the French Pyrenées, is one of the most important modern art centres. Why? In 1910, the Catalan sculptor Manolo Hugué – or simply Manolo – was the first artist to move to Céret, near the Spanish border. He invited his fellow countryman Pablo Picasso to join him there and soon artists such as Georges Braque, Juan Gris and Fernande Olivier (Picasso's lover at the time) followed in his footsteps. Picasso spent several months in Céret, between 1911 and 1913. He continued his cubist experiments there, with his inseparable companion Georges Braque, creating still lifes and collages for the most part. That is how Céret became the 'Mecca of cubism'. Between 1919 and 1922, the French-Jewish painter Chaïm Soutine lived in Céret and created more than 200 paintings here: portraits of local shop owners and craftsmen, as well as dramatically distorted, stormy landscapes and village scenes. In 1950, the painters Pierre Brune and Frank Burty Haviland decided that they wanted to establish a museum in Céret to bear witness to this remarkable history, with works by the painters who had worked in Céret during the 20th century. Most of these artists liked the idea and donated work to the museum. Picasso, for example, gifted a series of 28 ceramic bowls with bull fighting scenes while Matisse gave 14 drawings that he made in 1905 in the nearby town of Collioure. The result is a remarkably diverse modern art collection. Unfortunately, the museum is currently closed for renovation. Check the website for news about the reopening.

59 MUSÉE CANTINI

19 rue Grignan
13006 Marseille
Bouches-du-Rhône
+33 (0)4 13 94 83 30
musees.marseille.fr

A wonderful collection of 20th-century art in a stately 17th-century city palace. Marseille's Musée Cantini has works by such international giants as Francis Bacon, Alberto Giacometti and Balthus but it also highlights the works of artists who have a connection with Marseille. There are plenty of works by surrealists who fled the Nazis during World War II and lived in the Villa Air-Bel, just outside Marseille. This includes the circle around André Breton with Max Ernst, Wifredo Lam, Marc Chagall and André Masson, among others. The collection also has works by artists who painted Marseille, L'Estaque and the port, such as Raoul Dufy, André Derain and Matisse's friend and contemporary, Albert Marquet, whose work is still unjustly underrated.

60 MUSÉE PAUL VALÉRY

rue François
Desnoyer
34200 Sète
Hérault
+33 (0)4 99 04 76 16
museepaulvalery-sete.fr

The Musée Paul Valéry in Sète is located in a modernist building from the early seventies by the architect Guy Guillaume. In addition to a really good fine arts collection with a survey of French painting from the 19th century to the present, the museum is also home to an extensive collection of manuscripts and memorabilia of Paul Valéry. In 1920, he wrote a long poem titled *Le cimetière marin (The Graveyard by the Sea)*. The museum overlooks the seaman's cemetery where Valéry is buried by the way. The most interesting pieces in the museum are the stylistically diverse paintings featuring Sète, the lake and the old harbour, including work by Albert Marquet, François Desnoyer, Jean Hugo and Topolino. Finally, you can also see the collection of the Lebanese-French poet Salah Stétié here, which includes works by Pierre Alechinsky, among others. The top floor gallery is reserved for temporary contemporary art exhibitions.

62 MUSÉE D'ART MODERNE DE COLLIOURE

61 MUSÉE DES BEAUX-ARTS JULES CHÉRET

33 avenue des Baumettes
06000 Nice
Alpes-Maritimes
+33 890 31 52 34
musee-beaux-arts-nice.org

This quaint (albeit a little dusty and crumbling) museum is situated in a magnificent former palace that belonged to a Ukrainian princess. It was built in 1878. At the time, the Russian upper-class used to travel to Nice to spend the winter there. The museum has a nice collection of paintings by the Van Loo family of artists (18th century) as well as a handful of 19th-century orientalist paintings. The modernist works are the most interesting, however, with an entire room dedicated to the airy, almost phosphorescent urban scenes and landscapes of Raoul Dufy (1877-1953). Jules Chéret's drawings and posters are also worth checking out. More or less forgotten, the painter is the father of the modern poster, long before Toulouse-Lautrec burst on the scene. After training as a lithographer in London from 1859 until 1866, Chéret returned to Paris where he started designing colourful and frivolous posters for cabarets, music halls and theatres like the Folies Bergère and the Moulin Rouge, as well as for JOB, the popular brand of cigarette rolling papers. Chéret's posters are populated with dancing and smoking, free-spirited women and as such he played an indirect role in women's emancipation. Chéret died in Nice in 1932. The city's Musée des Beaux-Arts was named after him.

62 MUSÉE D'ART MODERNE DE COLLIOURE

AT: VILLA PAMS
4 route de Port-Vendres
66190 Collioure
Pyrénées-Orientales
+33 (0)4 68 82 10 19
museecollioure.com

Collioure's nice, little museum is located in the former Villa Pams, which also has a Gothic cloister. The museum's permanent collection includes one drawing by Henri Matisse, *Barques et poulets 'Collioure'*, which he made in Collioure in 1906. The real eye-catcher, however, is the gigantic panorama by Augustin Hanicotte, which he painted between 1925 and 1935 and which depicts the return of the fishing trawlers and the lives of the people who worked on the beach and in the port. The style is somewhere between a Pieter Bruegel painting and a modern comic strip. There are several smaller drawings and paintings of fishing boats, by Hanicotte and Édouard Pignon, and views of Collioure by Julien Descossy and Beatriz Garrigo. The temporary exhibitions focus on themes relating to water, the sea or Collioure, with a well-curated selection of contemporary French and international artists.

63 FONDATION BEMBERG

AT: HÔTEL D'ASSÉZAT
Place d'Assézat
31000 Toulouse
Haute-Garonne
+33 (0)5 61 12 06 89
fondation-bemberg.fr

Fondation Bemberg presents a magnificent collection of old and modern art in a stunning 16th-century Renaissance *hôtel particulier*, which was built for the woad merchant Pierre d'Assézat. The collection was donated to the city of Toulouse in 1995 by the collector Georges Bemberg. Worth a visit for the old masters alone: the art gallery has works by Cranach, Patinir, De Hooch, Clouet and Veronese. But the modern collection is even more impressive. The Bemberg Collection offers a fascinating overview of the main art movements of the late 19th and early 20th centuries, in addition to an outstanding ensemble of paintings by Pierre Bonnard (1867-1947), reflecting the evolution of his style from post-impressionism to his very personal take on fauvism. Other must-sees include an exceptional work by Berthe Morisot (an impressionist wild garden), a remarkable self-portrait from 1910 of the actress Sarah Bernhardt who was also a keen painter, and paintings by Fantin-Latour, Matisse, Marquet and Braque as well as drawings by Degas, Toulouse-Lautrec, Picasso and Modigliani. A museum you can't afford to miss.

64 MUSÉE DE VENCE

2 place du Frêne
06140 Vence
Alpes-Maritimes
+33 (0)4 93 58 15 78
vence.fr/musee-de-vence

This picturesque 17th-century castle in the old centre of Vence opened in 2018 and has a modest but interesting collection of works by Henri Matisse. The permanent exhibition features drawings for the most part (a series of delightful one-line portraits), an edition of the art book *Jazz* (1947) with large-format collages, sketches for an edition of Charles Baudelaire's *Les Fleurs du Mal*, and preliminary studies and designs for La Chapelle du Rosaire (the Chapel of the Rosary) that Matisse built in Vence in the early 1950s. By the way, you can see the chapel in the distance from the square in front of the museum. Also worth checking out: the portraits of Matisse by renowned photographers such as Henri Cartier-Bresson and Robert Capa, which were taken when Matisse lived and worked at Villa Le Rêve in Vence.

65 MUSÉE ALBERT-ANDRÉ

AT: HÔTEL DE VILLE
Place Auguste Mallet
30200 Bagnols-sur-Cèze
Gard
+33 (0)4 66 50 50 56
musees.gard.fr

A small museum with a moving history, in a surprising location – on the second floor of the town hall in Bagnols-sur-Cèze –, that has managed to stay largely under the radar. In 1917, the painter and curator Albert André started collecting artworks by his contemporaries, founding the first contemporary art museum outside Paris. Unfortunately, fire destroyed part of the museum in 1923. André set about rebuilding his collection, asking his artist friends for help. Pierre Bonnard, Maurice Denis, Albert Marquet and Claude Monet donated works. This explains why the museum was later nicknamed 'Le musée de l'amitié': the museum of friendship. In 1971, the collection was significantly expanded by a donation from the art critic George Besson, which included works such as *Le 14 juillet au Havre* by Albert Marquet and *Portrait d'Adèle Besson* by Kees van Dongen. Don't miss *La fenêtre ouverte à Nice* by Henri Matisse, *Le bouquet de roses* by Suzanne Valadon and *L'Implorante*, a bronze statue by Camille Claudel.

66 MUSÉE GRANET

Place Saint-Jean de Malte
13100 Aix-en-Provence
Bouches-du-Rhône
+33 (0)4 42 52 88 32
museegranet-aixenprovence.fr

If you've travelled to Aix-en-Provence, you'll obviously want to see some paintings by the most famous artist who lived and worked in the region: Paul Cézanne (1839-1906), who wanted to make "something solid and lasting out of impressionism". You can see ten of his works at the Musée Granet; unfortunately, no landscape with the Montagne Sainte-Victoire, the legendary mountain that overlooks the city. However, the Musée Granet has a nice variety of works: a still life, a preliminary study for *Les Grandes Baigneuses* – women bathing in the nude –, a portrait of Mrs Cézanne and an early portrait of Cézanne's best friend, the writer Émile Zola, who was also born in Aix-en-Provence. Don't miss the beautiful collection of works by Alberto Giacometti, the sculptor who is known for his fragile elongated human figures, as well as the room dedicated to Nicolas de Staël and the lesser-known artist Pierre Tal-Coat: two completely different painters who both created abstract landscapes. Look for Jean-Baptiste-Camille Corot's *Florence, vue du bord de l'Arno*, from 1834: a virtuoso, lyrical and breathtakingly modern work.

67 MUSÉE DE LA PHOTOGRAPHIE DE MOUGINS

67 rue de l'Église
06250 Mougins
Alpes-Maritimes
+33 (0)4 93 75 85 67
inexhibit.com

This small, intimate 'home' museum can be found next to the church of Mougins and is mostly known for its collection of black-and-white portraits of Pablo Picasso, which André Villers (1930–2016), the French photographer and founder of the museum, made during the last twelve years of the artist's life. Picasso lived in Mougins from 1961 to 1973. André Villers was a personal friend of Picasso's, which gave him the opportunity to photograph the artist at work and as he went about his daily life. Picasso's friendship, sympathy and complicity is palpable in every picture. The photos are presented in an almost domestic setting, in small rooms and on the staircase. The collection also includes portraits of Picasso by other well-known photographers such as Robert Doisneau, Jacques-Henri Lartigue and Edward Quinn.

OUT OF THE ORDINARY

68 FRANCIS BACON MB ART FOUNDATION

21 boulevard d'Italie
98000 Monaco
+377 93 30 30 33
mbartfoundation.com

It is a little-known fact that the Irish-British painter Francis Bacon (1909-1992) spent quite some time in Monaco. A true Francophile and an asthmatic, Bacon appreciated the sea air and the sophisticated ambiance of Monte-Carlo. This also explains why Monaco has a Francis Bacon Foundation. Founded in 2014 by avid Bacon admirer Majid Boustani, it now has a collection of approximately 3000 items belonging to or relating to Francis Bacon, including paintings, furniture designs, photos and an extensive library and archive.
Bacon lived and worked in Monaco from July 1946 until the early 1950s. He was already exploring the idea of his pope paintings – variations on Velázquez's magnificent portrait of Pope Innocent X (c. 1650) – at the Hôtel Ré (3 avenue Saint-Charles). But Bacon also loved to gamble at the famous casino in Monte-Carlo, spending several days at a time there. A risk taker, he enjoyed the element of chance, an element that was also inherent to his painting process. It was also in Monaco that he intensively studied portraiture, culminating in the creation of a series of searing *Heads* and establishing him as a leading figurative post-war artist. Bacon regularly returned to Monaco, with friends, family and lovers in the years after. His last visit was in 1990, two years before his death. The Francis Bacon Foundation is located in a beautifully restored belle-époque building. Unfortunately it is dwarfed by Monaco's many high-rises. The foundation's website includes an interactive map of places that Bacon liked to frequent. Free guided tours of the MB Art Foundation by appointment only.

69 MUSÉE INTERNATIONAL DES ARTS MODESTES

23 quai Maréchal de Lattre de Tassigny
34200 Sète
Hérault
+33 (0)4 99 04 76 44
miam.org

What does the label *'arts modestes'* cover? Almost everything according to this rather special museum in Sète. Arts that are forgotten, marginal, obscured, and the art of amateur painters, among others. So not 'Art' with a capital A but puppets, amateur cinema, pulp fiction and pornography, as well as punk, sci-fi novels, art brut and aspects of underground culture or toys and gadgets from popular and commercial culture. It's like Ali Baba's cave, only more surprising.

70 MUSÉE LES ARCADES

AT: CENTRE HOSPITALIER DE MONTFAVET
Avenue de la Pinède
84918 Avignon
Vaucluse
+33 (0)4 90 03 90 90
ch-montfavet.fr

The Centre hospitalier de Montfavet – a psychiatric hospital just outside Avignon – is also home to a small museum about the history of the hospital and the evolution of psychiatry and mental health treatments in general. Part of the museum is dedicated to the sculptor Camille Claudel, who was confined here from 1914 until her death in 1943. The artist, who had been the assistant and lover of the sculptor Auguste Rodin for ten years – from 1883 until 1893 – was committed because she exhibited signs of paranoia after Rodin refused to marry her despite making promises to the contrary. This signalled the end of their affair. She had at least one abortion, which soured her relationship with her ultra-Catholic brother Paul Claudel. Her physicians suggested reintegrating Claudel in her family environment as early as 1920, but her mother refused because she was 'the black sheep of the family'. The artist would live in the asylum for 30 years. The letters on display at Les Arcades attest to her tragic fate. Original furniture and photos of Camille and her work evoke her daily life in the hospital. You can see more of her compelling body of work at the Musée Camille Claudel in Nogent-sur-Seine and at the Musée Rodin in Paris. Musée Les Arcades is only open on Wednesday afternoons. A unique experience.

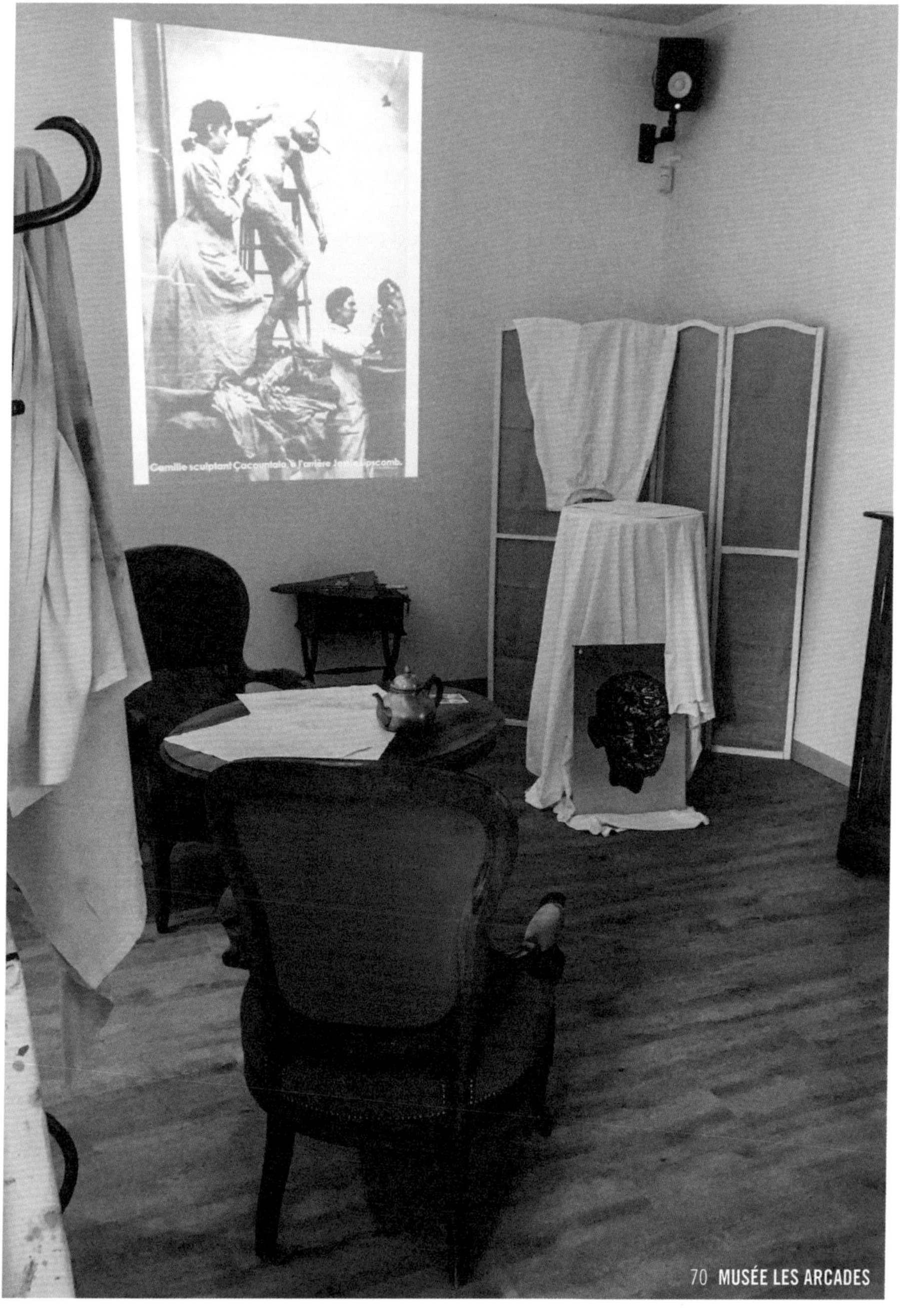
Camille sculptant Çacountala, à l'arrière

71 VILLA ARSON

20 avenue Stephen Liégeard
06105 Nice
Alpes-Maritimes
+33 (0)4 92 07 73 73
villa-arson.org

The Villa Arson is a one-of-a-kind national art institution: the art academy, arts centre, an artists' residence, and specialised library on the premises are all dedicated to contemporary art. The architecture is just as unique, however: the institution's activities revolve around the main building, an 18th-century vivid red ochre villa, which formerly belonged to a wealthy French merchant called Pierre-Joseph Arson. In the 1960s, Michel Marot built a singular labyrinthine concrete structure in the large Mediterranean garden: a small city with streets, squares and terraces. Here works by contemporary artists such as Dan Graham, Bertrand Lavier and Maurizio Nannucci engage in a dialogue with the vegetation and the architecture. Villa Arson has an excellent programme, exhibiting works by young, contemporary artists and the academy's own students.

72 MUSÉE D'ARTS BRUT

1 rue Beau Séjour
34000 Montpellier
Hérault
+33 (0)4 67 79 62 22
musee-artbrut-montpellier.com

An unconventional museum that is home to a dazzling array of works by equally unconventional artists. Creative spirits who live on the fringes of society, who lead an isolated life, who have no formal artistic training, who have been diagnosed with an autism spectrum disorder or even (temporarily) ended up in a mental health unit. Their works are qualified as *'art brut'* or 'outsider art'. The directness of expression, the spontaneity, and the natural roughness of these artworks make a big impression, often eliciting a strong emotional response. In many cases, they are created with simple means or (unusual) materials at hand. The museum's collection comprises approximately 2000 works, of which 750 are on display. A visual overload. Consider yourself warned.

73 **MUSÉE INTERNATIONAL D'ART NAÏF ANATOLE JAKOVSKY**

AT: CHÂTEAU SAINTE-HÉLÈNE

Avenue de Fabron
06200 Nice
Alpes-Maritimes
+33 (0)4 93 71 78 33
nice.fr/fr/culture

A bit of an outlier in Nice's cultural offering. This museum provides an overview of naïve art from the 18th century to the present. The collection features works by artists from around the world, including lesser-known and world-famous artists such as Le Douanier Rousseau – the French painter whose work can be found in all the leading art collections – and Grandma Moses, an American folk artist who began painting in earnest at the grand age of 78 and whose work has been reproduced on stamps and postcards. The museum was founded after Anatole and Renée Jakovsky donated their art collection to the city of Nice. Housed in Château Sainte-Hélène, the former residence of the perfumer François Coty, the museum is surrounded by a stunning garden with rare aromatic plants.

74 MUSÉE INGRES BOURDELLE

19 rue de l'Hôtel-de-ville
82000 Montauban
Tarn-et-Garonne
+33 (0)5 63 22 12 91
museeingres bourdelle.com

Two for the price of one. One museum dedicated to two artists who were both born in Montauban and who went on to enjoy a spectacular (inter)national career: the legendary painter Jean-Auguste-Dominique Ingres and the sculptor Émile-Antoine Bourdelle. Ingres (1780-1867) is mainly known for his extremely classical portraits – including that of the 'Emperor' Napoleon on his imperial throne – and his paintings of the backs of female nudes. But he was also an excellent violin player. As he opted to pursue a career in painting, he only played the violin in his spare time, however. In French, the expression *'un violon d'Ingres'* has become synonymous for a pastime or hobby. You can see his violin in the museum, along with other personal belongings and his paintings, of course. Ingres donated more than seventy canvases to his native city in addition to more than four thousand drawings. Bourdelle (1861-1929) is an entirely different cup of tea: a sculptor who was fascinated by (classical) heroes, great masters (including Beethoven) and human power. One of his best-known sculptures is that of the Greek mythical hero Hercules, as he draws his bow to kill the monstrous birds that feed on human flesh. The museum owns a plaster modello of this sculpture.

75 **MUSÉE MARCEL-LENOIR**
AT: CHÂTEAU DE MONTRICOUX
56 Grand'Rue
82800 Montricoux
Tarn-et-Garonne
+33 (0)5 63 67 26 48
marcel-lenoir.com

Marcel-Lenoir (1872-1931), the pseudonym of Jules Oury, was an interesting painter, who is a difficult artist to pin down. He was also a draughtsman and a jewellery designer, and a contemporary of Matisse, Braque and Modigliani. Although born in Montauban, he later moved to Paris, the then capital of the avant-garde, where he created works that held the middle between symbolism and art nouveau. Giacometti, who also lived in Montparnasse, admired his work and called him a 'giant of his time'. At his death, aged 59, in Montricoux, he was almost completely forgotten. Marcel-Lenoir was a difficult man. He also refused to be affiliated with any specific art movement, trying his hand at a wide range of styles. The castle in Montricoux, which has a cosy and somewhat old-fashioned ambience, offers an interesting survey of his remarkable oeuvre, with nudes and saints.

76 **MAISON ALEXANDRA DAVID-NÉEL**
27 avenue du Maréchal Juin
04000 Digne-les-Bains
Alpes-de-Haute-Provence
+33 (0)4 92 31 32 38
alexandra-david-neel.fr

Alexandra David-Néel (1868-1969) was a force of nature. Her life reads like an adventure novel. What's more, she lived to 100. The daughter of a French father and a Belgian mother, David-Néel trained as a pianist and opera singer, performing in the opera houses of Hanoi, Athens and Tunis. She then briefly worked as a journalist but soon found her true calling as an explorer, orientalist and feminist. She was the first western woman to visit Lhasa, the capital of Tibet, in 1922, after which she made her way to China, Japan, Mongolia and back to Tibet. She wrote dozens of books about her travels and was the first person to introduce the West to Buddhism, influencing the American beat poets, among others. Alexandra did most of her writing at her home in Digne-les-Bains, which she bought in 1928 and which she named *'Samten Dzong'* or fortress of meditation. You must book to visit her house and study and see all the books and art treasures that she brought back from her distant travels. The garden and museum are freely accessible.

77 **MUSÉE GASSENDI**

64 boulevard Gassendi
+33 (0)4 92 31 45 29
musee-gassendi.org

CAIRN
10 montée Bernard Dellacasagrande
+33 (0)4 92 62 11 73
cairncentredart.org

4000 Digne-les-Bains
Alpes-De-Haute-Provence

Art as a journey of discovery. Literally. First you visit the 17th-century house of the Musée Gassendi in Digne, where old and contemporary art are presented alongside cabinets of curiosities and objects relating to local history. The museum trail is conceived as a fictional mountain climb. After that, it's time for the real thing. The Musée Gassendi invites contemporary artists to work in situ, in nature. Since 2000, artists have created works in the mountains, with the support of the CAIRN (Informal Art Center for Nature Research, with a nod to the English word 'cairn'). They are inspired by nature, studying the relationship of man with his surroundings, while also taking climatological challenges and social change into account. Walk the trail to see their artworks – there are 20 different trails to choose from. You can even spend the night in some of the artworks, such as Andy Goldsworthy's 'Refuge d'Art', if you're on a multi-day hike. CAIRN exhibits works by David Renaud, herman de vries, Joan Fontcuberta and Richard Nonas, among others. Bring sturdy shoes.

78 **MUSÉE GOYA**

1 rue de l'Hôtel de ville
81100 Castres
Tarn
+33 (0)5 63 71 59 30
www.ville-castres.fr

You wouldn't expect to find a handful of paintings by the famous Spanish painter Goya (1746-1828) as well as the largest collection of Spanish art in France outside the Louvre in a town like Castres but there it is. In 1894, Pierre Briguiboul, the son of a painter and an art collector from Castres, bequeathed three canvases by Goya to the municipality. The Louvre then kindly loaned a series of Spanish artworks to the city, while the city continued to add to its Spanish collection, which now includes works by Velázquez, Miró and Picasso. The four famous series of prints by Goya, which include *The Disasters of War*, among others, are exhibited for short periods of time only because they are so fragile.

79 CHAPELLE SAINT-JEAN

AT: FERME DE FONT ROBERT

Avenue de la Bastide
04160 Château-Arnoux-Saint-Auban
Alpes-de-Haute-Provence
+33 (0)4 92 64 02 64

Surprising and groundbreaking. In the mountains above his native village of Château-Arnoux-Saint-Auban, the French sculptor Bernar Venet (b. 1941) designed the interior of the simple 17th-century Chapelle Saint-Jean. The artist only used corten steel, his trademark material. The church benches are made from enormous steel crossbeams, the cross behind the simple altar is tilted and leans against a wall, while some of the stained-glass windows look more dynamic in spite of the fact that they have been executed in austere black and white. The end result is a minimalistic, pure and breathtakingly homogenous design.

79 CHAPELLE SAINT-JEAN

79 CHAPELLE SAINT-JEAN

NEMAUSUS

BUILDINGS

MODERNIST
buildings

80 **MUSÉE FERNAND LÉGER**
255 chemin du
Val de Pôme
06410 Biot
Alpes-Maritimes
+33 (0)4 92 91 50 20
en.musees-nationaux-alpesmaritimes.fr

Expect the unexpected. This immense building, which is dedicated to the art of Fernand Léger, is located just outside the village of Biot (the 't' is pronounced). The French-Russian architect Andreï Svetchine designed this monumental museum, which opened its doors in 1960, five years after Fernand Léger died. Shortly before his death, he had purchased some land, hoping to turn it into an open-air museum for his sculptures. His wife Nadia Léger decided to build a proper museum to showcase her husband's work instead. The gigantic, colourful mosaics are just as eye-catching as the building's monumental dimensions. The façade has been decorated with an oblong, 500-square-metre mosaic, after a design by Léger for the stadium in Hanover. The museum – a bright, open and airy space – offers an excellent survey of Léger's oeuvre: the famous, boldly simplified treatments of workers and machines, which contributed to his fame, as well as his surprising, impressionist beginnings and the later abstract works. Léger's political commitment to labour and freedom is manifested in all the works on display.

80 MUSÉE FERNAND LÉGER

81 **VILLA NOAILLES**

Montée Noailles
83400 Hyères
Var
+33 (0)4 98 08 01 98
villanoailles-hyeres.com

This monumental, modernist hillside villa is situated in the hills that overlook Hyères, near the ruins of the old castle. It was built between 1923 and 1925, after a design by the architect Robert Mallet-Stevens. It is also one of the earliest examples of this modern style in France. The client, Vicomte Charles de Noailles, wanted an extremely functional home, stripped of any ornamentation, with as much daylight as possible. The many tiny rooms make it feel somewhat labyrinthine, however. Various influential designers contributed to the Villa, including Marcel Breuer, Theo van Doesburg, Eileen Gray and Charlotte Perriand. Since 2003, the Villa Noailles has become an exhibition space for architecture, fashion, design and photography. Parking near the villa can be quite complicated. The access roads are steep and narrow.

82 CHAPELLE MATISSE

466 avenue
Henri Matisse
06140 Vence
Alpes-Maritimes
+33 (0)4 93 58 03 26
chapellematisse.com

Henri Matisse regarded the Chapelle du Rosaire in Vence as his masterpiece and the crowning glory of his career. It is a *Gesamtkunstwerk*: the architecture, the large drawings on ceramic tiles, the stained-glass windows, the furniture and the liturgical robes have all been designed by Matisse. The simple but impressive chapel essentially is an ode to light, colour and space: the vivid yellow and blue stained-glass windows exquisitely reflect the light on the white marble floors. The story of how this chapel was built is also quite interesting. In 1942, Matisse underwent abdominal surgery, after which he advertised for a night nurse: Monique Bourgeois was a kindred spirit and soon became one of his models. Two years later, Monique entered the Dominican convent at Vence, a decision that greatly irritated Matisse, who was a liberal. They kept in touch, nonetheless. When the Dominican order of Vence wanted to build a new chapel, Matisse offered his assistance. He ended up taking on the entire project. His approach, the atypical architecture and, in particular, his unique, stripped-down and almost naïve treatment of the Stations of the Cross, with an emphasis on the brutality and horror of Christ's suffering, gave rise to conflicts with the higher clergy. Monique – or *soeur* Jacques-Marie as she was now known – continued to support him, however. Picasso also waded into the fray: he did not understand why an atheist like Matisse would want to design a chapel. The chapel was inaugurated in 1951. By then, Matisse was too ill to attend. A deeply moving, intensely personal masterpiece, that has lost none of its power.

83 **CITÉ RADIEUSE LE CORBUSIER**

280 boulevard
Michelet
13008 Marseille
Bouches-du-Rhône
+33 (0)4 91 77 80 74
citeradieuse-marseille.com

The French-Swiss architect Le Corbusier (pseudonym of Charles-Édouard Jeanneret) built this revolutionary, imposing and colourful block of flats between 1946 and 1952. It is 137 metres long, standing at a height of 56 metres and comprises 337 flats with 23 different layouts, for households of one to ten persons. Most flats are duplexes and extend from one side of the building to the other, meaning they get light and air, both from the city and the sea. Shortly after World War II, France had an acute housing shortage: an excellent opportunity for Le Corbusier to put his theories about a new way of living and the vertical city into practice. The concrete building rests on tall piles, ensuring people can circulate in the space beneath it. There are various shops on the third floor: a baker, the Le Ventre de l'Architecte restaurant, the Hôtel Le Corbusier and the Imbernon bookshop/publishing house, which sells an excellent selection of architecture books. The spacious rooftop terrace – an architectural gem with stunning panoramic views over Marseille and the sea – is occupied by a shallow paddling pool for children, a solarium, an open-air theatre and even a small school, which has since been converted into an artist's residence. Part of the building can be visited freely, but you must obviously respect the residents' privacy at all times. Request a guided tour and a visit of a model flat through the Office de Tourisme Marseille: *www.marseille-tourisme.com.*

83 CITÉ RADIEUSE LE CORBUSIER

84 VILLA E-1027 EILEEN GRAY, LE CABANON & LES UNITÉS DE CAMPING LE CORBUSIER

Sentier Massolin (Villa) / Avenue Le Corbusier
INFO: ASSOCIATION CAP MODERNE
Avenue de la Gare
06190 Roquebrune-Cap-Martin
Alpes-Maritimes
+33 (0)4 92 15 01 41
capmoderne.monuments-nationaux.fr

Is it a house or a small ocean liner at anchor? The Irish designer and architect Eileen Gray built her flat-roofed, concrete white villa – an icon of modernist architecture – between 1926 and 1929 among the rocks near the sea and Roquebrune-Cap-Martin, overlooking Monaco Bay. She designed the villa with her fellow architect and lover Jean Badovici, hence the villa's peculiar name: E-1027. E stands for Eileen, while the figures refer to the letters of the alphabet: 10-J(ean), 2-B(adovici) and 7-G(ray). The villa seems much larger than it actually is, because of its hyperrational layout, the ingenious use of movable partitions, the central open living area and the large windows with a sea view. Eileen Gray designed everything herself, from the sofa down to the rugs on the floor. For all the work she put into it, she did not get to enjoy it that much after her split from Badovici. He inherited the house and occupied it until his death in 1956. In the meantime, one of Badovici's good friends, the architect Le Corbusier frequently stayed at Roquebrune. He built his famous wooden Cabanon next to the villa: a simple 'hut' (measuring 3,66 by 3,66 metres), which was both primitive and ingenious, based on his anthropometric scale of proportions, called Modulor. He holidayed in his Cabanon for many years, in close proximity with nature. He would go on to build a series of colourful Unités de Camping, according to the same principles. The Villa E-1027, the Cabanon and the Unités de Camping can only be visited with a guide. You must book ahead. Parking near the meeting point – the train station of Roquebrune-Cap-Martin – is a perilous undertaking. You're better to take the train.

84 VILLA E-1027 – EILEEN GRAY

84 LE CABANON – LE CORBUSIER

85 ÉGLISE + CLOÎTRE SAINT-TROPHIME

HOLY *places and* **RELIGIOUS** *sites*

85 **ÉGLISE + CLOÎTRE SAINT-TROPHIME**

6 place de la République
13200 Arles
Bouches-du-Rhône
+33 (0)4 90 96 07 38
patrimoine.ville-arles.fr

The 12th-century Church of Saint-Trophime in the centre of Arles is a gem. The portal with its stunning sculptures is one of the finest examples of a breathtaking triumphant arch, while the cloister is the epitome of elegance and harmony. Take the time to admire the delicate columns and the beautifully sculpted capitals, with human figures, plants and flowers rendered in exquisite detail. You can also walk on the roof of the cloister, from where you have a view of the robust church tower and the town of Arles. Every summer, the annual Rencontres d'Arles photo festival hosts temporary exhibitions in the refectory and the convent.

86 **ÉGLISE DES JACOBINS**

Place des Jacobins
31000 Toulouse
Haute-Garonne
+33 (0)5 61 22 23 82
jacobins.toulouse.fr

The exterior of the 14th-century brick Church of the Jacobins in Toulouse looks forbidding, simple and massive. The interior, by contrast, is a superb example of exquisite architecture. At the far end of the 80-metre-long nave stands a 28-metre-tall column, called the palm tree, which supports the immense ribbed vault (22 ribs!) and to which all the ribs converge like the leaves of a stone palm tree. Quite unique!

87 CATHÉDRALE SAINT-NICOLAS

Avenue Nicolas II
06000 Nice
Alpes-Maritimes
+33 (0)9 81 09 53 45
sobor.fr

The Eastern (or Russian) Orthodox cathedral adds a surprising, exotic twist to the urban landscape of Nice, with its onion-shaped domes and gilded spires. What's more, it's also the largest Russian Orthodox church in Western Europe and undoubtedly one of the most beautiful. The wealthy Russian nobility liked to spend the winter in Nice, a custom that started in the 19th century. They formed a real enclave, prompting the need for a Russian church where they could profess their faith. In 1859, a first church was built at the initiative of Tsarina Alexandra Fedorovna but it soon proved too small for the congregation. Work on the current building started in 1903. Mikhail Preobrazhensky, an architect and an academic of the University of Saint Petersburg designed it. The cathedral was completed in 1912. Tsar Nicholas II financed its construction and costs nor efforts were spared to turn it into a real gem: gilded crosses and glazed roof tiles from Italy, brick from Germany and mosaics that were created in situ by Russian artists. The opulent interior has been decorated with frescoes, wood carvings and precious icons. The chapel next to the Cathedral is dedicated to Nicolas, the son of Tsar Alexander II, who died in Nice aged 20 in 1865 from meningitis.

88 ÉGLISE SAINTE-MARIE-MADELEINE

Place de l'Église
06410 Biot
Alpes-Maritimes
biot-tourisme.com

Keep your eyes peeled because before you know it you'll have walked past it. The Église Sainte-Marie-Madeleine is completely surrounded by buildings and seems to have been hiding at one end of Place des Arcades in Biot. The tiny, lovely village church was built under the street level, meaning you – exceptionally – have to walk down a staircase when entering the church. On the left side of this intimate church, you can see a nice altarpiece by Louis Bréa, one of the 'primitive' painters from Nice. He painted this altarpiece of *Our Lady of the Rosary (Vierge du Rosaire)* – one of his best works – with vivid colours and lots of gilt leaf, dating from c. 1510. In the centre panel, the *Virgin of Mercy (Vierge de la Miséricorde)* folds open her cloak to symbolically protect everyone – the pope and ordinary citizens – against bubonic plague.

87 CATHÉDRALE SAINT-NICOLAS

89 BASILIQUE NOTRE-DAME DE LA GARDE

Rue Fort du Sanctuaire
13281 Marseille
Bouches-du-Rhône
+33 (0)4 91 13 40 80
notredamedelagarde.fr

The Catholic basilica of Marseille, which was built between 1853 and 1864, is located on the city's highest natural point, on a hill to the south of the Old Port, at an altitude of 161 metres. The city's best-known symbol, it towers above Marseille, offering magnificent views over the docks, the islands offshore and the *calanques* (coves). The bell tower of Notre-Dame rises up to a height of 41 metres, topped by a 12,5-metre spire, which supports the monumental (11,2-metre) copper gilded statue of the Virgin and Child. The many ex votos in the basilica attest to the fact that it has always been a place of pilgrimage. Some of them are in the shape of ships or airplanes. Besides the traditional ex votos with supplications and expressions of gratitude for a (miraculous) recovery, you'll also find ex votos here for Olympique Marseille, the city's football team, pleading for a victory.

90 ABBAYE DE GELLONE

Place de la Liberté
34150 Saint-Guilhem-le-Désert
Hérault
saintguilhem-valleeherault.fr

This simple, 11th-century abbey is a heavenly haven in Saint-Guilhem and its bustling town centre. The abbey was founded by Guilhem, a knight in the entourage of Charlemagne, who withdrew here to live as a monk. The abbey later became a place to stop for pilgrims en route to Compostella. Only half of the former abbey has been preserved. After the French Revolution, the abbey was dismantled and sold at auction. Parts of the cloisters were subsequently acquired by John D. Rockefeller, who donated them to the Metropolitan Museum of Art in New York. And this is where you can still find them today, as part of The Cloisters in Washington Heights. A nice pond has since been added to the space where the cloisters once stood at Saint-Guilhem. Each summer, the abbey's lapidarium is transformed into a contemporary exhibition space.

91 CHAPELLE NOTRE-DAME DE VIE

501-869 chemin de la Chapelle
06250 Mougins
Alpes-Maritimes
+33 (0)4 92 92 14 00 (office de tourisme)
mougins-tourisme.fr

Notre-Dame de Vie at Mougins, which originally dates from the 12th century, was rebuilt in 1655. Winston Churchill painted this chapel on four occasions in the 1930s, while staying with the Guinness family, who owned the mas next door, before Picasso bought it from them. In 1931, a monumental tomb was erected in the chapel garden for the Guinness family. Bridget, the wife of Benjamin Seymour Guinness, is buried here. It was Benjamin who first spotted the Mas de Notre-Dame de Vie in 1925. The banker and philanthropist converted the traditional farmhouse into a luxurious villa. Picasso, who was a family friend, became a regular visitor and eventually ended up buying the house from their son Loel. He famously adored the cypress-lined path and the Italianate atmosphere of the chapel and grounds. After Picasso's death in 1973, his wife Jacqueline Roque lived in the house until she committed suicide in 1986.

92 CHAPELLE DE LA SANTONNE

Chemin de la Santonne
84400 Apt
Vaucluse
domainede lasantonne.com

This tiny chapel is completely unique. Built in stone, it seems to blend in almost organically with the surrounding landscape and the hillside on which it is built, with its curving, dynamic lines. The architect Roger Petit was an English teacher and a passionate lover of all things modern art. He resolved to build a chapel if he returned from the Algerian War alive. He kept his word. Construction started in 1960. Petit worked to his own design, building the church single-handedly, with the stones he found on his own land. The interior is equally surprising: a shell-like vault, an abstract Christ figure hewn from the wood of an olive tree and the light that is reflected through several stained-glass windows. As if the Catalan architect Gaudí had gone back to basics ...

93 SYNAGOGUE DE CARPENTRAS

15 place Maurice Charretier
84200 Carpentras
Vaucluse
+33 (0)4 90 63 39 97
synagoguedecarpentras.fr

In addition to being one of the oldest synagogues in France, the Synagogue of Carpentras is definitely one of the most extravagantly decorated. There has been a Jewish place of worship in this location since 1367. The current 18th-century building, which is still in use today, is an elaborate rococo affair. In addition to a place of prayer, this synagogue also has a *mikveh* – a bath with natural streaming water used for ritual immersion and cleansing – and a bakery where unleavened bread *(matzah)* was baked until the early 20th century.
There were Jewish settlements in Provence as early as the 1st century AD. In 1306, the French King Philip the Fair (not to be confused with the Duke of Burgundy who came much later) expelled the Jews from his realm, after which they moved to the papal lands at Avignon, among others. Jewish communities were thus established in Avignon, Carpentras, Cavaillon and L'Isle-sur-la-Sorgue. After 1450, Jews were only allowed to have pawn shops or secondhand shops and were forced to live in the same street, called a *carrière*, which was closed off at both ends by gates. That is how the ghetto of Carpentras was established in 1461. It was only abolished after the French Revolution (1789-1799). The synagogue is all that remains of this originally Jewish quarter.

CASTLES *and* FORTS

94 FORT SAINT-JEAN

Promenade Louis Brauquier
13002 Marseille
Bouches-du-Rhône
+33 (0)4 96 13 80 90
marseilletourisme.fr

Fort Saint-Jean resembles a small city: with streets, squares, a church and a hospital – a wonderful place to get lost. The large, impressive fortification dates from the 14th century, the distinctive square and round towers were added later. Fort Saint-Jean has undergone a radical restoration in recent years. The former glory of its sand-coloured stone has been restored, making it one of the most popular monuments in Marseille. A footbridge connects the fort with the city. A second, longer footbridge runs to the Mucem (Musée des Civilisations de l'Europe et de la Méditerranée) and offers breathtaking views over the port and the city. Fort Saint-Jean is actually part of the Mucem, which hosts exhibitions in various venues throughout the old fort.

95 LE CASTELLET

84560 Ménerbes
Vaucluse
menerbes.fr

The French-Russian painter Nicolas de Staël was a restless soul: he travelled to the coastline of the (English) Channel, the South of France, Spain, Sicily and even North Africa for inspiration, painting landscapes and nudes at the crossroads of figuration and abstraction. Following the success of his 1953 exhibition in New York and his representation by the leading gallerist Paul Rosenberg, de Staël bought Le Castellet, a manor house in Ménerbes, near the cemetery and the Église Saint-Luc. He renovated the rundown house himself, moved his studio there, and took his inspiration from the landscape and the light of the Luberon. He didn't live there for long, though. He regularly commuted between Le Castellet and his studio-flat in Antibes, where he committed suicide on 16 March 1955. De Staël's son Jérôme still lives at Le Castellet, which is why it is closed to the public.

 MUCEM (FORT SAINT-JEAN ON THE LEFT AND J4 ON THE RIGHT)

96 **CHÂTEAU DE PENNE**

Rue du Château
81140 Penne
Tarn
+33 (0)5 63 55 71 09
chateau-penne.com

The view is quite breathtaking: the ruins of the 12th-century Penne Castle seem to elude gravity, perched at the top of a promontory. The climb up to the château is gruelling but worth it. The restoration started in 2006: in the summer you can often see stonemasons at work here, in traditional medieval costumes. The informative signs around the site give visitors an excellent idea of medieval life. From the keep you have a splendid view over the village, the green valley and the meandering Aveyron.

97 **LE BASTION – MUSÉE JEAN COCTEAU**

Quai Napoléon III –
Bastion du Vieux Port
06500 Menton
Alpes-Maritimes
+33 (0)4 93 18 82 61
museecocteau menton.fr

In 1957, Menton wanted to forge closer links with Jean Cocteau (1889-1963) after the artist painted the new marriage room at the registry office. The city made the old bastion (a small 17th-century fort) available to him, for the Musée Jean Cocteau, which the artist was free to use as he saw fit. From 1962, Cocteau made plans for the building's restoration, designing the layout and drawing up a list of works that could be exhibited there. Following Cocteau's sudden death on 11 October 1963, the project briefly ground to a standstill. Édouard Dermit, Cocteau's adoptive son and heir, continued his work, based on the artist's plans and instructions. The modest museum – a stone and wood cocoon – opened its doors in 1966. What makes this museum so interesting is that Cocteau designed everything himself, including the display cabinets. Check out the pebble mosaics, that are integrated in the outside walls and floors, in keeping with the traditional pavements of Menton. The museum organises temporary exhibitions, with works from the Cocteau bequest, dedicated to one specific theme from this extraordinary artist's rich oeuvre: fashion, ceramics, textile design, film, literature…

98 **CITADELLE SAINT-ELME – MUSÉE VOLTI**

Chemin de Ronde
06230 Villefranche-sur-Mer
Alpes-Maritimes
+33 (0)4 93 76 33 27
villefranche-sur-mer.fr

It is an extraordinary sight. Dozens of sculptures by the sculptor Antoniucci Volti (1915-1989) are installed throughout the 16th-century citadel of Villefranche-sur-Mer, in particular in the large courtyard and in the casemates. The contrast between the polished elegance of his female nudes and the impregnable robustness of the military fortifications is quite something. But, in addition to the Musée Volti, the citadel is also home to a second museum: paintings and works on paper by Henri Bernard Goetz (1909-1989) and his wife Christine Boumeester (1904-1971) – explorations of figuration and abstraction – are exhibited in a number of the vaulted rooms of the old barracks. Goetz and Boumeester bequeathed their own works and their art collection to the city of Villefranche. Their collection includes works by friends such as Picasso, Picabia and Miró.

99 GARE SAINT-CHARLES

100 GARE D'AVIGNON TGV

Unique
RAILWAY STATIONS

garesetconnexions.sncf

99 **GARE SAINT-CHARLES**

Square Narvik
13232 Marseille
Bouches-du-Rhône

As you walk out of the railway station at Marseille-Saint-Charles, you will be amazed by the sweeping views over the city. The station is situated on a hill on the fringe of the city centre. In the old days, the station was an important stop for intercontinental travellers from European cities, who arrived here to take the boat to Africa, the Middle East or the Far East. These days are long behind us and we mostly rely on airplanes for this nowadays. But the monumental, baroque staircase that you have to walk down to get into the city is still there. It was officially inaugurated in 1925 and is decorated with sculptures of lions, children and allegorical figures that refer to the history of Marseille and its port, agriculture and fisheries, and the former French colonies in Africa and Asia.

100 **GARE D'AVIGNON TGV**

Place de l'Europe
84000 Avignon
Vaucluse

The TGV station of Avignon, which is situated 5 kilometres to the south-west of the city centre, resembles a huge, upturned canoe, made from concrete, glass and steel. Its elongated interior – 350 metres long and 14,5 metres tall – is reminiscent of a modern cathedral. The railway station was built in 2001 to a design by Jean-Marie Duthilleul and Jean-François Blassel. The platforms are located above the station hall because the high-speed line runs across the River Rhône on a viaduct. Moreover, the architects also took the potential of flooding in the area into account.

101 GARE DE MONACO-MONTE-CARLO

Place Sainte-Dévote
98000 Monaco

The railway station of Monaco-Monte-Carlo dates from 1999 and was built entirely underground: the station, which is made from polished concrete and clad with tropical hardwood, is situated in a 466-metre-long tunnel, which runs under the Principality. Originally, there were two stations above-ground, one of which was close to the port. But because tiny Monaco wants to utilise every square metre of its territory to construct housing on it, the decision to dig a tunnel under the Principality was made as early as the 1960s. The current station is located more inland, on the border with France. The result is a curious situation: half of the underground parking garage on the north side of the station is in French territory, the other half is on Monegasque land. The boundary is indicated with a dotted line in the ceiling and two inverted triangles. This means you will be driving back and forth between the two countries in the car park.

102 GARE DE PERPIGNAN

1 place Salvador-Dalí
66000 Perpignan
Pyrénées-Orientales

In 1963, the world-famous Catalan surrealist artist Salvador Dalí proclaimed Perpignan Station to be the cosmogonic centre of the universe. "I always have my most brilliant ideas in Perpignan Station", he famously said. Two years later, he painted the monumental canvas *La gare de Perpignan*, which is now in the Museum Ludwig in Cologne. According to legend, his students later added a Daliesque, psychedelic painting to the ceiling of the ticket office hall. In reality, however, the French railway company SNCF commissioned the design. Unfortunately, the painting was lost during the renovation in 2014. On the other side of Avenue du Général de Gaulle, in Place de Catalogne, you can see a monumental, fun tribute to Dalí by the French artist couple Les Pritchard's: *Dalí en lévitation* (2000). The artist veers up from a giant red chair, like a jack in the box, and gazes at his cherished station.

103 LA CIOTAT

866 avenue
de la Gare
13600 La Ciotat
Bouches-du-Rhône

This simple station building has written history. This is entirely the merit of two film pioneers, the Lumière brothers. Their father, Antoine Lumière, had a factory in Lyon that specialised in photographic equipment. His two sons, Louis and Auguste, shared his passion, developing a device that could simultaneously record, develop and project images: they called it the *cinématographe* and applied for a patent for their invention on 30 March 1895. So what does La Ciotat have to do with this, you ask? In 1893, Antoine had a holiday cottage built there, where the family spent their annual summer holidays. While the Lumière brothers shot their first film at factory gates in Lyon, approximately half of the first twenty films they made were shot in La Ciotat in the summer and autumn of 1895. Their most famous film undoubtedly is that of the steam train entering La Ciotat's station. Apparently, the first spectators in a cinema recoiled in fear because they thought that a real train was barrelling towards them. Because of the audience's reaction, this film, which lasts a mere 50 seconds, is often called the first 'horror film'. The many travellers that are getting on and off the train include Joséphine Lumière, the mother of the two inventors, and Suzanne, Louis's daughter. They pretended not to know each other. A memorial plaque in La Ciotat's station marks the occasion.

102 GARE DE PERPIGNAN

CONTEMPORARY ARCHITECTURE

104 LUMA ARLES TOWER

AT: PARC DES ATELIERS
**33 avenue
Victor Hugo
13200 Arles
Bouches-du-Rhône**
luma-arles.org

There is more to Arles than antique monuments and Vincent van Gogh. The Luma cultural centre is currently being built on the city's fringe, on a seven-hectare plot of industrial wasteland. The eye-catcher is a 56-metre-tall tower by the famous – and often-criticised – Canadian architect Frank Gehry. The façade, which is wrapped with 11.000 stainless steel panels, holds the middle between a glittering rock and a series of haphazardly stacked houses. Luma Arles was founded in 2013 by the Swiss art collector and art patron Maja Hoffmann. With her non-profit organisation Luma, Hoffmann studies the relationships between art, culture, human rights, education and the environment. In Arles, she hopes to offer artists a place to experiment, to collaborate with other artists, curators and scientists, and show their new work to the public. Luma Arles is also overseeing the transformation of the entire industrial site, le Parc des Ateliers. The German architect Annabelle Selldorf has already converted five industrial buildings into exhibition spaces, workshops and artist's residences. The park was developed by the Belgian landscape architect Bas Smets. Each year, Luma participates in Les Rencontres d'Arles, the annual photo festival, and the world music festival Les Suds.

105 LE COLISÉE

**Rue du Colisée /
Avenue de la Liberté
30000 Nîmes
Gard**

This semi-circular complex with housing, shops, offices and local government services can be found along one of the busy access roads into the centre of Nîmes. Its terrace structure resembles a contemporary Roman amphitheatre. Avenue de la Liberté cuts right through the building. The building, which dates from 1989-1995, was designed by the Japanese architects Mieko Inoue and Kisho Kurokawa.

106 MUCEM

7 promenade Robert Laffont (1 esplanade du J4)
13002 Marseille
Bouches-du-Rhône
+33 (0)4 84 35 13 13
mucem.org

The Mucem, the Musée des Civilisations de l'Europe et de la Méditerranée in full, is a striking symbol of the transformation that the old port of Marseille has undergone in recent years. The museum, which is located on reclaimed land near the former J4 port terminal, opened in 2013, when Marseille was designated as the European Capital of Culture. The French architect Rudy Ricciotti designed a monumental concrete cube, measuring 72 metres by 72 metres, which is clad with an eye-catching latticework of reinforced concrete. Footbridges extend between the cube and the latticework, from which you can also access the museum's roof, which has a restaurant and cafe. En route, you can enjoy views of the city and the sea. The Mucem mainly hosts temporary exhibitions that are usually related to European civilisation and Mediterranean culture, travel and migration, religion and citizenship. At night, the building is beautifully lit – a design by artist Yann Kersalé, like a new beacon in the port of Marseille.

107 VILLA MÉDITERRANÉE

Promenade Robert Laffont (Esplanade du J4)
13002 Marseille
Bouches-du-Rhône
tourisme-marseille.com
grotte-cosquer.com

The spectacular Villa Méditerranée – next door to the Mucem – was built in 2010 after a design by the Italian architect Stefano Boeri. The cantilevered exhibition floor hangs over the water feature beneath it. Boeri said that he wanted to design a building that 'welcomes the sea' and is a 'a gateway, rather than a barrier'. Interestingly enough, the city was unable to come up with a suitable purpose for this controversial building – it cost 70 million euro to build, financed by the Provence-Alpes-Côte d'Azur region. The proposals for a casino and a wine museum were nixed. Eventually, the decision was made to relocate the Assemblée Parlementaire de la Méditerranée to the building but the plans were abandoned at the last minute. In 2022, a replica of the prehistoric underwater Cosquer Cave will open here. Bizarre.

108 FRAC PROVENCE-ALPES-CÔTE D'AZUR

20 boulevard de Dunkerque
13002 Marseille
Bouches-du-Rhône
+33 (0)4 91 91 27 55
fracpaca.org

In 2013, Marseille was designated European Capital of Culture. Consequently, a lot of new cultural infrastructure was built in the city. Besides the Mucem and the Villa Méditerranée in the old port, a new building was also constructed for the Frac (Fonds Régional d'Art Contemporain). The design by the Japanese architect Kengo Kuma is a real eye-catcher. The corner building's façade is clad with hundreds of opaque glass rectangles that combine to create a chequerboard effect across the exterior of the six-storey building. The glass panes are arranged at different angles to create an impression of openness and transparency in addition to a wonderful chiaroscuro effect. The opening in the façade accommodates a terrace that can be used for exhibitions and events. The Frac was established in 1983 by the French Ministry of Culture. Today it consists of a network of 23 regional public collections of contemporary art across France.

109 MUSÉE JEAN COCTEAU – COLLECTION SÉVERIN WUNDERMAN

2 quai de Monléon
06500 Menton
Alpes-Maritimes
+33 (0)4 89 81 52 50
museecocteau menton.fr

Is it a giant sponge? Or a huge mollusc that washed up on the promenade at Menton? This futuristic building was designed by the French architect Rudy Ricciotti, who also created the Mucem in Marseille. The concrete and steel structure arouses the curiosity of passers-by with its bizarre openings and crevices. The museum, where you can see the extensive and versatile Jean Cocteau collection and which was donated to Menton by the American collector Séverin Wunderman, opened in 2011: approximately two thousand art objects in all, including paintings, drawings, books and posters, all created by the French poet Jean Cocteau, who also worked as a film director, draughtsman, painter, jewellery and fashion designer. Wunderman also collected work from artists who were friends of Cocteau, such as Picasso, Modigliani and De Chirico. Jean Cocteau (1889-1963) was born in Paris but ended up settling in Menton. Unfortunately the Wunderman collection has remained closed to the public since the heavy floods of October 2018. To see work by Cocteau in Menton, you will have to visit the nearby Bastion and the wedding room of the town hall *(La salle des mariages)*.

FRAC

110 NEMAUSUS 1 & 2

12-16 rue du Vistre
30000 Nîmes
Gard
jeannouvel.com/en/projects/nemausus

In 1986, the French architect Jean Nouvel built several striking social housing units just outside the centre of Nîmes: their name Nemausus refers to the city's Latin name. The two elongated, parallel buildings are reminiscent of ships moored in port. Nouvel positioned the buildings on tall piles, in accordance with Le Corbusier's design principles, which allowed him to create parking spaces under the housing. The flats can be accessed from the open galleries and often extend across two and even three levels, making them 30 to 50 percent more spacious than the average social housing facilities. Nouvel managed to keep the costs down by using concrete and aluminium construction elements. The robust, industrial design of the two buildings refers to the old electrical installation factory that once stood here.

110 NEMAUSUS 1 & 2

111 CARRÉ D'ART

Place de la Maison Carrée
30000 Nîmes
Gard
+33 (0)4 66 76 35 70
carreartmusee.com

What a challenge for the famous British architect Norman Foster to build a contemporary building opposite La Maison Carrée (5th century AD), a beautifully preserved Roman temple. In 1993, Foster's Carré d'Art opened to the public: a monumental but open, light and airy steel and glass building. The five slender columns that support the canopy are Foster's reinterpretation of the Roman columns of the Maison Carrée. The Carré d'Art has two underground floors, where you can find the public library, among others. This contemporary art museum *(musée d'art contemporain)* showcases its permanent collection with art from 1960 to the present in varying displays on the upper floors, with works by Gerhard Richter, Sigmar Polke, Claude Viallat, Arman and César. It also hosts temporary exhibitions of international contemporary art. Highly recommended.

112 MUSÉE DÉPARTEMENTAL DES ARTS ASIATIQUES

405 Promenade des Anglais
06200 Nice
Alpes-Maritimes
+33 (0)4 89 04 55 20
maa.departement06.fr

The city of Nice decided to work with a famous Japanese architect for its Musée des Arts Asiatiques. Kenzo Tange (1913-2005) wanted the white museum to resemble a snowflake or, better yet, a swan or a waterlily. In any event, the building seems to float on the water of the pond in Parc Phoenix, at the top of the Promenade des Anglais. The museum building from 1998 consists of two basic shapes, the circle and the square. In Japan, these refer to heaven and earth, respectively. The white marble façade and large windows accentuate the building's light, airy quality. The permanent display features artefacts from all over Asia, without distinguishing between ethnography, fine arts or decorative arts. Breakfast is served in the intimate tearoom where – *noblesse oblige* – you can also attend a traditional Japanese tea ceremony.

113 STADE VÉLODROME

3 boulevard Michelet
13008 Marseille
Bouches-du-Rhône
+33 (0)4 84 45 38 00
orangevelodrome.com/en/visits

The football stadium – its official name is the 'Orange Vélodrome' – is a real beacon on Marseille's skyline. Its origins date back to 1937. At the time, they already played football here, although Olympique Marseille shared the stadium with rugby teams. Moreover, there was also a cycling track here, hence the 'Vélodrome' in its name, and it was also used for boxing matches. The stadium has been renovated and expanded several times over the years. The most recent renovation dates from 2014, when the stadium was adapted to the strictest standards of UEFA, the European football organisation. This meant that the Euro 2016 cup matches could also be played here. The distinctive undulating fibreglass roof was added in 2014. You can see it from all over the city and it has since become an icon of Marseille. The roof was designed by SCAU architects. They used 5500 tons of metal for the roof's framework, roughly the equivalent of 80 percent of the Eiffel Tower. The stadium has a capacity of 67.000 spectators. You can visit it with a guide, on days when there are no matches scheduled.

NEW DISTRICTS

worth the detour

114 QUARTIER SEXTIUS-MIRABEAU IN AIX-EN-PROVENCE

13100 Aix-en-Provence
Bouches-du-Rhône

Over the past twenty years, a completely new district emerged to the west of the historic city centre of Aix-en-Provence. Part of it was built on a former railway marshalling yard. The Les Allées (2007) shopping centre links the redeveloped Rotonde – with plenty of space for pedestrians – with a cultural district with large new institutions in 'le quartier Sextius-Mirabeau', an urban design by Bohigas and Wilmotte. A lot of new buildings were constructed here: Le Pavillon Noir by Rudy Ricciotti (2006), devoted to dance productions and performances, contrasts with the round, sand-coloured Grand Théâtre de Provence by Vittorio Gregotti (2007), with 1400 seats. In 2014, the monolithic Conservatoire Darius Milhaud was added (a design by Kengo Kuma). The conservatoire trains musicians, dancers and actors. La Cité du Livre/Bibliothèque Méjanes has been here somewhat longer. The excellent historical library moved into a former match factory in 1989 and is a good example of the successful reconversion of an industrial building.

115 ANTIGONE IN MONTPELLIER

34000 Montpellier
Hérault
+33 (0)4 67 60 60 60
montpellier-france.com

Montpellier was looking to expand the city centre towards the east and the river. Between 1983 and 2000, the Catalan architect Ricardo Bofill designed a completely new district around a central axis that extends from Place de la Comédie in the city centre to the River Lez. An impressive neighbourhood was built on a former military training ground, with huge squares, symmetrical landscaped public gardens and monumental buildings in a theatrical style which is probably best described as neoclassical postmodernism. Stylised triumphal arches, colonnades, sculptures and fountains populate an urban setting that is reminiscent of Greek theatres, Bath's Royal Crescent and the Champs-Elysées in Paris. It is an interesting mix of blocks of flats, office buildings, government institutions, restaurants and cafes as well as an Olympic swimming pool and a media library. Whether you like it or not, there is no denying that it is an impressive achievement.

115 ANTIGONE IN MONTPELLIER

116 LA GRANDE-MOTTE

CONTACT: OFFICE DE TOURISME
55 rue du Port
34280 La Grande-Motte
Hérault
+33 (0)4 67 56 42 00
tourism-occitanie.co.uk

La Grande-Motte emerged out of nowhere in the 1960s. Not actually a district, but an entire city by the sea, near Montpellier. Mass tourism grew at a rapid pace in the sixties. In an attempt to counter the exodus to Spain's beaches, France built La Grande-Motte, a seaside resort for everyone. The architect Jean Balladur created a series of eye-catching pyramids: huge buildings in which each flat has a balcony with a wide view of the sea and the surroundings. Moreover, he added green areas, sports infrastructure, sandy beaches and plenty of space for pedestrians. At the time, the project met with a great deal of criticism. In 2010, however, it was declared 'Patrimoine du XXe siècle'.

117 MARINA BAIE DES ANGES

06270 Villeneuve-Loubet
Alpes-Maritimes

Marina Baie des Anges, along the sea between Nice and Antibes, consists of four 70-metre-tall blocks of flats, which are all shaped like waves and enclose a bay and a marina. This prestigious, megalomaniac project by the French architect André Minangoy, dates from 1968 and took 25 years to complete. There are 1300 homes in the buildings. Like La Grande-Motte, this architectural ensemble was designated 'Patrimoine du XXe siècle' in 2010.

118 PORT GRIMAUD

83310 Port Grimaud
Var
grimaud-provence.com

Grimaud is an old, fortified hilltop town. Port Grimaud is a port, born from the imagination of an architect and situated in the Bay of Saint-Tropez. François Spoerry (1912-1999) designed a mini-Venice or mini-Murano in a swampy area in 1966, with entrance gates, fishermen's houses, canals, arched bridges and jetties. A fun, picturesque-looking harbour. Spoerry even built a simple church here, called Saint-François d'Assise, where you can see stained-glass windows by Victor Vasarely.

Remarkable art in
OLD CHURCHES

119 LA CHAPELLE DES PÉNITENTS BLANCS

Place Jean Boyer
13100 Aix-en-Provence
Bouches-du-Rhône
+33 (0)4 42 52 88 32
museegranet-aixenprovence.fr

The Chapelle des Pénitents Blancs, around the corner from Musée Granet to which it belongs, dates from 1654. The spacious chapel has a turbulent history as a storage and school. After renovation, it reopened in 2013 as a modern art space where the 20th-century art collection of the Fondation Jean et Suzanne Planque is on permanent display. Born in 1910, Jean Planque was a painter and an art expert, working for the Fondation Beyeler in Basel. His love for Cézanne's paintings led him to Aix. Through contacts with such artists as Dubuffet, Giacometti and Picasso and through his work as an art dealer, he acquired an excellent collection, with paintings by Cézanne, Bonnard, Picasso, and de Staël among others, which are beautifully presented in the chapel.

120 ÉGLISE LOUISE BOURGEOIS

Rue Aristide Briand
84480 Bonnieux
Vaucluse
+33 (0)4 90 75 80 54
egliselouise bourgeois.com

While the Église Louise Bourgeois, just outside Bonnieux, may not exactly be easy to find, your visit will more than make up for the difficulty. In 1998, the famous French-American artist Louise Bourgeois (1911-2010) added five works to this empty, snow-white monastery chapel: a bronze spider, a pink baptismal font made from Carrara marble, a 'cell' as an idiosyncratic confessional, a Virgin and Child in textile and a bronze cross consisting of two arms and hands. While this may not seem like much, the result is – in all its minimalist purity – simply mind-blowing. The artworks are chock-full of personal references, with the spider as a central symbol of the mother who weaves her beautiful yet suffocating web. A visit to this chapel is an overwhelming and emotional experience.

120 ÉGLISE LOUISE BOURGEOIS

121 MUSÉE DES AUGUSTINS

21 rue de Metz
31000 Toulouse
Haute-Garonne
+33 (0)5 61 22 21 82
augustins.org

The Musée des Augustins was established in the former Augustinian monastery of Toulouse in 1793, shortly after the creation of the Louvre in Paris. As such, it was one of the first major museums outside of Paris. Romanesque and Gothic sculptures were displayed in the cloister and wing with remarkable round arches, while the Gothic monastery church was perfectly suited for exhibiting religious paintings by Rubens, Perugino, Vouet and Murillo, among others. The museum is currently being renovated and will probably reopen in 2022. We'll have to wait and see what has changed.

122 MUSÉE DE L'ANNONCIADE

2 place Georges Grammont
83990 Saint-Tropez
Var
+33 (0)4 94 17 84 10
saint-tropez.fr/culture/musee-de-lannonciade

This charming, colourful museum was established in 1955 in Notre-Dame de l'Annonciade, an old chapel from 1568. The art collector Georges Grammont donated 56 paintings from his rich collection for the chapel. The museum offers a wonderful and very homogeneous survey of figurative art between 1890 and 1950 with works by great painters who worked in or near Saint-Tropez, including Matisse, Bonnard, Dufy, Derain, Marquet, Van Rysselberghe and Friesz. It all started with Paul Signac, who moored his yacht *L'Olympia* in Saint-Tropez in 1892. The artist was immediately enamoured with the sea and the light, sensing that he had found 'the perfect place' to paint. In 1897, he bought a house here, which became a meeting place for many like-minded painters and where he also set up his studio, La Hune. The house is located at 32 avenue Paul Signac behind the citadel of Saint-Tropez but is closed to the public. Fortunately, you can see Signac's paintings in the Musée de L'Annonciade.

123 ABBAYE DE LAGRASSE

4 rive gauche
11200 Lagrasse
Aude
+33 (0)4 68 43 15 99
abbayedelagrasse.aude.fr

The old Benedictine abbey of Lagrasse, whose earliest traces date back to the 8th century, is worth a visit in itself. Since 2016, a contemporary artist has been invited to work here every summer. The French-Swiss artist Christian Jaccard created a monumental work with smoke and fire on a wall of the former dormitory. This work is on permanent display. In 2019, Abdelkader Benchamma (France) exhibited his geometric black and white paintings here, while Nadia Naveau (Belgium) surprised visitors with her neo-baroque sculptures in 2020.

124 NOTRE-DAME DES SABLONS

Place Saint-Louis
30220 Aigues-Mortes
Gard
+33 (0)4 66 53 73 00
ot-aiguesmortes.com/eglise-notre-dame-des-sablons

The oldest building of Aigues-Mortes is decorated with 20th-century art. The Notre-Dame des Sablons chapel – presumably *sablons* refers to the sandy marshland in the region – dates back to the 13th century. The chapel was thoroughly restored in the 1960s, and the simple, natural stone interior returned to its original glory. In 1991, the artist Claude Viallat's colourful, abstract stained-glass windows were installed here. Viallat, who was born in 1936 in Nîmes, originally started out as a painter. Gradually, however, he developed a keen interest in the support of his paintings: canvas or panel. He began to experiment, painting on the back of his canvases and then on shirts, tarpaulin and umbrellas until he became intrigued by the transparency of glass. His stained-glass windows in Aigues-Mortes are an ode to light and pure colour.

Old buildings, NEW USES

125 CRAC OCCITANIE

26 quai Aspirant Herber
34200 Sète
Hérault
+33 (0)4 67 74 94 37
crac.laregion.fr

Near the Canal Royal in the fishing port of Sète, an old cold store for fish has been converted into a contemporary art centre with impressive white spaces: the Centre Régional d'Art Contemporain Occitanie. In 1997, the architect Lorenzo Piqueras stripped this industrial building to its essence. Three immense loading bays still bear witness to the building's original use. The CRAC hosts temporary exhibitions in which French and foreign artists work with themes that also have local relevance.

126 LA VIEILLE CHARITÉ

2 rue de la Charité
13002 Marseille
Bouches-du-Rhône
vieille-charite-marseille.com

La Vieille Charité is a beautiful homogeneous complex on the Butte (hill) des Moulins in the heart of Marseille's old Panier quarter. It was built c. 1670 by the architect Pierre Puget as an almshouse for Marseille's poor and beggars. The atmospheric architectural ensemble is built in a simple Italian baroque style: a courtyard, enclosed by four wings, with arcade galleries on three storeys and a domed central chapel. The architect only used pink stone from the nearby quarry. The complex remained vacant for many years but was carefully restored in the 1990s. Currently it is home to a number of museums and cultural institutions, including the Musée d'Archéologie Méditerranéenne, Musée des Arts Africains, Océaniens, Amérindiens (MAAOA), and the Centre International de la Poésie Marseille. The building, the courtyard and chapel can be accessed at no charge.

127 **MAISON DE LA PHOTOGRAPHIE**

Rue Nicolas Laugier / Place du Globe
83000 Toulon
Var
+33 (0)4 94 93 07 59
toulontourisme.com

The small but fascinating Maison de la Photographie, which was founded in 2002, is located in a former hammam that is tucked away in the city centre of Toulon. Unfortunately, all that remains of the former bathhouse is its round structure. The museum relies on the photo collection of its larger sister institution, the Musée d'Art de Toulon, with work by such artists as Henri Cartier-Bresson, Robert Doisneau and Marc Ribou for its often-fascinating exhibitions. They sometimes also show work by Gilbert & George and Dennis Oppenheim because photos are an intrinsic part of their work.

126 **LA VIEILLE CHARITÉ**

128 LES ABATTOIRS

76 allées Charles-de-Fitte
31300 Toulouse
Haute-Garonne
+33 (0)5 34 51 10 60
lesabattoirs.org

Built between 1826 and 1833, the former slaughterhouse of Toulouse is now home to a modern and contemporary art centre. The austere but monumental brick building hosts temporary exhibitions, including 'Picasso et l'exil' (in 2019) as well as an exhibition of the work of the contemporary video artist Laure Prouvost (in 2020). Its permanent collection includes work by Jean Dubuffet, Lucio Fontana, Sam Francis, Antoni Tàpies and Victor Vasarely, among others. In the basement you can admire the massive stage curtain *La dépouille du Minotaure en costume d'Arlequin*, which Pablo Picasso painted in 1936 for Romain Rolland's play *Le Quatorze Juillet*.

129 LE CHÂTEAU D'EAU

1 place Laganne
31300 Toulouse
Haute-Garonne
+33 (0)5 61 77 09 40
galeriechateaudeau.org

On the left bank of the Garonne near Toulouse's Pont Neuf stands an old water tower from 1822, which has been home to one of France's most important photo museums since 1974. The three floors of the tower, which supplied Toulouse with fresh drinking water until 1870, is used for exhibitions from the museum's own collection in addition to the work of leading French and international photographers. Le Château d'Eau also has an excellent photo documentation centre and library. Head to the top floor – an open gallery 30 metres above the city – to enjoy sweeping views over Toulouse.

130 LAVOIR VASSEROT

1 rue Joseph Quaranta
83990 Saint-Tropez
Var
visitvar.fr/fr/fiche/lavoir-vasserot-4078033

This *lavoir*, or a communal place for washing clothes, was built in 1862 after a design by the architect Charles Albert Vasserot. For decades, the women of Saint-Tropez came here to do their laundry. You can still see the three wash basins here: one for white clothes, one for coloured clothes and a place to rinse the laundry. In 1981, the building was listed as a monument. Since 1991, it is used for temporary art exhibitions. The Lavoir exhibits all kinds of art.

129 LE CHÂTEAU D'EAU

131 **FRICHE LA BELLE DE MAI**
41 rue Jobin
13003 Marseille
Bouches-du-Rhône
+33 (0)4 95 04 95 95
lafriche.org

La Friche la Belle de Mai is a huge cultural warehouse in Marseille. La Friche, which means 'the wasteland' in French, moved into an old tobacco warehouse in the Belle de Mai district, where the Gitanes and Gauloises cigarette brands were once produced. In 1990, the tobacco factory closed. La Friche la Belle de Mai has studios and workspaces for artists, as well as rehearsal spaces, exhibition spaces, theatre and concert halls and a gigantic rooftop terrace. La Friche is shared by more than sixty artistic and cultural institutions, bands and projects, which work in all kinds of different disciplines, including theatre, dance, music, and contemporary visual arts. Two radio stations also broadcast from here. But that's not all: this cultural beehive is also home to a nursery and a primary school, to ensure its integration in the neighbourhood. There is also a large restaurant in the building, a small coffee bar and a bookshop. Check the exciting and unexpected programming.

Reinvented

CITY PALACES

132 HÔTEL DE CAUMONT

3 rue Joseph Cabassol
13100 Aix-en-Provence
Bouches-du-Rhône
+33 (0)4 42 20 70 01
caumont-centredart.com

The Hôtel de Caumont is a stunning mansion in Aix-en-Provence. This beautifully restored 18th-century city palace is situated near Aix's largely car-free, chic avenue, the Cours Mirabeau. In 2015, Caumont became an art centre, hosting excellent exhibitions, where you can also visit the original opulent private rooms of Pauline, Marquise de Caumont. In recent years, the museum has organised temporary exhibitions with work by William Turner, Marc Chagall, the collection of the Guggenheim Museum in New York, Nicolas de Staël and Joaquín Sorolla, among others. Caumont also has a garden and a cafe-restaurant.

133 CAMPREDON CENTRE D'ART

20 rue du Docteur Tallet
84800 L'Isle-sur-la-Sorgue
Vaucluse
+33 (0)4 90 38 17 41
campredon centredart.com

The Hôtel Donadéï de Campredon is a venerable, monumental dwelling from 1746, in the French classicist style. Its original owner, Charles-Joseph de Campredon, belonged to old, landed gentry. Since 1982, the art centre has organised some excellent exhibitions (usually three a year). Previous exhibitions have featured work by leading modern and contemporary artists and photographers, such as Henri Cartier-Bresson, Anne and Patrick Poirier, Robert Doisneau, Vivian Maier, Jacques-Henri Lartigue and Jessica Lange – yes, that's right, the American actress also works as a photographer when she's not shooting films.

134 MUSÉE RÉATTU

10 rue du
Grand Prieuré
13200 Arles
Bouches-du-Rhône
+33 (0)4 90 49 37 58
museereattu.arles.fr

More fortified bastide than city palace. The Musée Réattu is housed in the former commandery of the Knights of Malta in Arles. They chose to settle in this strategic location along a bend of the Rhône and were based here from the 15th to the 17th century. In 1796, the painter Jacques Réattu acquired the building and set up his home and studio here. Réattu died in 1833 without having realised his dream of founding an artists' colony in the huge complex: L'Atelier du Midi. In a sense, Musée Réattu has now accomplished this for him. Réattu's academic paintings are confronted with the work of modern and contemporary artists, often commissioned by the museum. Musée Réattu also invites artists to curate exhibitions: this was the case, for example, in 2008 for the Arles-born fashion designer Christian Lacroix (b. 1951). The museum owns sculptures and paintings by Pierre Alechinsky, Pol Bury, Marino Marini, Germaine Richier and Ossip Zadkine, among others. In 1971 (two years before his death), Pablo Picasso donated 57 drawings to the museum, which provide a nice overview of his oeuvre.

135 MUSÉE DE LODÈVE

Square Georges Auric
34700 Lodève
Hérault
+33 (0)4 67 88 86 10
museedelodeve.fr

This 18th-century city palace of Cardinal de Fleury, who served as prime minister under Louis XV, underwent far-reaching renovations between 2015 and 2018. The architects of Projectiles created a direct and well-executed confrontation between contemporary architecture and heritage, combining exposed concrete with natural stone. They also developed the stripped-down scenography and aesthetic presentation of the museum's mainly archaeological treasures. Every year, the Musée de Lodève hosts an exhibition of art from the pivotal years between 1860 and 1930. Artists that have been previously featured include Théo Van Rysselberghe, Pierre Bonnard and Louis Valtat, often in collaboration with private collections.

136 MO.CO.

13 rue de la République
34000 Montpellier
Hérault
+33 (0)4 99 58 28 00
moco.art

In 2019, Montpellier Contemporain (MO.CO.) opened its doors in Hôtel Montcalm, a 19th-century city palace that is just a short walk from Place de la Comédie. The Hôtel des Collections mainly features international contemporary art, from public or private collections. Because the Mo.Co. has no art collection of its own, it has already organised exhibitions with art from the London-based Cranford Collection and the State Tretyakov Gallery in Moscow on such themes as permafrost and the Amazon Forest. The French artist Bertrand Lavier has created a fun fountain in the garden. The museum has a restaurant and a museum shop. MO.CO. La Panacée, its other location in the city centre, essentially is a lab for new and experimental art in Montpellier's former Royal College of Medicine.

137 MUSÉE ESTRINE

8 rue Estrine
13210 Saint-Rémy-de-Provence
Bouches-du-Rhône
+33 (0)4 90 92 34 72
musee-estrine.fr

A small museum, in a typical Provençal-style city palace from 1749, that is mainly dedicated to local artists. The eye-catcher is the well-executed Centre d'Interprétation Vincent van Gogh. Don't expect any paintings by Van Gogh, however. What you will find is a series of documents and images that chart his life and give visitors an interesting biographical overview. Quotes from his letters are illustrated with the works that he made on the spot while a film confronts Van Gogh's paintings with the landscapes around Saint-Rémy. An interesting introduction to this legendary painter.

138 VILLA DATRIS

7 avenue des Quatre Otages
84800 L'Isle-sur-la-Sorgue
Vaucluse
+33 (0)4 90 95 23 70
fondationvilladatris.fr

Since 2011, Danièle Kapel-Marcovici organises an annual exhibition, from June till September, with works by international contemporary artists, in a 19th-century Provençal villa, in the centre of L'Isle-sur-la-Sorgue. The four floors and garden of the magnificent Villa have already hosted exhibitions on such themes as light (2012), nature (2017), textile (2018), animals in sculpture (2019) and recycling (2020). In 2013, the work of 70 female artists was on display here, including Camille Claudel, Louise Bourgeois, Rebecca Horn and Niki de Saint Phalle. No admission charged.

139 VILLA TAMARIS

295 avenue de la Grande Maison
83500 La Seyne-sur-Mer
Var
+33 (0)4 94 06 84 00
villatamaris.fr

An imposing 19th-century hillside villa that overlooks the Bay of Tamaris near Toulon. It was built by Marius Michel, an officer in the French merchant navy, who earned a reputation for himself as the director-general of the lighthouses along the coastline of the Ottoman Empire. The Turkish sultan granted him the honorary title of 'Pacha'. Upon his return to France, Marius Michel 'Pacha' transformed the Bay of Tamaris into a seaside resort from 1870 onwards, designing 50 villas in an oriental style and even setting up a ferry service between La Seyne and Toulon. Unfortunately almost all of the villas, including that of the novelist George Sand, have since been demolished. The Villa Tamaris remained unfinished. In 1991, it became a contemporary arts centre, focussing on the latest trends in painting.

MUSÉE MASSÉNA

140 **VILLA MASSÉNA**

65 rue de France
06000 Nice
Alpes-Maritimes
+33 (0)4 93 91 19 10
nice.fr

Villa Maséna is a magnificent gem. A visit to the neighbour of Nice's legendary Hôtel Negresco becomes a journey back in time: you have travelled to the belle époque, with its red plush, lavish gold decorations and rustling ball gowns. The Villa – it's actually more of a palace – was built between 1898 and 1901 by the Danish architect Hans-Georg Tersling in a neoclassical style with a distinctly Italian flourish. Prince Victor d'Essling, the grandson of Marshal André Masséna, made it his winter residence. The villa was donated to the city of Nice in 1919, which turned it into a city museum. On the ground floor you can still admire the original, opulently decorated salons. The first floor traces the history of Nice, with paintings, costumes and documents (don't miss Napoleon's death mask!), from roughly 1800 to World War I: Nice as a pawn between Italy and France, and the city's development as a seaside resort. The magnificent, historic garden borders on the Promenade des Anglais. A memorial has been erected at the entrance to commemorate the horrific terrorist attack on 14 July 2016, which killed 86 when a truck ploughed into the unsuspecting crowd on the Promenade des Anglais as they watched the annual fireworks display.

THE CLASSICS
but differently

141 VILLA KÉRYLOS

Rue Gustave Eiffel
06310 Beaulieu-sur-Mer
Alpes-Maritimes
+33 (0)4 93 01 01 44
villakerylos.fr

You won't believe your eyes. A lonely white villa sparkles in the sun against the azure blue sea on a rocky outcrop near Beaulieu-sur-Mer: sleek art deco on the outside, whereas the interior is a reconstruction of a sumptuous ancient Greek villa. This really is a unique experience and a journey back in time: on the one hand, you feel as if you have been immersed in the world of ancient Greece. On the other hand, the villa is equipped with all the mod cons. Théodore Reinach commissioned this villa from the architect Emmanuel Pontremoli. Reinach was a bit of a *homo universalis*: an archaeologist, lawyer, historian, musicologist, mathematician and politician. He was inspired by the houses that he had seen on the Greek island of Delos. It took him six years to build his dream villa, from 1902 until 1908, together with Pontremoli, using the most precious marble, alabaster and exotic wood. He furnished his holiday home with authentic Greek mosaics, furniture, amphoras and lamps and had frescoes copied. Reinach regarded his villa as an ode to democracy, which had its birthplace in ancient Greece, and to a civilisation that revolved around man.

142 MUSÉE DE LA ROMANITÉ

16 boulevard des Arènes
30000 Nîmes
Gard
museedelaromanite.fr

Twenty-five centuries of Nîmes's city history in a brand-new setting. In 2018, the French architect Elizabeth de Portzamparc built a dazzling building – in every sense of the word – opposite the city's famous 2000-year-old amphitheatre. The confrontation between the arena and the Musée de la Romanité is quite striking: a round, heavy and firmly anchored stone volume with distinctive arches that create verticality as opposed to a light, almost floating, horizontal building, which appears to be draped with a fluttering glass toga. The Musée de la Romanité showcases an extensive collection of archaeological finds in an innovative and clear manner, using 65 multimedia displays. It also highlights the great influence of Roman civilisation on Nîmes – 'the French equivalent of Rome'.

143 THE BARBEGAL AQUEDUCT AND MILLS

Route de l'Aqueduc
13990 Fontvieille
Bouches-du-Rhône
+33 (0)4 90 54 67 49
petit-patrimoine.com

Not a well-preserved monument, but the unique remains of ancient times. Look for the 'Aqueduc romain' road sign about three kilometres south of Fontvieille, near the intersection of the D33 and D82. In the fields you can see the remains of a double, 1st-century Roman aqueduct. The aqueduct supplied fresh, clean water from the north of the Alpilles – near Eygalières – to Arles. A second canal powered an impressive flour mill consisting of two rows of eight smaller water mills built one above the other on the southern flank of the hill. Recent archaeological research points to the very first industrial complex, a unique remnant from Roman antiquity. The flour that was produced here was probably used to make the hard biscuits for ships to supply the seaports in the Rhône Delta. You can find a model of the mill in the Musée départemental Arles antique.

144 PONT DU GARD

400 route du Pont du Gard
30210 Vers-Pont-du-Gard
Gard
+33 (0)4 66 37 50 99
pontdugard.fr

A sight that never fails to impress, especially when you can get very close to it or even stand under it. The Pont du Gard – which towers 49 metres above the Gardon River and is 274 metres long – is the tallest and one of the best-preserved Roman aqueducts. It is also the most famous one, attracting one million visitors a year. A state-of-the-art museum was built nearby, combining a multimedia exhibition, film projection and 3D animation in a minute depiction of the history of the bridge's construction. Do visit it! One of its most distinguishing features? The rocks that were used to build the bridge – some of which weigh up to six tons – were hewn and cut in such a way that they fit together like the pieces of a puzzle. Two thousand years later, the bridge is still as sturdy as it ever was. The Romans were ingenious engineers, that much is obvious. Originally, the aqueduct was 50 kilometres long and was built to supply water, partly underground, from the springs near Uzès to the large Roman city of Nîmes.

145 AQUEDUC DE ROQUEFAVOUR

Route de Roquefavour / D65
13122 Ventabren
Bouches-du-Rhône
+33 (0)4 42 28 76 47
aixenprovence tourism.com/fr/fiche/5793

Although this structure, with its arches on three levels, takes its inspiration from the Pont du Gard, it is not a Roman aqueduct. The magnificent Aqueduc de Roquefavour was built between 1842 and 1847, some 40 kilometres to the north of Marseille, by the engineer Franz Mayor de Montricher. It is part of the 80-kilometre-long Canal de Marseille, which still supplies water from the Durance River to Marseille and which currently accounts for 80 percent of the city's drinking water. The gigantic structure, with a total length of 393 metres and a height of 82,6 metres, is the tallest and longest stone aqueduct in the world.

Famous houses:

WRITERS

None of these houses is open to the public. Of course, you can always take a chance.

146 **VILLA MAURESQUE – SOMERSET MAUGHAM**

52 boulevard
Général de Gaulle
06230 Saint-Jean-Cap-Ferrat
Alpes-Maritimes

The famous British writer William Somerset Maugham lived and worked in this magnificent villa from 1927 until 1965, the year in which he died aged 91. The Villa Mauresque was built soon after 1900 in the Moorish style for Leopold II, King of the Belgians. He owned various properties and villas nearby, which he financed with the profits from the infamous 'red rubber' from his personal colony, the Congo Free State. One of these properties was the Villa Saint Second, which was built as a residence for his mistress Baroness de Vaughan, née Caroline Delacroix, who was fifty years younger. King Leopold II went on to build four more villas: La Banana, La Boma, La Matadi and La Mauresque. In 1927, Somerset Maugham acquired the latter and had it 'modernised' by the American architect Barry Dierks, who stripped it of all the original neo-oriental elements. The Villa Mauresque became a meeting place for all the celebrities that visited the South of France, from Winston Churchill and the Aga Khan to T.S. Eliot, H.G. Wells, Ian Fleming, Noël Coward and Virginia Woolf. Maugham lived there with his successive partners. His last partner, Alan Searle, inherited his estate and villa. We can only guess what the villa looks like today. You can catch a glimpse of the house and the large garden over the tall hedge but you won't get past the entrance gate. But it doesn't matter because driving around Cap Ferrat is like driving through paradise anyway.

147 VILLA DE LA PLAGE – VLADIMIR NABOKOV

57 promenade des Anglais
06000 Nice
Alpes-Maritimes

The Russian-American novelist Vladimir Nabokov (1899-1977) had spent time in Nice as a child. He only returned in 1960, however, at the height of his fame, to write a novel he had been mulling over for years: *Pale Fire*. This remarkable book consists of the poem *Pale Fire* by the fictional writer John Shade, with an introduction and an extensive commentary by the equally fictional and mad scientist Charles Kinbote. Nabokov always used index cards and the first one is dated 29 November 1960, Hôtel Negresco in Nice. Soon the Nabokovs swapped the famous hotel for a spacious flat on the third floor of Villa de la Plage, a Victorian white wedding cake-style villa at 57 promenade des Anglais. Here Nabokov was able to concentrate on his work, in addition to giving frequent interviews – a French translation of his autobiography had just been published – and indulging in his favourite pastimes: playing tennis and catching butterflies in the nearby hills of Grasse and Vence.

148 VILLA JULES – LOUIS COUPERUS

Corner of Avenue Alfred Borriglione and Avenue Romain Rolland
06100 Nice
Alpes-Maritimes

The Dutch novelist Louis Couperus lived and worked in the Villa Jules in Nice from 1900 until 1908. Couperus wrote naturalistic works, which were often set in affluent, upper class circles. Oscar Wilde read the English translation of his novel *Noodlot (Footsteps of Fate)* from 1890 and loved it. Louis Couperus and his wife Elisabeth had discovered Nice when travelling to relatives in the Dutch East Indies, a Dutch colony consisting of what is now Indonesia. After spending a year in Java, they relocated to Nice, drawn by the warm climate and the cosmopolitan lifestyle. Louis Couperus greatly enjoyed sensuous Nice, experiencing one of his most productive periods there. Nice is also featured in his novels: from the elegant balls at the Palais Masséna to the strolls up and down the Promenade des Anglais. The Villa Jules is still there, but the magnificent garden has since been built up.

149 VILLA ISOLA BELLA – KATHERINE MANSFIELD

2 avenue Katherine Mansfield
06500 Menton
Alpes-Maritimes
katherinemansfieldsociety.org

The New Zealand short story writer Katherine Mansfield (1888-1923) lived in Europe all her adult life. She spent three years in France, recovering from tuberculosis on the French Riviera, like so many other winter visitors. Her first sojourn was at Bandol. She later moved to Menton at the age of 31. In the spring of 1920, she stayed at the Hôtel de l'Hermitage and from September 1920 to May 1921 at the Villa Isola Bella, on the corner of Chemin Fleuri and (what is now called) Avenue Katherine Mansfield, close to Menton's Garavan railway station. The Villa Isola Bella, which was owned by her father, a prosperous banker and businessman, proved fertile ground for Mansfield, inspiring such short stories as *The Singing Lesson, The Young Girl, The Stranger* and *The Daughters of the Late Colonel*. Mansfield also commented on her life in Menton in her notebooks and diaries. In a letter to her husband, John Middleton Murry, she wrote: 'You will find Isola Bella in pokerwork on my heart', and: 'This darling little town, these mountains – It is simply a small jewel.' Mansfield died two years later in Fontainebleau.

150 VILLA HU(X)LEY / VILLA LES FLOTS – ALDOUS HUXLEY

340 allée Thérèse
83110 Sanary-sur-Mer
Var

Still a well-kept secret: the English author Aldous Huxley wrote his famous, dystopian science fiction novel *Brave New World* in Sanary-sur-Mer. He worked at a furious pace: he started writing in May 1931 and completed it in August. The novel, which anticipated on in vitro fertilisation, eugenics and mass manipulation through advertising, medication, sex and entertainment, was published in 1932 and is widely considered one of the most influential novels of all time. Huxley and his Belgian wife Maria Nys lived in the Villa Huley from 1930 until 1937. This should of course read Villa Huxley, but the façade painter forgot the 'x'. The villa is called 'Les Flots' these days. Huxley enjoyed living in this remote villa, among the pine trees, overlooking the Bay of Bandol. The writer and his wife made contact with the exiled artists who fled Germany and Austria, following Hitler's rise to power, and who settled in Sanary for a short or longer time.

151 PAVILLON JEAN RACINE

Promenade des Marronniers (Start at Rue de l'Évêché)
30700 Uzès
Gard
terresdecrivains.com

The famous French playwright Jean Racine is said to have lived and worked in the pavilion in Promenade des Marronniers next to Saint-Théodorit Cathedral in Uzès for several years. Said to, because very little is known about his short stay at Uzès. Racine was orphaned early on and moved in with his uncle Antoine Sconin, who was the vicar-general of the diocese of Uzès, at the age of 22. Jean Racine was a literary talent, without an income. So the intention was for the young man to give up his bohemian lifestyle, far from Paris and its temptations, and experience a religious vocation. In vain, it would seem. Racine wrote 24 letters in Uzès, in which he expresses his optimism and joy as well as his loneliness and melancholy. In May 1663, Jean Racine returned to Paris and began writing his first plays.

152 LA SOUPE DE L'ESPACE – JOSEPH CONRAD

9 avenue des Îles d'Or
83400 Hyères
Var
+33 (0)4 94 66 84 03
terresdecrivains.com/Joseph-CONRAD-a-Marseille-Hyeres

The Polish-British novelist Joseph Conrad wrote about the sea, but also had a maritime career. In 1874, 17-year-old Conrad travelled from Poland to Marseille, from where he would sail multiple times to the Antilles, Mexico and Venezuela on merchant ships, to supply weapons to Colombian revolutionaries. He lived in Hyères, in the boarding house of Thérèse Chodzko, at 9 boulevard (now: avenue) des Îles d'Or. The building is now occupied by a bookshop – there is no such thing as coincidence. Conrad set two of his later novels in the South of France: *The Arrow of Gold* (1919) in Marseille in the 1870s, while *The Rover* (1923) takes place against the backdrop of the French Revolution, Napoleon's rise to power and the French-English rivalry in the Mediterranean.

153 VILLA MARIE – F. SCOTT FITZGERALD

155 avenue des Pins
83700 Saint-Raphaël
Var

The American writer F. Scott Fitzgerald, his wife Zelda and their two-year-old daughter left the United States to escape their financial troubles. Life in France was much cheaper and there was no 'Prohibition' there. The glamorous Fitzgeralds had a busy social life … In the spring of 1924, they arrived at Hyères, where they spent some time with Charles and Marie-Laure de Noailles, art patrons and financiers of surrealist films. Here they met Salvador Dalí, Man Ray and Jean Cocteau. They then ended up renting the 19th-century Villa Marie in Saint-Raphaël. With servants. It was here that Fitzgerald finished his successful novel *The Great Gatsby*. While the book is set in Long Island, it was most certainly inspired by the carefree, decadent lifestyle of the French Riviera and the couple's marital woes. The ochre-coloured Villa Marie with its open tower still looks resplendent among the pine trees. It was built in 1883 for the French actress Suzanne Reichenberg.

154 FRIEDRICH NIETZSCHE IN NICE

38 rue Catherine Ségurane
06300 Nice
Alpes-Maritimes

Friedrich Nietzsche, the philosopher with the hammer, first travelled to Nice in November 1883. He found a place to live near the port, on Rue Catherine Ségurane. A plaque on the house, at number 38, commemorates this fact. Nietzsche was looking for 'a landscape where he could think' and a mild climate because of his health problems. Nice ticked all the boxes, offering light, sun, and heat, in addition to a cosmopolitan environment and freedom. But he also experienced periods of great loneliness and anguish there, after Lou Andreas-Salomé had dumped him, after his fall-out with Wagner and when his books received a poor reception. A restless mind, he moved often. He had a love-hate relationship with Nice but returned nonetheless to spend the winter there. He also completed several major works there, including *Thus Spoke Zarathustra, Beyond Good and Evil* and *The Gay Science*. In April 1888, he left Nice definitely and moved to Turin, where he suffered a mental breakdown on 3 January 1889.

Famous houses:
PAINTERS

155 **HÔTEL RÉGINA – HENRI MATISSE**

71 boulevard de Cimiez
06000 Nice
Alpes-Maritimes

Henri Matisse, who was born in 1869 in the Département du Nord near the Belgian border, discovered the vibrant colours and dazzling light of the south early on in his career. In 1917, he relocated to Nice, initially living in hotels, after which he found a flat at 1 place Charles-Félix, in the old city centre, near the flower market. But the most important address in Nice is the former Hôtel Régina, where Matisse lived from 1938 in a spacious flat with a studio. It is there that he created his enormous collages: a garden with plants and animals, as well as his *Blue Nudes (Les Nus Bleus)*, made from painted paper cut-outs. The Hôtel Régina was a monumental hotel, with 400 rooms. It was built in 1897 on the hill of Cimiez at a time when luxury tourism was booming and affluent Europeans travelled to Nice to spend the winter in the city's mild climate. It was originally built for the British Queen Victoria, who spent three holidays there, between 1897 and 1899, bringing her court of more than 100 with her. There is a monument in front of the hotel's garden in her memory. The rise of mass tourism and the Wall Street Crash of 1929 contributed to the hotel's bankruptcy. By the time Matisse moved in, the 400 rooms had been converted into spacious flats. The Matisse Museum is just across the street.

156 CHÂTEAU DE VAUVENARGUES – PABLO PICASSO

4 rue René Nicol
13126 Vauvenargues
Bouches-du-Rhône
aixenprovence tourism.com/en/fiche/5685

The gates to the Château de Vauvenargues swing open only rarely, but usually this 13th-century fortified bastide remains closed to visitors. In 1958, Pablo Picasso acquired the castle and 1100 hectares of land. He wanted to leave the Villa Californie in Cannes because the construction of new buildings concealed the sea view. When he first saw Vauvenargues, he was immediately taken by the view of the Mont Sainte-Victoire, the mythical mountain that Paul Cézanne had painted dozens of times. Picasso regarded Cézanne as his spiritual father. When Picasso told Daniel-Henry Kahnweiler that he had bought Cézanne's Mont Sainte-Victoire, the art dealer famously responded: "Which one?". Picasso replied with satisfaction: "The real one". Ultimately Picasso only lived here for three years, from 1959 until 1962, after which he relocated to Mougins. The Picasso family still owns the property, however, and the artist is laid to rest in its garden, alongside his last wife Jacqueline Roque.

157 MAISON NICOLAS DE STAËL

Corner of Promenade Amiral de Grasse and Rue du Revely
06600 Antibes
Alpes-Maritimes

From autumn 1954, the French-Russian painter Nicolas de Staël rented a studio-flat in Antibes on the top floor of a building on the corner of Promenade Amiral de Grasse and Rue du Revely. He was drawn to the light, and possibly also the immense Fort Carré, which he painted several times. But he also wanted to be alone here: away from his wife and children and close to his new, but complicated love. De Staël worked tirelessly, painting day and night, as if he foresaw that the end was drawing near. He painted *Le Fort-Carré d'Antibes, Nu couché bleu* and the monumental *Le Concert* (3,5 by 6 metres), his last canvas, here. You can see these three works at the Musée Picasso, which is just a short walk from this studio. On 16 March 1955, De Staël committed suicide, leaping to his death from the rooftop. He was only 41 years old. There are two commemorative plaques on the façade: one in French and one in Russian.

Famous houses: MUSICIANS

158 VILLA NELLCÔTE – ROLLING STONES

10 avenue Louise Bordes
6230 Villefranche-sur-Mer
Alpes-Maritimes

In the spring of 1971, the Rolling Stones went into tax exile in France. Mick Jagger, who had just married Bianca, moved to Paris, while each of the other band members rented a house in the South of France, in Grasse, Arles and Biot, respectively. The best place to record a new album proved to be Villa Nellcôte in Villefranche-sur-Mer, however. This luxurious mansion from 1854 ('a mini Versailles') was the temporary residence of Rolling Stones guitarist Keith Richards, along with his partner Anita Pallenberg and their son Marlon. From June 1971, the basic tracks for *Exile on Main St.*, the band's most storied album, were recorded in the basement. Their mobile recording studio was outside. The recording was complicated by the fact that so many guests drifted in and out, spending shorter or longer periods of time in the mansion, including such characters as William S. Burroughs, Gram Parsons and John Lennon. The plentiful supply of drugs didn't help matters: Keith Richards and his wife – and many others – were addicted to heroin. Mick Jagger (recently married) and Bill Wyman (who felt ill at ease there) were often absent. The Villa Nellcôte currently has Russian owners. These days, you won't get past the very heavy, black baroque gates. Unless you rent a boat: you can spot the mansion from the sea. A must-do if you're a diehard Stones fan.

159 LA MADRAGUE – BRIGITTE BARDOT

Chemin de l'Estagnet (Sentier littoral)
83990 Saint-Tropez
Var

Saint-Tropez is almost synonymous with Brigitte Bardot (b. 1934), better known as BB. The French film star, singer and sex symbol of the late 1950s and 1960s rose to stardom with Roger Vadim's *Et Dieu... créa la femme* (1956) – which was shot in Saint-Tropez – and with songs by Serge Gainsbourg such as *Bonnie and Clyde* (1968). In 1958, BB bought Villa La Madrague along the Route des Canebiers in Saint-Tropez. In 1963, she was given permission to build a wall around her property, which extends to the beach, to keep the paparazzi at bay. In 1973, she retired from acting. Since then, she has used her fame to promote animal rights. Rumour has it she shares her house with 30 cats. You can only see La Madrague from the sea. Boat trips are organised from Saint-Tropez for anyone wishing to catch a glimpse of this mythical property and perhaps even of the legendary diva.

160 MAISON PAGANINI

23 rue de la Préfecture
06300 Nice
Alpes-Maritimes

In 1838, the famous violinist and composer Niccolò Paganini (1782-1840) died in Nice, after travelling there from Paris after Christmas. He had fallen on hard times financially and his health was declining. In Nice, which belonged to the Kingdom of Sardinia at the time, his friend, the Count of Cessole offered him a flat at 23 rue de la Préfecture in the old city centre of Nice. Paganini no longer played the violin himself by then. Instead he set up a trade in rare string instruments. He died on 27 May 1840, aged 57. The Church denied his body a Catholic burial in Genoa because he was accused of selling his soul to the Devil in exchange for his virtuoso skills and because the last rites had not been administered before his death. Paganini's body was kept in a barrel of oil. It was finally buried 36 years later, in a cemetery in Parma.

CINEMAS

with a story

161 CINÉMA EDEN THÉÂTRE

25 boulevard
Georges Clémenceau
13600 La Ciotat
Bouches-du-Rhône
+33 (0)4 88 42 17 60
edencinemalaciotat.com

The Eden Théâtre in La Ciotat is the oldest public cinema in operation in the world. While the very first commercial film was shown in the Salon Indien in the basement of the Grand Café in Paris on 29 December 1895, the brothers Lumière organised a private screening in the Eden Théâtre in La Ciotat that same year, on 14 October. The hall, which was built in 1889, was mainly used for plays, musicals and events. The then owner Raoul Gallaud and Antoine Lumière, the brothers' father, knew each other well. A few years earlier, the Lumières had built their holiday residence 'Le Palais Lumière' in La Ciotat. On 21 March 1899, 250 spectators paid to see 19 short films by the Lumière brothers in the Eden Théâtre, including *The launching of a ship in la Ciotat* and *A transatlantic leaving Marseille harbour*. This screening marked the real start of the Eden as a cinema. And now, 120 years later, you can still see films at the Eden or take a guided tour of this cinema. Plush red velvet and plenty of nostalgia!

EDEN

TRE

162 STUDIOS DE LA VICTORINE

16 avenue Edouard Grinda
06200 Nice
Alpes-Maritimes
+33 (0)4 97 25 81 80
studiosdelavictorine.fr

At one time, Nice used to be the French equivalent of Hollywood. In 1919, two film producers acquired La Victorine, a 7-hectare leisure property, from the Masséna family and built film studios there. Initially they were drawn to the fabulous daylight and sunshine in Nice. They only began to work with electrical lights and Tungsten studio lights much later. The studio had its heyday, under the management of the Hollywood producer Rex Ingram, who lived in Nice from 1924 until 1930 and who expanded the studios significantly. La Victorine also experienced difficult times, however, changing hands frequently. Today you can still find the studios in their original location, near Nice Airport. Films that were made here include *Et Dieu… créa la femme* by Roger Vadim (1956), *Mon oncle* by Jacques Tati (1958), *La Nuit américaine* by François Truffaut (1973) and *Magic in the Moonlight* by Woody Allen (2014) in addition to a series of French and international TV series such as *Riviera*. In 2017, the city of Nice bought the studios, giving them a new lease of life. While the studios are not open to the public, the city organises an open house every now and then.

163 MUSÉE DU CINÉMA / CINÉMARTIGUES

4 rue Colonel Denfert
13500 Martigues
Bouches-du-Rhône
+33 (0)4 42 10 91 30
cinemartigues.com

A tiny museum with a phenomenal collection that is entirely dedicated to film-making. In 2007, film fan Prosper Gnidzaz bequeathed his amazing collection of 900 film reels and antique projectors to the town of Martigues. This paved the way for the creation of the Cinémathèque Gnidzaz, where the history of film is brought to life, where Gnidzaz discusses his passion and where the role of Martigues as a film set is highlighted. The tiny cinema in the museum can seat 35 spectators. The city of Martigues also supports the larger arthouse Cinéma Jean Renoir in Allée Renoir.

164 **CINÉMATHÈQUE DE TOULOUSE**

69 rue du Taur
31000 Toulouse
Haute-Garonne
+33 (0)5 62 30 30 10
lacinemathequede toulouse.com

France's second most important Cinémathèque relocated to a 16th-century abbey in 1997. In addition to being one of three national film archives, the Cinémathèque de Toulouse also hosts temporary exhibitions as well as screening all kinds of films. During the summer months, the films are shown in open air in the courtyard of the renovated abbey. Check out the film library, in the former chapel, where you can see the remarkable rediscovered fresco from 1933, that praises the virtues of socialism. In a religious institution, nonetheless!

165 **LE GENDARME DE SAINT-TROPEZ**

MUSÉE DE LA GENDARMERIE ET DU CINÉMA DE SAINT-TROPEZ
2 place Blanqui
83990 Saint-Tropez
Var
+33 (0)4 94 55 90 20
saint-tropez.fr/culture/mgc

The scenes in the headquarters of the gendarmerie in Louis de Funès's comedies were actually filmed in the real building of the Gendarmerie Nationale in Saint-Tropez. In 2016, it became a museum dedicated to the history of the gendarmerie and film-making in Saint-Tropez. Obviously, the museum dwells at length on the series of extremely popular *Gendarmerie* comedies starring Louis de Funès, which kicked off with *Le Gendarme de Saint-Tropez* in 1964. Six films were made in all. The interactive exhibition, which includes rebuilt sets, features all kinds of props from the *Gendarmerie* films. The temporary exhibitions focus on other film icons in the city, such as Brigitte Bardot. She rose to fame with the film *Et Dieu… créa la femme*, which was largely shot in Saint-Tropez in 1956.

THEATRES
in unusual places

166 HALLE AUX GRAINS

Place Dupuy
31000 Toulouse
Haute-Garonne
+33 (0)5 61 63 13 13
onct.toulouse.fr/halle-aux-grains

Originally, this concert hall was a cereal storage and market, which was built in 1864 in the pink brick that is so typical of Toulouse. It is situated near the Canal du Midi, so that barges could easily unload grain here. The building briefly became a sports hall, where boxing competitions were once held. Since 1974, it has been the residence of the renowned Orchestre National du Capitole. The hexagonal building is famous for its superb acoustics. The hall has an innovative layout, meaning the audience – maximum 2200 spectators – is seated around the orchestra.

167 THÉÂTRE DE LA CRIÉE

30 quai de Rive Neuve
13007 Marseille
Bouches-du-Rhône
+33 (0)4 91 54 70 54
theatre-lacriee.com

In 1981, the Théâtre National de Marseille moved into the old fish market, near the Vieux Port, where fish was sold at auction between 1909 and 1976. The fish market has since moved to l'Estaque, outside the city. Unfortunately, all that remains of the original building is its façade. The Théâtre de la Criée styles itself as 'a theatre, art, visual and fantasy factory'. The building has two theatres: one that can seat 800 spectators and one with 280 seats. The foyer, which often hosts exhibitions, is open to the public during the day.

168 THÉÂTRE DU CAPITOLE DE TOULOUSE

Place du Capitole
31000 Toulouse
Haute-Garonne
+33 (0)5 61 63 13 13
theatreducapitole.fr

The 18th-century city hall of Toulouse is an imposing and majestic building, which also has quite a surprise in store for visitors: it is also home to a theatre! The 'performance hall' in the right wing dates from 1736, was destroyed by fire in 1917, and rebuilt as a neo-baroque gem. The Théâtre du Capitole owes its excellent reputation to its world-class opera and ballet productions.

169 THÉÂTRE GALLI

80 avenue Raoul Henry
83110 Sanary-sur-Mer
Var
+33 (0)4 94 88 53 90
theatregalli.com

A place where you would least expect to run into a striking, sleek and modernist building but there you have it. The Théâtre Galli, which is situated on the fringe of the old city centre of the seaside resort of Sanary-sur-Mer, has a remarkable history. It is named after its founder Georges Galli, a lawyer and star of the silent movie era, who entered a religious order after retiring from acting. In 1957, Galli, who was the abbot of Sanary by then, had the 'Cité de la Jeunesse' built in the town. It was France's first youth centre. The art deco building was subsequently used as a sports centre and performance venue. Since then, it has undergone a radical renovation and has become a theatre and concert hall. In 1991, trompe l'oeil paintings of famous locals and washashores, such as the writer Thomas Mann, the artists Alma Mahler and Franz Werfel, and the architect Marius Michel (who is better known as Michel 'Pacha'), were added.

169 THÉÂTRE GALLI

Unique

BRIDGES

170 VIADUC DE MILLAU

Along the motorway A75/E11
12100 Millau
Aveyron
+33 (0)5 65 75 40 12 (office du tourisme)
leviaducdemillau.com

The spectacular Millau Viaduct, which was officially inaugurated on 14 December 2004, is the world's tallest bridge. Pylon P2 (the piers are numbered from north to south) is the highest of seven: 343 metres. This is a record-breaking bridge in every sense of the word: the viaduct's total length is 2460 metres, the roadway is situated 245 metres above the River Tarn, and the distance between each of the pylons is 342 metres, which is taller than the Eiffel Tower (324 metres). The bridge deck is made from steel and weighs an amazing 50.000 tons. The top half of the pylons is split in two to counter flex and expansion of the material. The British architect Norman Foster designed this remarkably elegant bridge, together with the French engineer Michel Virlogeux. The structure was built by Eiffage, a French group that can trace its roots to Gustave Eiffel, the designer of the Eiffel Tower in Paris. Construction was extremely complicated: the Belgian engineering firm Greisch was in charge of the resistance calculations. They also developed the innovative launching devices used to build the deck high above the valley. The Millau Viaduct connects Clermont-Ferrand in the north with Béziers and Montpellier in the south. For many decades, the Tarn Valley was a bottleneck because the old road ran through the town of Millau.

171 PONT SAINT-BÉNÉZET

Boulevard de la Ligne
84000 Avignon
Vaucluse
+33 (0)4 32 74 32 74
(office du tourisme)
avignon-tourisme.com

This is probably one of the most famous bridges in the world. And it is not even a 'complete' bridge at that. Most French speaking children are taught this little ditty: *'Sur le pont d'Avignon / on y danse on y danse…'*. According to legend, the bridge was built by a young shepherd, who claimed that an angel had commanded him to build it in a dream. It was completed in 1185. Fortunately, the young man got a lot of help. Originally the bridge was 900 metres long, had 22 arches, and connected Avignon with Villeneuve-lès-Avignon, where you can still see the 13th-century tower of the French King Philippe le Bel today. The bridge was an important link between Lyon and the Mediterranean. It was also of strategic importance, which explains why it was destroyed and rebuilt several times over the centuries. Around 1650, the bridge collapsed because the river was often in flood. Since then, only four arches remain standing and the bridge stops in the middle of the river… Apparently, the famous song refers to the shepherds who were dancing on the river banks. In which case, the lyrics should be *'Sous le pont…'* There are chapels on and under the bridge, where you can see a small documentary exhibition about 'le pont d'Avignon'.

172 PONT DU DIABLE

Route d'Aniane
34150 Aniane
Hérault
+33 (0)04 67 57 58 83
saintguilhem-valleeherault.fr/en/pont-du-diable

This bridge, which is situated just a short distance from Saint-Guilhem-le-Désert, is said to date from the 11th century and supposedly is one of the oldest bridges in France. It connected the abbey at Aniane, with Gellone Abbey at Saint-Guilhem. Legend has it that it owes its name, the Devil's bridge, to the pact that the bridge builders signed with the devil. The devil would let them continue to build the bridge. In return, he could claim the soul of the first person to walk across the completed bridge. The builders chased a cat across, after which the furious devil attempted to destroy the bridge, in vain.

173 PONT VIEUX

Rue des Tineries
11220 Lagrasse
Aude

This 14th-century arched bridge connects Lagrasse, one of France's most beautiful villages, with the abbey on the opposite bank of the Orbieu River. Originally, the bridge also had two towers. Explore the narrow, cobbled streets of this quiet village and houses such as Maison Maynard (14th century) and Le Presbytère (15th century), where the tourist office is located. The large, open market hall dates from the 14th century: ten stone columns support its wooden roof.

FONDATION MAEGHT

LANDSCAPES

SCULPTURE
parks

174 **CHÂTEAU LA COSTE**
2750 route de
la Cride
13610 Le Puy-
Sainte-Réparade
Bouches-du-Rhône
+33 (0)4 42 61 89 98
chateau-la-coste.com

Château La Coste is a vast open-air museum for contemporary art and architecture in a vineyard, 15 kilometres to the north of Aix-en-Provence. In 2004, the Irish art collector Paddy McKillen decided to give artists and architects free rein in the grounds. The Japanese architect Tadao Ando built the elegant art centre with a water feature. A large bronze spider by Louise Bourgeois hovers over the water, greeting visitors, along with a colourful mobile by Alexander Calder. Wear sturdy shoes and protect yourself against the heat and the sun with a hat and a bottle of water because the walk takes at least two hours, the trail is hilly but it's definitely worth it. En route, you'll get to see sculptures by such leading artists as Franz West, Richard Serra, Jenny Holzer, Liam Gillick, Michael Stipe (yes, the lead singer of R.E.M.), Sophie Calle, Tracey Emin, Sean Scully and Ai WeiWei. Tadao Ando has converted the hilltop village chapel into an intimate, minimalistic space for reflection. Every year, new sculptures are added to the collection. The old wine storehouses host temporary exhibitions. There are a number of excellent restaurants in the grounds, for a quick snack or a full meal.

175 **POPPY AND PIERRE SALINGER FOUNDATION**

AT: LA BASTIDE ROSE

99 chemin des Croupières
84250 Le Thor
Vaucluse
+33 (0)6 13 72 43 99
pierresalinger.org

Pierre Salinger became internationally famous, serving as the White House Press Secretary under US President John F. Kennedy after which he managed the Robert F. Kennedy's presidential campaign. He then went on to work as a journalist and was appointed to the US Senate. In 2000, he moved to France: he had always said that he would leave the USA if George W. Bush was elected president. At Le Thor, near Avignon, Salinger mainly concentrated on art, founding the Poppy and Pierre Salinger Foundation. Since 2004, they have been sponsoring annual contemporary sculpture exhibitions in the grounds of their estate La Bastide Rose. Sometimes the exhibitions are dedicated to the work of one artist, such as Keith Haring in 2006 and Alexander Calder in 2009. Other years, the exhibitions focus on a theme such as L'Amour (2018) or Totem (2016). Pierre Salinger did not get to enjoy the South of France for long: he died in 2004 in Le Thor and is buried in Arlington National Cemetery, near Washington D.C., near the graves of JFK and Bobby Kennedy. There is an intimate Musée Pierre Salinger at La Bastide Rose, that offers an overview of his life and career in documents and pictures.

176 LA COMMANDERIE DE PEYRASSOL

RN 7
83340 Flassans-sur-Issole
Var
+33 (0)4 94 69 71 02
peyrassol.com

In addition to being a vineyard estate that produces outstanding wines, La Commanderie de Peyrassol, which is situated 40 kilometres to the north of Hyères, also has an excellent collection of 50 monumental sculptures in the grounds. Philippe Austruy, the entrepreneur who acquired the Commanderie in 2001, joined forces with Valérie Bach, who runs the Brussels-based gallery La Patinoire Royale, for this initiative. Their dream was to restore this estate, which was founded in the 13th century, to its former glory and have it engage in a dialogue with modern art. Among the vines you can see whimsical works by Arman, Carsten Höller, Anne and Patrick Poirier, Philippe Berry and Niki de Saint Phalle, a modern-day Icarus disguised as Michael Jackson by Panamarenko, corten steel sculptures by Bernar Venet, paintings by Antoni Tàpies and Bertrand Lavier, and a glass installation by Dan Graham. They recently added a striking pavilion – a monumental sculpture in its own right – to permanently exhibit more fragile artworks.

177 VENET FOUNDATION

Chemin du Moulin des Serres
83490 Le Muy
Var
venetfoundation.org

Monumental, minimalistic and conceptual. This is the Venet Foundation, the crowning glory of the career of Bernar Venet, the French sculptor who is mainly famous for his large-scale, often curved wood and corten steel sculptures. It's not the kind of place you can visit on the spur of the moment, however. Venet was born in 1941 in France but spent most of his life in New York. He moved back to France in 2014, creating the perfect setting for his own sculptures on a 7-hectare estate near Le Muy. He confronts his own work with the minimalistic and conceptual works of such internationally famous artists as Sol LeWitt, Donald Judd, Dan Flavin, Tony Cragg and James Turrell. The open 'chapel' that Venet designed for Frank Stella's relief sculptures is awe-inspiring. This is the most important French private collection of minimalist and conceptual art. You must book ahead, however, after which you will be allocated a slot and the exact address details of the Venet Foundation. The tour takes about two hours.

178 **FONDATION MAEGHT**

623 chemin des Gardettes
06570 Saint-Paul-de-Vence
Alpes-Maritimes
+33 (0)4 93 32 81 63
fondation-maeght.com

A solid reputation and a museum as *Gesamtkunstwerk*. Marguerite and Aimé Maeght were much-praised and visionary art dealers, based in Paris, who conceived the idea of building their own private museum in Saint-Paul-de-Vence. It opened in 1964 as the first European foundation dedicated entirely to contemporary art. The Catalan architect Josep Lluís Sert designed an iconic building, working closely with a number of distinguished artists to incorporate their works in the museum: Georges Braque created a water feature with a fish mosaic, Joan Miró designed a labyrinth with 'organic' artworks while Alberto Giacometti's elongated, life-sized sculptures grace the courtyard. There are several works by leading modern sculptors on the lawn outside in front of the museum building: a whimsical fountain by Pol Bury, a monumental work by Alexander Calder and a wind sculpture by Takis, in addition to works by Jean Arp, Barbara Hepworth and Eduardo Chillida. And, of course, there is the museum itself, where part of the enormous collection (13.000 works) is shown with highlights including Pierre Bonnard, Marc Chagall, Joan Mitchell and Ellsworth Kelly alongside an annual roster of temporary exhibitions. Don't forget to check out the Chapelle Saint-Bernard with stained-glass windows by Georges Braque and Raoul Ubac.

Seen through the
PAINTER'S EYE

179 **TERRAIN DES PEINTRES – PAUL CÉZANNE**
Chemin de
la Marguerite
13100 Aix-en-Provence
Bouches-du-Rhône
aixenprovence tourism.com/en/ fiche/2664

The Terrain des Peintres – or Field of the Painters – is situated one kilometre to the north of Atelier Paul Cézanne, or a 10-minute walk. It boasts stunning views of the Mont Sainte-Victoire, the mountain that overlooks Aix. Copies of nine of Cézanne's paintings are placed in this specially designed vantage point. The artist often came here to paint the Mont Sainte-Victoire in the years between 1901 and 1906: he was obsessed by the mountain, producing no less than 87 paintings and watercolours between 1886 and 1906. Cézanne waged a battle with the mountain: he wanted to capture it in a more 'solid and durable' impressionist style, using a more organised and structured approach, with lines and bold strokes. The mountain continued to elude him, becoming increasingly abstract in form in his canvases.

181 ESPACE VAN GOGH

180 PONT DE LANGLOIS – VINCENT VAN GOGH

At the top of Rue Gaspard Monge, along the canal from Arles to Bouc
13200 Arles
Bouches-du-Rhône

In May 1888, Vincent van Gogh painted a drawbridge, the first bridge on the canal that connects Arles with the Mediterranean. The bridge reminded him of the typical drawbridges in his home country. Unfortunately, the Pont de Langlois, which is named after the keeper's name, has since been moved to the top of Rue Gaspard Monge, downstream along the canal from Arles to Bouc, which is situated a few kilometres to the south-west of the city. In fact, the 'Pont Van Gogh' is not even the bridge that the painter immortalised in his canvas: the original bridge and the keeper's house were destroyed by the Germans during World War II. In 1962, the current bridge, an identical copy from Fos-sur-Mer, was installed in a location that is fortunately similar to the landscape that Van Gogh painted. A sign near the bridge features a reproduction of the painting. You'll have to use your imagination and add the carriage and the women washing clothes in the river to the scene yourself.

181 ESPACE VAN GOGH – VINCENT VAN GOGH

Place Félix Rey
13200 Arles
Bouches-du-Rhône

This is the former hospital at Arles – now the city's media library – where Vincent van Gogh stayed twice between the end of December 1888 until May 1889, following his first mental health crisis. After cutting off his left ear on 23 December 1888, he was in a generalised state of delirium, recognising nobody and talking incoherently. Doctor Félix Rey – after whom the square in front of the hospital is named – was finally forced to confine him to a small, locked room. Once Vincent had recovered, he was allowed to return home – to 'la Maison Jaune' in Place Lamartine (which was destroyed in 1944 by the Germans), taking up his brushes again: he painted the lovely courtyard of the Espace Van Gogh, which you can still visit. Unfortunately his mental health soon declined again: he had four serious mental breakdowns. Finally, the locals had had enough and launched a petition: they wanted him to leave because he was 'crazy', drank too much, groped women and made inappropriate and obscene remarks. Vincent ended up voluntarily admitting himself to Saint-Paul-de-Mausole, an asylum in Saint-Rémy.

182 L'ARBRE DE VENCE – CHAÏM SOUTINE

Place du Frêne
06140 Vence
Alpes-Maritimes
vence.fr/le-grand-frene-preserve

This enormous, stately ash tree in front of the Musée de Vence is said to be almost five hundred years old. Legend has it that is was planted by King François I in 1538. The French king stopped at Vence en route to Nice, where he was supposed to sign a peace treaty with Emperor Charles V to end the war in Italy. The legendary tree has inspired many an artist. The French-Jewish painter Chaïm Soutine painted it no less than twenty times in 1929, translating his inner torment in his depiction of the tree as a tortuous, tormented figure in a storm. One of the paintings is reproduced on a sign near the colossal tree.

183 LA FONTAINE DE VENCE – RAOUL DUFY

Place Antony Mars
06140 Vence
Alpes-Maritimes
vence-tourisme.com/fr/decouvrir/art-et-culture/la-route-des-peintres

Raoul Dufy was fascinated by this fountain from 1822, painting this urban landscape several times around 1920. Although Dufy painted in oils, his works often resemble watercolours because of the light, airy compositions and washes he used. His style is simple, somewhat naïve even, yet so beautiful. He often uses vivid, sunny colours, but here he elected to use soft pastels to render the fountain and the houses in the square. The painting, which is reproduced on a sign in front of the fountain, is in the collection of the Centre Pompidou. Dufy's painting is part of the 'Route des Peintres' in Vence, which consists of six works in all: in addition to Dufy, there is a tree by Chaïm Soutine, a landscape by Jean Dubuffet, and urban scenes by lesser-known artists such as Alexis Mossa, Maurice Cahours and Georges William Thornley. You can find a map on the website of the Office du Tourisme.

182 L'ARBRE DE VENCE – CHAÏM SOUTINE

184 DESPAIR / THE SCREAM – EDVARD MUNCH

Promenade des Anglais
06000 Nice
Alpes-Maritimes
munchmuseet.no

The Norwegian painter Edvard Munch returned to Nice several times, where, surprisingly enough, he was inspired to create his world-famous work *The Scream* (1893). At the end of 1891 or in early 1892, he made the first pen drawings for this work in his sketchbook, immediately after several sketches of passers-by on the Promenade des Anglais. He developed the motif, using charcoal, drawing a man with a bowler hat, leaning on a balustrade. There are two figures walking in the distance and you can see the mountains and the sea in the background. Munch added a blood-red sky in oils. At the time, the work was still called *Despair*. On 22 January 1892, Munch wrote the following in his diary: "I was walking along / the road with two / friends when the sun / went down / The Sky suddenly / turned blood-red / I paused, leaned / against the fence tired / to death above the / blue-black fjord and city / blood in flaming tongues hovered / My friends walked / on and I stayed / behind quaking / with angst / and I felt as though a / vast endless / scream passed through / nature". On the Promenade des Anglais in Nice, Munch probably relived an experience that had befallen him a few months earlier at sunset in Oslo. It is unclear where Munch was staying in Nice at the time. His correspondence lists addresses of hotels and a villa that no longer exist. Upon his return to Oslo, he further developed the concepts of *Despair*, culminating in the world-famous *The Scream*.

Le Midi in LITERATURE

185 MÉNERBES – PETER MAYLE

84560 Ménerbes Vaucluse

When Peter Mayle, who previously worked as a creative director for a large ad agency, relocated from the UK to Ménerbes in 1987, his intention was to write a novel. But he never managed to get down to writing, due to the problems with the renovations of his house, the unexpectedly cold mistral wind, and the difficulties and misunderstandings he encountered in his dealings with local plumbers, builders and lawyers. Until he had the brilliant idea to chronicle his adventures in Provence. After a somewhat hesitant start, *A Year in Provence* (1989) became a massive hit and was translated in dozens of languages. Thanks to Peter Mayle, British people and the world discovered Provence. Even the French translation was a success. Mayle wrote a number of sequels to his first novel, with *A Year in Provence* paving the way for a new literary genre. In 1997, Mayle moved to Long Island, in the USA, to get away from the many fans and sightseers who turned up at his front door… He ended up returning, nonetheless, living at Vaugines and Lourmarin. He died in 2018 in Ménerbes.

186 ÈZE – GEORGE SAND, JEAN COCTEAU AND FRIEDRICH NIETZSCHE

JARDIN EXOTIQUE D'ÈZE

Rue du Château
06360 Èze
Alpes-Maritimes
+33 (0)4 93 41 10 30
www.jardinexotique-eze.fr

A must-see. The village of Èze is perched on a rocky outcrop 429 metres above the sea. The bus journey from the railway station at Èze-sur-Mer up to the village is quite an adventure: the route is spectacular, as are the hairpin bends. The town's Jardin Exotique – with its many exotic plants, ponds, waterfalls and sculptures – offers breathtaking views in every direction. It's easy to see how this panorama inspired so many lyrical descriptions from various writers. In her *Nouvelles lettres d'un voyageur*, George Sand called the view 'enchanting': "possessing the most beautiful view from the road, the view with the best composition; where grace competes with harshness". Jean Cocteau wrote: "There is no place more exotic or more eccentric than this. It seems to float in nothingness". And the German philosopher Friedrich Nietzsche was inspired to write his book *Also sprach Zarathustra* (1883-85) here.

186 ÈZE – GEORGE SAND, JEAN COCTEAU AND FRIEDRICH NIETZSCHE

187 **FONTVIEILLE – ALPHONSE DAUDET**

LE SENTIER DES MOULINS DE DAUDET
INFO: OFFICE DE TOURISME
Avenue des Moulins
13990 Fontvieille
Bouches-du-Rhône
+33 (0)4 90 54 67 49
fontvieille-provence.fr/en/accueil-gb

Alphonse Daudet's *Lettres de mon moulin (Letters from my Windmill)* (1869) is a collection of short stories and one of the most popular works in French 19th-century literature. While Daudet lived in Paris, he regularly returned to his native Provence. He did not have a mill and he did not write his stories there, however. He was a regular guest at the Château de Montauban, just outside Fontvieille, where his cousin's family lived. From there, he often liked to take a walk to the nearby windmills, smelling the flowers and the scent of the wheat and using his imagination and all his senses to commit these bucolic scenes and all of Provence to paper in short tales. From the village, you can take a walk which leads past Daudet's mill and Château de Montauban.

188 **AUBAGNE – MARCEL PAGNOL**

MAISON NATALE DE MARCEL PAGNOL
16 cours Barthélémy
INFO: OFFICE DE TOURISME
8 cours Barthélémy
13400 Aubagne
Bouches-du-Rhône
+33 (0)4 42 03 49 98
tourisme-paysdaubagne.fr

The eminent writer, playwright and film director Marcel Pagnol (1895-1974) is still very popular with French readers. His books inspired two very successful films, i.e., *Jean de Florette* and *Manon des Sources*. Pagnol was born in Aubagne, grew up in Marseille, and lived and worked in Paris. He is best known, however, for his Provençal novels and plays. His satire *Topaze* from 1928, on general themes such as honesty and dishonesty which are still very relevant today, was adapted several times as a film. With *Marius* (1929), Pagnol returned to his Provençal roots and Marseille. He founded his own film production company in the 1930s, making his films with several great French actors, including Fernandel. In 1962, Pagnol wrote a series called *L'Eau des Collines*, based on his own film from 1951. The film adaptation, *Jean de Florette* (1986), and its sequel *Manon des Sources*, starring Gérard Depardieu, Yves Montand and Emmanuelle Béart, was an international hit. In Aubagne, you can visit the house where Pagnol spent his childhood years. There is an exhibition with photos and documents and a reconstruction of the flat where his family lived. You can also follow in Pagnol's footsteps, taking the 'Childhood memories' walking tour.

189 MARSEILLE – MARCEL PAGNOL

ROUTE DE LA TREILLE
13011 Marseille
Bouches-du-Rhône
tourisme-marseille.com/fiche/circuit-marcel-pagnol-marseille

If you want to learn more about the writer and playwright Marcel Pagnol, take this long walk on the fringe of Marseille, which starts from his grave. Pagnol died in 1974 in Paris, aged 79, but was buried in his native Provence. The trail takes you to several sites where he spent part of his childhood or where the family spent their holidays, as described by the writer himself in his autobiographical novel *La Gloire de mon père* from 1957. Other places include locations where he shot films such as *Regain*, *Angèle* and also *L'Eau des Sources*. Over the years, La Treille has changed significantly, however, forcing director Claude Berri to look elsewhere for locations to shoot his films *Jean de Florette* and *Manon des sources* in 1986. Berri ended up settling on Mirabeau and Vaugines.

190 GRASSE – PATRICK SÜSKIND

06130 Grasse
Alpes-Maritimes

The perfume capital of Grasse plays an important role in *Perfume* (1985), the international bestseller by the German writer Patrick Süskind. In this historical fantasy novel, Jean-Baptiste Grenouille, an orphan who is born in Paris in 1738, realises that he does not possess any scent himself. He thus resolves to create the ultimate, irresistible scent for himself, from the human body. He travels to Grasse where he learns the most important techniques to become 'the world's greatest perfumer' after discovering the entrancing scent of a young virgin. And thus begins a campaign of killing teenage girls to preserve their scent and achieve his goal, plunging Grasse into crisis.

191 MARSEILLE – JEAN-CLAUDE IZZO

13001 Marseille
Bouches-du-Rhône

Marseille can be a bit rough around the edges, which also explains why it was used as the backdrop for a series of detective novels. In 1995, Jean-Claude Izzo published *Total Khéops*, translated into English as *Total Chaos*, the first part of his Marseille Trilogy. It was an instant hit. Former police officer Fabio Montale, the son of working-class immigrants who moved to Marseille, just like Izzo, and who has a passion for poetry, jazz and beautiful women, investigates the violent deaths of two of his childhood friends. Montale becomes embroiled in a web of intrigue and corruption in the underworld and within Marseille's police force. In the sequels (*Chourmo* and *Soléa*), Montale comes out of retirement to further investigate the impact of the mafia in Marseille, as characters drop like flies.

192 MONIEUX – STEFAN HERTMANS

84390 Monieux
Vaucluse

The Flemish writer Stefan Hertmans sets the story of his internationally praised novel *The Convert (De Bekeerlinge* in Dutch, 2016) in the village of Monieux, which he knows inside and out as he has been living there for several years already. In 11th-century France, Vigdis Adelaïs, a young woman from a prosperous Christian family from Rouen, falls in love with David Todros, the son of a rabbi from Narbonne. They leave the city, pursued by her father's knights, ending up in Monieux, in the foothills of the Mont Ventoux. Until they are forced to flee the vicious wave of anti-Semitism that sweeps through Europe with the onset of the First Crusade. A book about (in)tolerance, migration and identity. Monieux has largely retained its medieval characters, with the odd trace here and there of the Jewish presence in the Middle Ages.

193 ÎLE DE PORQUEROLLES – GEORGES SIMENON

83400 Hyères
Var

The Belgian crime writer Georges Simenon (1903-1989) – the only writer to write more quickly than his publisher could publish and who has thrilled many mystery lovers with his *Inspector Maigret* series – first travelled to Porquerolles in 1926. His wife – the painter Régine Renchon, whom he called Tigy – wanted to get away from the bohemian and sometimes lawless lifestyle of Montparnasse. It was she who discovered the peace and quiet of the relatively unknown island of Porquerolles in May 1926. Tigy was the breadwinner at the time, Georges's books would only really start to sell from 1933 onwards when he signed with the Parisian publisher Gallimard. Georges and Tigy lived at Mas du Langoustier (which still exists) for quite some time. In 1935, they bought their own house near the harbour: Les Tamaris with a distinctive turret along Chemin du Langoustier. Simenon had a jetty built near the house for his own fishing boat. It is around this time that he created the character of the ingenious police detective Maigret (like Simenon he always carried a pipe) and that he started work on several novels. Porquerolles was first mentioned in his books after World War II, served as the setting for the novel *Le cercle des Mahé* (1946), a tragic love story. Simenon's inspector travelled to Porquerolles three years later to solve a murder. In *Mon ami Maigret* (1949, translated into English as *My Friend Maigret)*, Maigret is observed by a detective from Scotland Yard, Inspector Pyke, who has travelled to France to study the famous detective's unconventional methods. Much to Maigret's annoyance, Pyke follows him everywhere he goes, like a shadow. Maigret's departure from the island also signalled Simenon's departure. After the 1950s, he never returned to Porquerolles. By then, the world was at his feet: one of Belgium's most celebrated writers, Simenon had more than 400 novels to his name, having sold more than 550 million copies of his books worldwide, which were translated in 55 languages.

Le Midi in
MUSIC

194 LIGNE 3
BY: LÅPSLEY
34000 Montpellier
Hérault

The British singer and songwriter Låpsley (stage name of Holly Lapsley Fletcher) spent two months in Montpellier with her then boyfriend. *Ligne 3* is a reference to Montpellier's tram network and the tram that her boyfriend took to get to work from where they lived. The song, which was released in 2019, is about one specific day in the French city and documents the hours immediately after a long-term relationship comes to its end. "I wrote it a few days after I split up with my boyfriend. It's about the complexity of a break-up and actually I wanted to paint a picture of the day that we broke up", Låpsley explained.

195 ROUTE NATIONALE 7
BY: CHARLES TRENET
INFO: MUSÉE MÉMOIRE DE LA NATIONALE 7
3405 avenue de Provence N7
84420 Piolenc
Vaucluse
+33 (0)4 90 40 32 70

The French singer Charles Trenet knew exactly what he was doing when he released the jazzy song *Route Nationale 7* in 1955. The 966-kilometre long N7 trunk road connected Paris with the South of France, and in a sense is just as iconic as Route 66. As cars became more affordable in the 1950s, the Côte d'Azur suddenly seemed a lot closer, and France a lot smaller. In his song, Trenet even sings that Paris has become a suburb of Saint-Paul-de-Vence. The song was an instant hit. The Route Nationale 7 still attracts nostalgic drivers today, who appreciate its mythical status, even though you can now get to Le Midi much faster thanks to the Autoroute du Soleil. There is an N7 museum in Piolenc, near Orange.

196 LA MADRAGUE

BY: BRIGITTE BARDOT

La Madrague
Sentier Littoral
83990 Saint-Tropez
Var

In *La Madrague* (1963), Brigitte Bardot sings about the villa that she bought in Saint-Tropez in 1958, where she had shot the film *Et Dieu... créa la femme* two years earlier. The lyrics are by Jean-Max Rivière, while Gérard Bourgeois composed the music. Bardot loved the song because it was so personal. She explained: "Jean-Max Rivière had the brilliant idea to put simple, upbeat and nostalgic feelings to music. He was inspired by the place and saw it through my eyes". The song starts with memories of the summer that has just ended: the beach is deserted, everyone's gone home, people have returned to their jobs in the city and autumn is in the air.

197 LA MER

BY: CHARLES TRENET

Étang de Thau
34200 Sète
Hérault

In effect, Charles Trenet's famous song *La mer* was not inspired by the sea. The idea for the tune came to him while he was on a train in 1943, travelling from Montpellier to Perpignan and gazing out of the window at the Étang de Thau: a lagoon, not the Mediterranean Sea. He wrote the lyrics and the tune in just 20 minutes. The song was only recorded much later. Trenet didn't think it was a hit. Other artists turned it down, saying it was 'too ordinary'. Ultimately, Trenet recorded it in 1947. That same year, the French singer toured the United States, where the American version, *Beyond the Sea*, written by Jack Lawrence, became a huge hit. The English version is different: it is about a past love, while *La mer* is an homage to the never-ending movement of the waves and the ever-changing colour of the water. In 1959, Bobby Darin had a huge hit with *Beyond the Sea*, which was reinterpreted in 2003 by Robbie Williams for the soundtrack of *Finding Nemo*. Rod Stewart, George Benson and Barry Manilow also recorded their own versions. The French original was used in the closing scene of the 2007 film *Mr. Bean's Holiday*. By the time Charles Trenet died in 2001, there were 400 different recordings, with over 70 million copies sold.

198 **C'EST UNE GARONNE**

BY: CLAUDE NOUGARO

Pont Neuf
31000 Toulouse
Haute-Garonne

Toulouse pays tribute to the singer/songwriter Claude Nougaro with a statue. But you can also find the lyrics of his homage to the River Garonne on a corten steel artwork on one of the piers of the Pont Neuf, near 112 quai de Tounis, where Nougaro lived from the late 1980s onwards. He is said to have written the song on his balcony, with a view of the river. After his death in 2004, his ashes were partly dispersed in the river.

198 C'EST UNE GARONNE

199 **DOULIOU DOULIOU SAINT-TROPEZ**
BY: GENEVIÈVE GRAD
83990 Saint-Tropez
Var

The twist, but in French! The song was composed by the band leader Raymond Lefebvre for the comedy *Le Gendarme de Saint-Tropez* (1964), spawning a series of six extremely successful Gendarmes sequels. *Douliou douliou Saint-Tropez* is performed and danced by Geneviève Grad, the actress who played the role of the daughter of 'gendarme' Louis de Funès. The film, which revolves around the extremely uptight, scheming gendarme Ludovic Cruchot, is a succession of misunderstandings, as the gendarmes hunt down and chase a group of naturists at Plage des Canebiers and a Rembrandt is stolen from Musée de l'Annonciade – while the conflict between the 'serious' father and the daughter who defies her father's authority also plays a role.

200 **LES MARCHÉS DE PROVENCE**
BY: GILBERT BÉCAUD
Cours Lafayette
83000 Toulon
Var

In this song, the famous French chansonnier Gilbert Bécaud *(Nathalie, Et maintenant)* returns to Toulon, the city where he was born in 1927 as François Silly. He later took his adopted father's name 'Bécaud'. Gilbert was his second name. Bécaud moved to Paris after World War II, after having attended the Conservatoire in Nice. In *Les Marchés de Provence* he describes the scents and colours in a market in Provence and the singsong way in which the stallholders peddle their wares to passers-by. The song was inspired by the popular daily fruit and vegetable market in Cours Lafayette in Toulon.

201 UNE BELLE HISTOIRE

BY: MICHEL FUGAIN AND LE BIG BAZAR

Autoroute du Soleil
A6/A7
26000 Valence
Drôme

The early seventies. Freedom, happiness, free love and sexual liberation. In 1972, the French singer Michel Fugain sought to capture this atmosphere in a song about the brief encounter of a boy and a girl on a hot summer's day on the side of the motorway. They are each travelling in different directions, they catch each other's eye, and they are briefly carried away, for an instant, hiding in a wheat field. In Fugain's imagination, the scene took place along Route 66. Perhaps he was inspired by Janis Joplin's *Me and Bobby McGee* from 1971. But Fugain's French songwriter Pierre Delanoë relocated the story to France. The boy is on his way home, to the north, while the girl is en route for le Midi. We have no idea where their encounter took place, although the A6/A7, 'l'autoroute des vacances', is a likely contender.
What rhymes with "c'était sans doute un jour de chance?" "Valence!", of course. Did they meet there? Either way, *Une belle histoire* was a huge hit and many different versions were recorded over the years.

202 CÉZANNE PEINT

BY: FRANCE GALL

13100 Aix-en-Provence
Bouches-du-Rhône

This song from 1985 is an homage to the painter Paul Cézanne. It was performed by France Gall and written by her husband Michel Berger when they were holidaying in Aix-en-Provence. They were staying in a house with a view of Cézanne's studio and Mont Sainte-Victoire. The song ends as Cézanne is caught in an unexpected Provençal thunderstorm. As he scurried back to his studio, he collapsed. Several hours later, he was found by a passer-by, who carried him back into the town on his laundry cart. Cézanne died of pneumonia two days later, aged 67.

GARDENS
as works of art

203 VILLA ET JARDINS EPHRUSSI DE ROTHSCHILD

1 avenue Ephrussi de Rothschild
06230 Saint-Jean-Cap-Ferrat
Alpes-Maritimes
+33 (0)4 93 01 33 09
villa-ephrussi.com

A journey back in time. A palatial villa, that is an incredible artwork, and a park that resembles the Garden of Eden. This rose-coloured palazzo was built for Béatrice Ephrussi de Rothschild between 1907 and 1912. She was the slightly eccentric and idiosyncratic daughter of Baron Alphonse de Rotschild, a banker and art collector, and his wife Leonora, also a Rotschild but from the English branch of the family. Béatrice married François Ephrussi but ended up divorcing him because he was an inveterate gambler, which caused financial woes for the couple. Fortunately, her father left her a fortune upon his death in 1905. Béatrice was thus able to fulfil her dream and build a villa for her phenomenal art collection. The villa is situated on a promontory on the isthmus of Cap Ferrat, offering amazing views in all directions. But there's more: Béatrice had a seven-hectare park built around her sumptuous, Venetian-style villa with a ceiling painting by Tiepolo and marble columns from a palace in Verona. There are nine gardens in all, each on a different theme: a rose garden, Japan, Florence ... The large basin with dancing, musical fountains is the main feature. The view from the Temple of Love above it is amazing. This is a truly memorable experience: you feel as if you have somehow been transported to the belle époque.

204 JARDIN DU PALAIS DE CARNOLÈS

3 avenue de la Madone
06500 Menton
Alpes-Maritimes
menton.fr

The Musée des Beaux-Arts of Menton is currently closed for renovation but its stupendous garden with its remarkable sculptures – including an avenue lined with busts – and no fewer than 137 (!) varieties of citrus trees remains open. Menton is the lemon capital of France, after all. The estate's history dates back to the 17th century, when the Grimaldis, the princes of Monaco, used the palace as a summer residence. The first lemon and orange trees were planted in the garden in 1725, with the beds laid out in artful patterns. The current garden, with its wide range of varieties, dates from 1970, when the Jardin du Palais de Carnolès became part of the San Guiliano research centre (Corsica). The intention is to create the largest citrus collection in Europe. Menton has several other stunning tropical gardens: Serre de la Madone, Val Rahmeh, Fontana Rosa and Maria Serena are all worth visiting.

205 CHÂTEAU DE LA NAPOULE

Boulevard Henry Clews
06210 Mandelieu-la-Napoule
Alpes-Maritimes
+33 (0)4 93 49 95 05
chateau-lanapoule.com

Fairy tales do exist. Expect the unexpected when you visit this neo-Gothic castle. The somewhat eccentric American couple Henry and Marie Clews began building their home on the ruins of a medieval fortress in 1919. The garden alone, which can be visited separately, has plenty of surprises in store for visitors, including a maze with sculptures of bizarre people and fantastic creatures, ponds, fountains, gates and vistas of the Bay of Cannes through 'medieval' arches. All these statues were designed by Henry Clews himself. Look for the giant lizard who is trying to get into the castle through one of its windows or the man who is trying to escape from the tower by sliding down a rope. Scattered throughout the garden you will also find imaginative work by contemporary artists, including an elephant made from rubber tires by Serge Vandeput. The castle and Henry Clews's studio can only be visited during a guided tour.

206 JARDIN DU CASTEL SAINTE-CLAIRE

Avenue Edith Wharton
83400 Hyères
Var
+33 (0)4 94 00 78 65
hyeres-tourisme.com

It was a friendship that drew the American writer Edith Wharton to Hyères. In 1893, she had met the French writer Paul Bourget in Newport, permanently moving to Paris after she divorced her husband. After visiting Bourget's home in Costebelle, Wharton relocated to Hyères because of the sun and the pleasant climate. From 1920, she rented Castel Sainte-Claire, an old hillside monastery under the castle of Hyères, using it as her winter residence. It was here that she also wrote her famous novel *The Age of Innocence* (1921). She acquired the property seven years later, designing its botanic garden, which has an excellent collection of exotic plants. The garden also offers magnificent views over the city and harbour. Wharton lived here until her death in 1937. Interesting detail: the villa's previous owner, the archaeologist Olivier Voutier who found the *Venus de Milo*, is buried in the garden.

207 DOMAINE DU RAYOL

Avenue Jacques Chirac
83820 Rayol-Canadel-sur-Mer
Var
+33 (0)4 98 04 44 00
domainedurayol.org

Around the world in ten gardens … Domaine du Rayol is a large park near the sea, which is planted with trees and plants from California, the Canary Islands, New Zealand, South Africa, Chile and Asia. Agave, yucca, eucalyptus, protea, mimosa, palm trees, bamboo: all in one place for you to discover. The origins of this park date back to 1910, when the Parisian banker Alfred Courmes had a house built here with an exotic garden. Unfortunately, the Wall Street Crash of 1929 put a stop to its further expansion. The property was then acquired by the aeronautical engineer Henri Potez, who restored the buildings, added a striking staircase that leads from the pergola to the beach and expanded the garden to 400 species. In 1989, the Conservatoire du Littoral bought the estate. The landscape architects Gilles Clément and Philippe Deliau designed the current garden. The park organises kids' activities, an underwater discovery tour (the eleventh garden!) and workshops for people with a green thumb. It also has a cafe and a specialised bookshop.

208 PLATEAU DES POÈTES

21 rue de la Rotonde
34500 Béziers
Hérault
+33 (0)4 67 76 84 00
plateaudespoetes.toile-libre.org

This particularly lovely English landscape park at one end of the Allées Paul Riquet, Béziers' main boulevard, was designed in 1867. The five-hectare park is planted with more than seventy exotic plant species, which are irrigated by a number of streams that all flow into a Swan Lake. The sculptor Jean-Antoine Injalbert, to whom the Hôtel Fayet museum in the city is dedicated, created the busts and monuments in the park. The main eye-catcher, however, is his baroque Titan fountain.

208 PLATEAU DES POÈTES

209 VILLA EILENROC

460 avenue
Mrs Beaumont
06160 Antibes
Alpes-Maritimes
+33 (0)4 93 67 74 33
antibesjuanlespins.com

A magnificent rose garden and a luxurious villa. Villa Eilenroc was built between 1860 and 1867 for Hugh Hope Loudon, a Dutchman with British roots, who had made a fortune in the Dutch East Indies. He hired none other than Charles Garnier, the architect of the Opéra Garnier in Paris, to design his home. Eilenroc is an anagram of Cornélie, Loudon's wife. The garrigue or wild scrubland that is so typical of this area has since been replaced with a beautifully landscaped garden, with olive trees and an abundance of roses in a tribute to the tradition and expertise of Antibes, which is renowned for its roses. Several films have been shot in and around the elegant Villa Eilenroc, including *Under the Cherry Moon* (1986), the black and white musical starring Prince and in which Kristin Scott Thomas DBE made her debut, as well as Woody Allen's romantic comedy *Magic in the Moonlight* (2014), with Colin Firth and Emma Stone. Do check the opening hours before going: the villa is currently undergoing renovation work and the garden and/or the building is often closed.

209 VILLA EILENROC

Inspiring

BEACHES

210 **GRUISSAN PLAGE**
LES CHALETS
SUR PILOTIS
11430 Gruissan
Aude
www.odyssea.eu

The legendary erotic film, *37°2 Le Matin*, better known as *Betty Blue* (1986), by the French director Jean-Jacques Beineix, opens with a long, steamy sex scene in a small hut on the beach at Gruissan. The protagonist Zorg (Jean-Hugues Anglade) lives on the beach in a wooden chalet on stilts. No need to look for the house: Betty, a volatile free spirit (Béatrice Dalle) set it on fire. There are still more than a thousand of these chalets on the beach today. They were built from the end of the 19th century onwards, as simple summer residences without water or electricity. Since then, most of these chalets have undergone extensive renovation and have been expanded. The government is hoping to maintain a dozen or so of these chalets in their original state and list them as protected monuments. Take your time to discover this place: a bit of American suburbia, albeit in France. Follow the road signs for Plage des Chalets.

211 LA PLAGE DES CANEBIERS

83990 Saint-Tropez
Var

Plage des Canebiers is one of many sandy beaches in Saint-Tropez. The bay is famous for several reasons. Along Chemin de l'Estagnet, just behind the coastline, you can visit La Treille Muscate, the cottage where the French writer Colette spent her summers between 1925 and 1939. The house and garden, which extends to the sea, is only open to the public occasionally, however. Brigitte Bardot's Villa La Madrague is situated further to the east. The nudist scenes in the film *Le Gendarme de Saint-Tropez* were shot at Plage des Canebiers.

212 PLAGE DU PALAIS DES FESTIVALS

Promenade Robert
Favre le Bret
06400 Cannes
Alpes-Maritimes

Mr. Bean's Holiday (2007) was filmed in several places in the South of France but the climax is the final scene, which was filmed in and around the Palais des Festivals in Cannes, during which the actor Rowan Atkinson walks out of the building and onto the beach. While this may seem simple, they had to build a temporary scaffolding for this scene. Moreover, Promenade Robert Favre le Bret is usually a pedestrian zone but cars were allowed to enter once-only to create a traffic jam and enable Mr. Bean to walk over the roofs of the cars and onto the sand to the tune of Charles Trenet's *La mer*.

213 RUHL PLAGE

1 promenade
des Anglais
6000 Nice
Alpes-Maritimes
+33 (0)4 93 87 09 70
ruhl-plage.com

Unfortunately, the stately belle époque Hôtel Ruhl has been demolished but you can still visit Ruhl Casino in the – rather uninspiring in my opinion – new build from 1960. Just outside the casino is the pebble beach of Ruhl Plage, where you can still gaze at the sea – and the beautiful people – on blue and white striped sunbeds. Expensive, but elegant. You can also dine on this private beach, like the American writer F. Scott Fitzgerald and his wife Zelda used to in the 1920s. Zelda wrote: "Stars fell in our plates … and we were alone with the deep blue grandeur and the filet de sole Ruhl, and the second bottle of champagne." Chin-chin.

VINEYARDS & CHÂTEAUX

214 **CHÂTEAU MIRAVAL**
Miraval
83570 Correns
Var
miraval.com

Hollywood stars Angelina Jolie and Brad Pitt acquired Château Miraval in Correns, to the north of Brignoles, in 2008. They got married six years later in the castle chapel of this 600-hectare estate but have since split up. In addition to the fine wines that are produced here on some thirty hectares and which are usually bottled in design bottles, Miraval has a number of other claims to fame. One of the previous owners, the French jazz pianist Jacques Loussier, had a recording studio built in 1977. Pink Floyd recorded some of the tracks of their album *The Wall* (1979) here. Many artists have since used this famous and well-equipped studio, including Sade, AC/DC, The Cranberries, Steve Winwood, The Cure, Bryan Ferry and Chris Rea. The studio is still here but no longer in use. Château Miraval is closed to the public.

215 **CHÂTEAU LA CANORGUE**
Route du Pont Julien
84480 Bonnieux
Vaucluse
+33 (0)4 90 75 81 01
chateaulacanorgue.com

After his international bestseller *A year in Provence* (1989), Peter Mayle penned a few sequels as well as *A Good Year* (2004). Two years later, Ridley Scott made a film of it, starring Russell Crowe and Marion Cotillard. Crowe plays a ruthless stock market trader in London, who inherits a vineyard. He travels to Provence, expecting to make a quick sale but once there is confronted with his own childhood and the past of his recently deceased uncle. The film was largely shot on the beautiful wine estate of Château La Canorgue, near Bonnieux. You can visit it but the owners – 5th-generation vintners – want people to respect the estate and pay attention to their excellent (organic!) wines. No groups, individual wine addicts only. Contact the estate before you visit.

216 CHÂTEAU VOLTERRA

Route de Camarat
83350 Ramatuelle
Var
+33 (0)4 94 49 66 83
chateauvolterra.com

In the summer of 1972, the (in)famous French singer Serge Gainsbourg rented Château Volterra in Ramatuelle near Saint-Tropez for a holiday with his family and that of his new girlfriend Jane Birkin. Unfortunately, his idea backfired and the get-together was anything but pleasant. Gainsbourg's mother was less than impressed by Birkin's brother's behaviour (and drinking). Things came to a head. The weekly magazine Paris Match, which had been invited to take idyllic photos of the family reunion, published a huge spread about the conflict. Jane Birkin was able to escape the unpleasant situation because the director Roger Vadim cast her in his film *Don Juan* (or *Si Don Juan était une femme*), which was shot in Paris, among others, starring Brigitte Bardot in the leading role. Serge Gainsbourg also ended up leaving the castle, following the film crew and – piquant detail – witnessed the love scenes of his old flame Brigitte Bardot with his new girlfriend Jane Birkin. Château Volterra is open to the public.

217 CHÂTEAU DE FONTCREUSE

13 route Pierre Imbert
13260 Cassis
Bouches-du-Rhône
+33 (0)4 42 01 71 09
fontcreuse.com

The British writer Virginia Woolf (1882-1941) stayed at Cassis several times between 1925 and 1929, escaping the harsh London winters with her husband Leonard Woolf. After her first visit in March 1925, the writer, who was troubled by mental illness throughout her life, noted: "Nobody shall say of me that I have not known perfect happiness." In a letter, she praised Cassis for its "heat and light and colour and real sea and real sky". The art critic Roger Fry probably introduced the painter Vanessa Bell, Virginia's sister, to Cassis. In March 1925 and April 1927, Virginia Woolf stayed in hotels. Her walks to the lighthouse of Cassis may have inspired her to write her novel *To the Lighthouse* (1927), which is set on the Scottish Isle of Skye, however. In 1927, Vanessa Bell rented La Bergère (the shepherdess), a small, disused farmworker's cottage amid the vineyards of Fontcreuse. For the next ten years, Vanessa Bell spent several months of the year painting at Cassis. Virginia and Leonard Woolf joined her in 1928 and 1929, renting a room in the Château de Fontcreuse, enabling Virginia to spend time with her sister. Fontcreuse and La Bergère can still be visited.

GRAVE OF JEAN MARAIS

DISCOVERIES

Beautiful
PAINTED INTERIORS

218 FONDATION CARZOU

7-9 boulevard
Elémir Bourges
04100 Manosque
Alpes-de-Haute-Provence
+33 (0)4 92 87 40 49
fondationcarzou.fr

You may blink at the sight that meets your eyes when you enter the neoclassical chapel in Manosque, whose walls are painted with a contemporary Apocalypse. It took the French-Armenian painter Jean Carzou (1907-2000), born Karnik Zouloumian in Aleppo, six years to complete his life's work. He has painted the fall of mankind against a vivid blue-green backdrop, including references to the two World Wars, genocides and dictators, environmental pollution, nuclear plants and industrialised society. But there is a glimmer of hope, nonetheless: Carzou also painted the tree of life and the renaissance of earth.

219 CHAPELLE FOLON

Place de l'Église
06570 Saint-Paul-de-Vence
Alpes-Maritimes
+33 (0)4 93 32 41 13
saint-pauldevence.com/en/fiches/musees-et-lieux-de-visites/the-folon-chapel-2

The Belgian artist Jean-Michel Folon created eight paintings, a monumental mosaic, four stained-glass windows and two sculptures for the Chapelle des Pénitents Blancs in Saint-Paul-de-Vence. He completed the designs shortly before his death in October 2005, after which they were carefully executed by craftsmen. The Chapelle Folon, which opened in 2008, is a *Gesamtkunstwerk* that showcases what a versatile artist Folon was. Here you step into his poetic, colourful and light-filled world. Folon's work is a tribute to mankind and to humanity. In all these works, he emphasises giving and sharing, and the importance of dreams and poetry.

219 **CHAPELLE FOLON**

220 HÔTEL DE VILLE – SALLE DES MARIAGES

221 CHAPELLE COCTEAU

220 HÔTEL DE VILLE – SALLE DES MARIAGES

17 rue de la République
06500 Menton
Alpes-Maritimes
+33 (0)4 92 10 50 00
museecocteaumenton.fr/La-salle-des-mariages.html

Jean Cocteau discovered the sunny Mediterranean charm of Menton in the 1950s, during his on and off stays in the villa of his rich admirer Francine Weisweiller in nearby Cap Ferrat. Cocteau therefore leapt at the opportunity when the then mayor of Menton asked him to create murals for the new marriage room in the town hall. From April 1956 until March 1958, Cocteau singlehandedly decorated the walls and the ceiling with his designs, taking inspiration from the ancient myth of Orpheus and Eurydice on the one hand and adding exotic characters, brimming with joie de vivre, on the other. He executed his paintings in a colourful, graphic style, with elegant arabesques and clean lines, which he dubbed *'le style de Menton'.* Cocteau also designed the bright red chairs, the cast iron 'palm tree' floor lamps and the wall-to-wall carpet with a panther pattern. The marriage room has a joyous, cheerful feel to it. Request the keys to the room at the town hall's reception desk. With a bit of luck, you'll have it all to yourself.

221 CHAPELLE COCTEAU

AT: LA CHAPELLE NOTRE-DAME-DE-JÉRUSALEM
Route de Cannes (DN7)
83600 Fréjus
Var
+33 (0)4 94 51 34 31
frejus.fr

In 1960, the artist Jean Cocteau was asked to design a chapel for a new neighbourhood that was scheduled to be built to the north of Fréjus. Unfortunately, the plan was abandoned following the untimely death of the urban planner. Cocteau's sudden death in October 1963 also threw a spanner in the works. The chapel, which is tucked away in a forest, remained unfinished and forgotten, even though Cocteau had produced 150 (!) sketches for its decoration. The murals, featuring the Passion of Christ, were executed by Édouard Dermit, Cocteau's adopted son. In 1989, the city of Fréjus acquired the chapel and had the octagonal building restored, after which Cocteau's grand design could finally be completed. Six lustrous mosaics featuring Old Testament scenes adorn the outside walls. The three monumental chapel doors, with six stained-glass windows, refer to the Crusades. A colourful *Gesamtkunstwerk*, in Cocteau's distinctive fluid style, right in the middle of nowhere.

222 MUSÉE NATIONAL PABLO PICASSO

Place de la Libération
06220 Vallauris
Alpes-Maritimes
+33 (0)4 93 64 71 83
en.musees-nationaux-alpesmaritimes.fr/picasso

Pablo Picasso painted two large allegorical representations of war and peace for the 12th-century Romanesque chapel of the museum in Vallauris. He did this in 1952, just after the end of World War II, when world peace was under threat because of the Cold War and nuclear weapons. Picasso created two monumental murals, each measuring 4,70 by 10,20 metres. These two powerful masterpieces hang opposite each other in the rather small barrel-shaped chamber. Black (death) and red (blood) are the dominant colours in the War mural, in which the symbols of civilisation, including books, are destroyed. The colour palette of the Peace mural, on the themes of harmony and fertility, is more vivid, with people dancing and playing music. You can see the sculptures, bowls and platters that Picasso mainly created in Vallauris in the adjoining Musée de la Céramique.

223 CHAPELLE DE SAINT-PIERRE DES PÊCHEURS

4 quai de l'Amiral Courbet
06230 Villefranche-sur-Mer
Alpes-Maritimes
+33 (0)4 93 76 90 70
villefranche-sur-mer.fr/cocteau-et-villefranche-en-anglais

The French poet, film director and artist Jean Cocteau (1889-1963) is everywhere on the French Riviera. He created several artworks in Menton and Saint-Jean-Cap-Ferrat. His first chapel can be found in Villefranche, however. This 'fishermen's chapel' probably dates from the 16th century. By the 1950s, it was used as a storage for fishing nets. Cocteau, who had already spotted the chapel in the 1920s when staying at the nearby Welcome Hôtel, lobbied hard for its restoration from 1956 onwards, painting the interior and exterior of the building. The walls are decorated with scenes from the life of Saint Peter, to whom the chapel is dedicated, in Cocteau's distinctive 'cartoon'-like style, supplemented with paintings of local fishermen's wives, musicians and friends, including one of his many patrons, Francine Weisweiller.

224 VILLA SANTO SOSPIR

14 avenue Jean Cocteau
06230 Saint-Jean-Cap-Ferrat
Alpes-Maritimes
+33 (0)4 93 76 00 16
santosospir.com

With more than 200 drawings (or 'tattoos' as Jean Cocteau called them) on its walls, there's no denying that Villa Santo Sospir is a *Gesamtkunstwerk*. The artist met the then owner, Francine Weisweiller, in 1949, when he was shooting his film *Les Enfants Terribles*. Nicole Stéphane, who was a niece of Francine's husband Alec Weisweiller, played the female lead in the film. Francine invited Cocteau to come stay with them at Villa Santo Sospir. Inevitably the artist felt bored and asked whether he could trace a drawing on the white wall above the fireplace. He ended up drawing the head of Apollo, the Greek god of art and music. Ultimately, Cocteau would cover all the villa's walls with his art. In 1952, he made a 35-minute documentary about the house, titled *La Villa Santo Sospir*. Eight years later, the villa also had a role in his feature film *Le Testament d'Orphée* (1960). Currently the villa is closed for restoration. It is scheduled to reopen in 2022.

WRITERS' HOMES

225 **MAISON JOË BOUSQUET**

53 rue de Verdun
11000 Carcassonne
Aude
+33 (0)4 68 72 45 55
tourism-carcassonne.co.uk

A unique and slightly bizarre house, where time seems to have stopped. Joë Bousquet, whose poetry is associated with the surrealists, spent the larger part of his life in bed. He was only 21 years old, when an enemy bullet smashed into his spine during one of the last battles of World War I and he became paralysed from the waist down. He lived in this house in Carcassonne from 1924 onwards and would never leave it again during his lifetime. He lived a bedridden life, always keeping the shutters of his room closed. He was in constant pain and spent a lot of time thinking, living in his own imaginary world. He also wrote poems and letters, receiving important painters and writers in his home, including René Magritte (who had fled Brussels at the beginning of World War II and ended up in Carcassonne). Other famous guests were Salvador Dalí, Louis Aragon, Max Ernst and Simone Weil. After Joë Bousquet's death in 1950, the house was preserved as he left it, with all his belongings including his opium pipe.

225 MAISON JOË BOUSQUET

226 MUSÉE MAISON FRÉDÉRIC MISTRAL

11 avenue Lamartine
13910 Maillane
Bouches-du-Rhône
+33 (0)4 90 95 84 19
museemistral.fr

Although Frédéric Mistral was awarded the Nobel Prize for Literature in 1904, his star has since faded. Mistral led the 19th-century revival of Occitan or Provençal, the language of Provence. He spent years working on a comprehensive Provençal dictionary and wrote the long poem *Mirèio* (1859), drawing on the language and love songs of the medieval troubadours for inspiration. The Musée Mistral is located in the beautifully maintained home that Mistral had built in 1876 in the run-up to his marriage: a bourgeois townhouse, where he wrote his works and where he had a view from his garden of the Provençal landscape that he loved so much.

227 MUSÉE-BIBLIOTHÈQUE FRANÇOIS PÉTRARQUE

Rive gauche de la Sorgue
84800 Fontaine-de-Vaucluse
Vaucluse
+33 (0)4 90 20 37 20
vaucluse.fr/culture-et-patrimoine

Obviously, this is not the original house where the Renaissance poet Francesco Petrarch (Petrarca) (1304-1374) lived and worked in the 14th century. But the museum is located more or less in the same place. The Italian writer was born in Arezzo but spent a lot of time at the papal court in Avignon, where he met Laura de Noves in 1327. It was love at first sight for Petrach, Laura – the virtuous wife of a French count – was less enthused, however. Petrarch poured his feelings for this ideal, elusive love into more than 300 love poems, paving the way for an entirely new genre: lyrical, romantic poetry. He mainly wrote his *Canzoniere* in Fontaine-de-Vaucluse, where the murmuring stream provided him with the peace and calm that he needed. The Sorgue still flows through the lovely garden of the Musée-Bibliothèque François Pétrarque. Its collection includes Petrarch's drawings and prints of Petrarch and 'his' Laura in addition to a series of old editions of his work. In 1336, Petrarch climbed the nearby Mont Ventoux, thus becoming the symbol of the 'new' man, who discovers, explores and describes the landscape.

228 ESPACE MUSÉAL WITOLD GOMBROWICZ

AT: VILLA ALEXANDRINE, 2ND FL.
36 place du Grand Jardin
06140 Vence
Alpes-Maritimes
+33 (0)4 93 58 06 38
vence-tourisme.com

Few people will be aware of the fact that the famous Polish writer Witold Gombrowicz spent the last years of his life in Vence. The author of grotesque/absurd prose such as *Ferdydurke* (1937), *Pornografia* (1960) and *Cosmos* (1965), who is often compared with Kafka and Beckett, lived in the Villa Alexandrine in the city centre from 1964 until 1969 with his wife Rita. The Office de Tourisme is located on the ground floor of this belle époque house from 1911. There is a nice documentation centre on the second floor. Here you won't find a reconstruction of Gombrowicz's former flat. Instead quotes on the walls, display cases with books, translations and special editions, photos and videos give visitors a good idea of the fascinating world and ideas of this remarkable writer.

SZACHY

229 CENTRE JEAN GIONO

AT: HÔTEL RAFFIN
3 boulevard Élémir Bourges

LE PARAÏS ET SES JARDINS
Impasse du Paraïs
04100 Manosque
Alpes-de-Haute-Provence
+33 (0)4 92 70 54 54
centrejeangiono.com

Jean Giono (1895-1970) is sometimes likened to William Faulkner. Like the American writer, Giono created an 'imaginary Midi' with a series of novels, in which he celebrates a mythical Provence and man's relationship with nature in poetic prose. In the 1930s, Giono was a prominent pacifist. After refusing to perform his military service, he was arrested and imprisoned at the beginning of World War II. In 1953, he wrote one of his most famous stories, *L'Homme qui plantait des arbres (The Man Who Planted Trees)*, in which a shepherd plants thousands of trees in his region in the Haute-Provence, with the sole aim of restoring life and harmony. An ecological manifesto, long before the term was invented. His story has been translated in several languages and turned into (animated) films and used for puppet shows. Jean Giono was born in Manosque, rarely leaving the town. In 1930, he bought a house called Le Paraïs, a green oasis where he wrote most of his works. The house opened to the public in 2016. You can also visit the Jean Giono documentation centre and a permanent exhibition on the writer's life and work in Hôtel Raffin up the road. An intriguing figure.

ARTISTS' STUDIOS

230 **FONDATION HARTUNG-BERGMAN**
173 chemin du Valbosquet
06600 Antibes
Alpes-Maritimes
+33 (0)4 93 33 45 92
fondationhartung bergman.fr

In 1973, the abstract painters Hans Hartung and Anna-Eva Bergman decided to move to the hills above Antibes. They built a modern, white villa in a minimalist, radical style, along with two artists' studios here in the 1960s. Hans Hartung designed it. After their deaths in the late 1980s, a foundation was established, in accordance with their will, which maintains their studios and promotes their work. You can visit this remarkable house and the two studios, which is set in an orchard of olive and pine trees. Booking compulsory.

231 **ATELIER PAUL CÉZANNE**
9 avenue Paul Cézanne
13090 Aix-en-Provence
Bouches-du-Rhône
+33 (0)4 42 21 06 53
cezanne-en-provence.com

Paul Cézanne's original studio is situated just 1,5 kilometres outside the city centre of Aix. The painter built it in 1902 and worked there until his death in 1906. While there are no original works, the atelier's unique ambience has been preserved. You feel as if the painter left just seconds before you arrived. The objects that he captured in his still-lifes are still there: apples, skulls and a plaster Cupid. Note the large windows, through which the daylight, which the painter found so important, falls in. Also note the vertical slot that Cézanne had built into the wall to be able to get monumental paintings such as his *Les Grandes Baigneuses* safely out of his studio. The neighbourhood around the atelier has been built up in the past 100 years. During Cézanne's lifetime, he would have had a view of the surrounding countryside. It was from this studio that he often set out on foot, his easel on his back, walking up the hill to paint the mythical Mont Sainte-Victoire.

232 MAISON DORA MAAR

58 rue du
Portail Neuf
84560 Ménerbes
Vaucluse
+33 (0)4 90 72 54 70
maisondoramaar.org

Henriette Theodora Markovitch, or Dora Maar as we know her, was Pablo Picasso's lover, muse and model for several years. The Croatian artist was already a well-known surrealist photographer when she met Picasso in 1935 in Paris. They became lovers, but Picasso also asked her to photograph the successive stages of the creation of his famous work, *Guernica*. Shortly after they split up in 1943, he bought an 18th-century house for her in Ménerbes. Dora Maar spent all her summers in the town, living like a hermit, until she died there in 1997, aged 89. It was at Ménerbes that she first began to paint still-lifes and semi-abstract landscapes. Upon her death, the American art patron Nancy Brown Negley bought the house and studio, turning it into a residence for artists and writers. Maison Dora Maar is only open to the public during presentations and exhibitions.

233 MAISON JANE EAKIN

Rue Sainte-Barbe
84560 Ménerbes
Vaucluse
+33 (0)6 14 75 50 33
menerbes.fr/menerbes

The American painter Jane Eakin (1919-2002) made her second home in Ménerbes, living and working in the town for over 40 years. She occupied a narrow, tall house, which was partly built into the rock face. Eakin was married to the New York journalist Robert Kleiman, who was based in Paris. She ended up divorcing him because she did not feel comfortable living the life of a society hostess. At the end of the 1950s, a friend introduced her to the Provençal village of Ménerbes. At the time it was a quiet village and tourists had yet to discover it. Understandably she was sold on it the minute she saw it. She left Paris and became a popular and active member of the local community. She left her house and paintings to the town after she died. There are about 100 paintings in all – sun-drenched landscapes and portraits that glow with colour and light for the most part – on display in all the rooms. Her studio is on the top floor, offering superb views of the mountains.

234 ATELIER FOLON

8 quai Antoine Ier
98000 Monaco
+377 93 50 06 10
fondationfolon.be

Most people remember the Belgian artist Jean-Michel Folon (1934-2005) for his slightly surrealistic, poetic vision of man and the world. In France, however, he is mostly famous for having created the closing credits of TV channel Antenne 2. In 1983, he moved to Monaco, where he had a studio in a former warehouse in the port. The studio looks as if the artist has just stepped out for a walk: the table is strewn with drawings and designs. There are sculptures, paintings, posters and drawings everywhere you look in the spacious studio. You can watch a few interviews and a short, silent movie, which Folon made in 1983 with Woody Allen. Monaco has several sculptures by Folon on its streets. He also produced stained-glass windows for the Hôtel Monte-Carlo Bay and a mosaic for the Église des Carmes. Folon is buried in Monaco.

235 VILLA THÉO

19 avenue Van Rysselberghe
83980 Le Lavandou (Saint-Clair)
Var
+33 (0)9 63 51 32 28
villa-theo.fr

In the spring of 1904, the Belgian neo-impressionist painter Théo Van Rysselberghe (1862-1926) travelled by bike from Hyères to Monaco, making his way along the coastline. He was looking for a place to build his new house and was accompanied by his good friend and colleague, the painter Henri-Edmond Cross. Van Rysselberghe ended up setting on Saint-Clair, where Cross had been living since 1895. Like Cross, Van Rysselberghe was instantly taken with the pristine landscape and the phenomenal light. Théo's brother, the architect Octave Van Rysselberghe, designed him a new house and studio in 1910. After the painter died, his daughter Elisabeth stayed on until she sold the property in 1933. In 2007, Le Lavandou bought the 'Villa Théo' to preserve the house's architectural and cultural value. After a thorough renovation during which some of the interior elements were maintained, the former studio is now used as a space for temporary exhibitions on Théo Van Rysselberghe and Le Lavandou. Villa Théo is also the place to start if you want to go on the 'Chemin des Peintres' walk. Théo Van Rysselberghe is buried in the local cemetery, near Henri-Edmond Cross, who died young and for whose grave Van Rysselberghe designed a bronze medallion.

236 MUSÉE RENOIR

19 chemin des Collettes
06800 Cagnes-sur-Mer
Alpes-Maritimes
+33 (0)4 93 20 61 07
cagnes-sur-mer.fr

Perhaps Renoir is not your cup of tea, but we highly recommend visiting his studio and garden. The painter Pierre-Auguste Renoir – whose prolific output of paintings of buxom, young beauties may put off some – moved to Cagnes-sur-Mer in 1903. In 1907, he had a large house built for his wife and three sons, as well as a large studio. He would live and work there for 11 years. By the end of his life, his arthritis became so painful that he was almost unable to paint. It is said that they tied the brushes to his wrists so he could paint nonetheless. In his studio you can still see his easel, his wheelchair and the sofa on which models could lay down. There are sixteen paintings (portraits and landscapes) and thirty sculptures in the house. Renoir created his first sculptures in Cagnes. One of his most famous statues, the *Venus Victrix*, still stands in the garden among the centuries-old olive trees. The stunning orchard was one of the main reasons why Renoir bought this property.

237 MUSÉE MAILLOL

Vallée de la Roume
66650 Banyuls-sur-Mer
Pyrénées-Orientales
+33 (0)4 68 88 57 11
banyuls-sur-mer.com

The sculptor Aristide Maillol, who is mainly known for his larger than life, monumental bronze female nudes, was born in 1861 in Banyuls-sur-Mer. He moved to Paris to train at the École Nationale Supérieure des Beaux-Arts. From 1910, he returned to his native Banyuls, living like a hermit in a simple house just five kilometres from the town. La Métairie (the farm) also had a studio. There are still a number of paintings and drawings on display, but it's the dozens of small bronze and terracotta sculptures that immediately catch the eye as well as the table and kitchen where Maillol prepared his meals. The artist grew vegetables and herbs in his own garden. He died in 1944 and is buried in the front garden, under a mournful sculpture, called *La Méditerranée*. The statue alone is worth following the long, winding road to La Métairie.

238 SAINT-PAUL-DE-MAUSOLE

Chemin Saint-Paul
13210 Saint-Rémy-de-Provence
Bouches-du-Rhône
+33 (0)4 90 92 77 00
saintpauldemausole.fr

A visit to the asylum where Vincent van Gogh was voluntarily hospitalised on 8 May 1889 is always a unique experience. You can see his spartan room and simple bed and the tubs that were used for hydrotherapy in Saint-Paul-de-Mausole hospice in Saint-Rémy. The painter spent one whole year here. They still care for patients here by the way. Vincent was given oils, brushes and canvases, a room that he could use as a studio and another room to store his paintings. He was also allowed short, supervised walks, during which he could paint outside. The walled garden fascinated him: you can still see it today and there are reproductions of his paintings on the walls. Van Gogh's output was prolific: he painted 150 paintings and created 100 drawings during his year of confinement, despite suffering several debilitating attacks. After his first attack in Saint-Rémy, he wrote to his brother Théo at the end of August 1889: "For many days I've been absolutely distraught, as in Arles, just as much if not worse, and it's to be presumed that these crises will recur in the future, it is ABOMINABLE.' On 16 May 1890, the painter left for Paris, travelling on to Auvers-sur-Oise, where he tried to shoot himself on 27 July 1890. He died two days later.

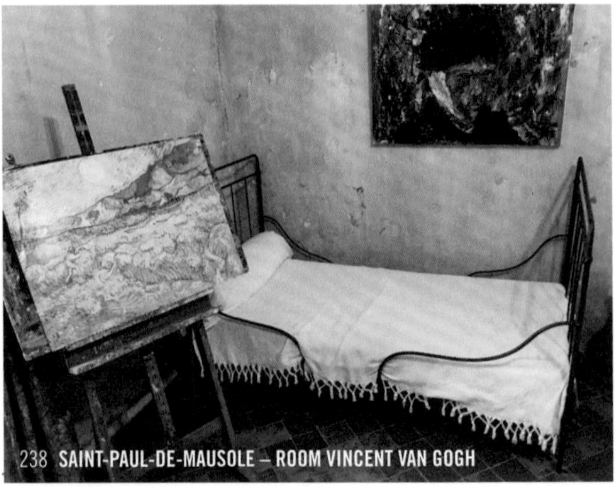

238 SAINT-PAUL-DE-MAUSOLE – ROOM VINCENT VAN GOGH

WALKS
in artists' footsteps

239 PAUL CÉZANNE IN AIX-EN-PROVENCE

INFO: OFFICE DE TOURISME D'AIX-EN-PROVENCE
300 avenue Giuseppe Verdi
13605 Aix-en-Provence
Bouches-du-Rhône
+33 (0)4 42 16 11 61
aixenprovencetourism.com

A walk 'In the steps of Cézanne' will take you to 31 locations that are related to life and work of this amazing painter. The trail starts from the statue of Paul Cézanne by the Dutch sculptor Gabriël Sterk, which was installed in Place du Général de Gaulle in 2006. On your walk, you will pass the houses where the painter was born and died, the houses where he lived with his family, the cafes and the faculty of law, where the painter originally enrolled. His studio, which is definitely worth visiting, is not included in this trail.

240 VINCENT VAN GOGH IN SAINT-RÉMY-DE-PROVENCE

INFO: OFFICE DE TOURISME ALPILLES EN PROVENCE
Place Jean Jaurès
13210 Saint-Rémy-de-Provence
Bouches-du-Rhône
+33 (0)4 90 92 05 22
alpillesenprovence.com

On 8 May 1889, Vincent van Gogh arrived in Saint-Rémy, where he was voluntarily committed to Saint-Paul-de-Mausole, a mental health institution located 1,5 kilometres to the south of the city centre. He spent one year in the hospital – until May 1890 – and created 150 paintings and 100 drawings there, including his world-famous work *Starry Night*, which now hangs in the Museum of Modern Art in New York. Vincent was allowed on supervised walks, during which he could paint. The walking trail that leaves from Musée Estrine in the city centre and leads to Saint-Paul-de-Mausole provides an overview of Vincent's work in Saint-Rémy: 19 panels with reproductions of paintings, including *A Wheatfield with Cypresses* and *Irises*. You can download a leaflet and an app from the website of the Office de Tourisme.

241 VINCENT VAN GOGH IN ARLES

INFO: OFFICE DE TOURISME ARLES CAMARGUE
9 boulevard des Lices
13200 Arles
Bouches-du-Rhône
+33 (0)4 90 18 41 20
arlestourisme.com/fr/circuit-van-gogh.html

The legendary Dutch painter Vincent van Gogh lived and worked in Arles from February 1888 until May 1889. It was one of his most productive periods: he created no less than 300 paintings and drawings here. It was at Arles that he painted some of his most famous works, including *Café Terrace at Night, Starry Night over the Rhône* and *Bedroom in Arles*. It was also here that he mutilated his ear (severing the ear and not just the lobe) on 23 December 1888, after a violent altercation with Paul Gauguin in a fit of madness. He was subsequently taken to the local hospital in Place Félix Rey. This first attack was caused by his illness: probably a combination of epilepsy and bipolar disorder, which was aggravated by his alcoholism or a sexually transmitted disease. In Arles, you can follow in Van Gogh's footsteps. The city has mapped a trail where you can see reproductions of his works: from Place Lamartine and the 'Maison jaune', where he lived with Gauguin and which unfortunately was destroyed by bombs during World War II, to Place du Forum where he painted his cafe terrace at night and the hospital, which is now called Espace Van Gogh. You can download the app with the walk from the website of the Office du Tourisme.

242 ARISTIDE MAILLOL IN BANYULS

INFO: OFFICE DE TOURISME BANYULS-SUR-MER
4 avenue de la République
66650 Banyuls-sur-Mer
Pyrénées-Orientales
+33 (0)4 68 88 31 58
banyuls-sur-mer.com

'Dans les pas d'Aristide' is a signposted walk in French and English through 'Le Cap d'Osna', an old neighbourhood in Banyuls, where the sculptor Aristide Maillol was born in 1861. The nice walk past fifteen signs with biographical information and photos starts from the beach, on the corner of Place du Général Bassères and Rue Aristide Maillol, taking you through a picturesque Catalonian neighbourhood with steep streets and small houses, often with a front garden and a wrought iron gate. The Maison Rose, where Maillol was born, is situated near sign number 5 but is not open to visitors. Don't forget to look out for Maillol's sculptures and a stele that was put up in memory of the sculptor in Avenue de la République, near the beach and the Office de Tourisme.

243 PIERRE BONNARD IN LE CANNET

AT: MUSÉE BONNARD
16 boulevard
Sadi Carnot
06110 Le Cannet
Alpes-Maritimes
+33 (0)4 93 94 06 06
museebonnard.fr

After visiting the Musée Bonnard, you can continue to explore Le Cannet in the painter's footsteps. This interesting walk takes you past twelve panels with reproductions of his paintings, always at a viewpoint. You also walk past the house where Pierre Bonnard lived with his wife Marthe: Le Bosquet at 29 avenue Victoria. The house is still occupied by the painter's descendants and is therefore closed to the public. Check the museum's website for the virtual peek behind the walls of Le Bosquet. Warning: 'Sur les pas de Bonnard' is a steep walk, with plenty of steps, that takes about two hours. Bring water, a hat and some sunscreen. You can download the walk in the free Guidigo app, but it is only available in French. More information under the 'Pierre Bonnard' tab on the museum's website.

244 LE CHEMIN DES PEINTRES IN L'ESTAQUE

INFO: OFFICE DE TOURISME ET DES CONGRÈS DE MARSEILLE
11 La Canebière
13211 Marseille
Bouches-du-Rhône
+33 (0)826 500 500
toutsurmarseille.fr/ balade-a-lestaque

L'Estaque is one of the birthplaces of cubism. The neighbourhood is situated in the 16th arrondissement or district of Marseille, even though it's 10 kilometres outside the city. Between 1870 and 1914, many painters descended on the fishing village, dazzled as they were by the bright light and the colourful cottages. But they also noticed the first small factories that were established there. Paul Cézanne visited often between 1870 and 1882, staying in a small house in Place de L'Église, from where you still have a stunning view of the port and Marseille in the distance. There is a commemorative plaque on the wall. Many painters followed in his wake, including Dufy, Derain and Marquet. Georges Braque stands out, however, because he painted the earliest cubist landscape, *Houses at l'Estaque*, here in 1908, after creating several fauvist works. The imposing railway viaduct of l'Estaque is a frequent feature of his cubist paintings. The two-hour walk takes you on a tour of eight sites with reproductions of paintings by different artists.

245 LE CHEMIN DU FAUVISME IN COLLIOURE

INFO: MAISON DU FAUVISME
10 rue de la Prud'Homie

INFO: OFFICE DE TOURISME
Place du 18 Juin
66190 Collioure
Pyrénées-Orientales
+33 0(4) 68 82 15 47
www.collioure.com

When the painter Henri Matisse arrived in Collioure in May 1905, which was a small and relatively unknown fishing village at the time, he was almost blinded by the blazing sunlight and the bright, dazzling colours. He tried to capture these sensations in his canvases, by using 'unrealistic' colours, painting pink hills, orange roofs and a green sea. A few months later, André Derain joined Matisse at Collioure. They painted side by side, inspiring each other to paint more freely. Their fierce, wild paintings shocked people at the Salon d'Automne in Paris. And that is how 'fauvism' was born overnight. You can still take a fascinating walk, called' Le Chemin du Fauvisme', in Collioure, which takes you past the many places where the two artists set up their easels. It includes vantage points, with reproductions of their paintings, at the top of Rue Bellevue and Rue des Caranques. Don't forget to walk along Boulevard du Boramar and follow the footpath along the Château Royal to see several reproductions on the old city walls. The Hôtel de la Gare, where Matisse and Derain stayed initially, was situated at 19 avenue Aristide Maillol, near the railway station. The house is still there and a commemorative plaque reminds passers-by of the hotel's famous guests. Pick up a leaflet from the Office de Tourisme or book a tour with the Maison du Fauvisme.

245 **LE CHEMIN DU FAUVISME IN COLLIOURE**

246 LE SENTIER FRIEDRICH NIETZSCHE

From SNCF station
Èze-sur-Mer to
Èze-Village
06360 Èze
Alpes-Maritimes

The German philosopher Friedrich Nietzsche was a keen walker, who spent several winters in Nice between 1883 and 1888. He often walked from Èze-sur-Mer to Èze-Village, one of the most beautiful villages in the South of France. Èze-Village is perched on a rock near the sea and can be reached on foot via what is now called the 'Sentier Friedrich Nietzsche' ('Nietzsche Footpath'). The steep, rock path will take you past some breathtaking views to the summit, 429 metres above sea level. During these walks, Nietsche was inspired to write the third part of his famous book, *Thus Spoke Zarathustra* (1883-'85). In *Ecce Homo* (1908), he wrote that the "decisive chapter, entitled 'Old and New Tables', was composed during the arduous ascent from the station to Eza – that wonderful Moorish village in the rocks. During those moments when my creative energy flowed most plentifully, my muscular activity was always greatest… I could then walk for seven or eight hours on end over the hills without a suggestion of fatigue." Don't underestimate the climb uphill, on a gravel path or bare rock. It takes about one and a half hours to complete. The trail starts opposite the railway station of Èze-sur-Mer. There is a commemorative plaque en route. Bring sturdy shoes and a set of healthy hiking lungs.

247 THE EXILES IN SANARY-SUR-MER

INFO: OFFICE DE TOURISME DE SANARY-SUR-MER
1 quai du Levant
83110 Sanary-sur-Mer
Var
+33 (0)4 94 74 01 04
sanary-tourisme.com

From 1933 until 1944, Sanary-sur-Mer became a refuge for German and Austrian writers and artists who had fled Hitler's Nazi regime. On 10 May 1933, the first book burnings took place in Germany, marking the start of an exodus of writers and artists, who were accused by the Nazis of having anti-German, amoral and decadent ideas. The German novelist Thomas Mann, whose works include *The Magic Mountain* and *Death in Venice*, lived in Villa Tranquille, at 442 chemin de la Colline, from 12 June until 22 September 1933. He returned to Sanary in 1935 and 1936. In the summer of 1938, Alma Mahler, the widow of the composer Gustav Mahler, and the writer-artist Franz Werfel moved into Le Moulin Gris, an old watchtower, at number 9 on the same street. Klaus Mann, Thomas's eldest son, stayed at Hôtel de la Tour (24 quai Charles de Gaulle), where he wrote his letters and a novella. The exiled writers would meet in cafes like La Nautique, La Marine and Café de Lyon. There is a commemorative plaque with 68 names of exiled artists who fled to Sanary, including Bertolt Brecht, Stefan Zweig and Joseph Roth, at the entrance of the Office de Tourisme. Here you can also pick up a map titled 'In the steps of exiled writers'. The walk takes you past the 33 houses where these artists lived. A sign with a photo and a brief explanation in French, English and German marks each address.

Sur les pas d'Auguste Chabaud
La Roubine à Graveson, 70 cm x 92 cm, 1912
Région PACA

248 SUR LES PAS D'AUGUSTE CHABAUD

INFO: OFFICE DE TOURISME
41 cours National
13690 Graveson
Bouches-du-Rhône
+33 (0)4 90 95 88 44
graveson-provence.com/graveson-en-provence/graveson-loisirs/a-visiter/sur-les-pas-d-auguste-chabaud

Auguste Chabaud (1882-1955) is a forgotten painter, who combined fauvism with expressionism. After World War I, he moved back to his native region. He would often pitch his easel at Graveson to paint the village and its residents in his typical angular, colourful style. You can follow Chabaud as he made his way through the village: you start from the Cours National, near the small museum that is dedicated to him and where you can pick up a nice brochure with the walk. There are fifteen signs in the town, with reproductions of his paintings. Although the village has changed over the years, the River Roubine still flows through the village and the plane trees and the narrow streets around the church are still there. A charming way to explore Graveson.

249 LE CHEMIN DES PEINTRES IN LE LAVANDOU

INFO: LA MAISON DU LAVANDOU
Quai Gabriel Péri
83980 Le Lavandou
Var
+33 (0)4 94 00 40 50
ot-lelavandou.fr

Between 1892 and 1926, many painters and writers were drawn to Saint-Clair, a neighbourhood of Le Lavandou. After Henri-Edmond Cross, the Belgian neo-impressionist painter Théo Van Rysselberghe also set up his studio in the town. Both artists were captivated by the light and the colours of the pristine landscape and the azure sea. Many artists followed in their footsteps, such as the painters Paul Signac, Maurice Denis and Maximilien Luce and the writers André Gide and Emile Verhaeren. A 2,5-kilometre 'Chemin des Peintres / Painters' Trail' (which takes approximately 1,5 hours to complete) winds its way through Saint-Clair and along the beach. There are 16 panels en route, with reproductions of landscapes and marine paintings that Van Rysselberghe, Cross, Signac and the others painted on the spot. A fascinating confrontation between the past and present. Van Rysselberghe's restored house and studio, the Villa Théo, is also included in the trail and is open to the public.

CEMETERIES
with famous residents

250 GRAVE OF ALBERT CAMUS

AT: CIMETIÈRE DE LOURMARIN
D27 (south of Lourmarin)
84160 Lourmarin
Vaucluse

The writer and philosopher Albert Camus was born to French-Algerian parents. He spent his childhood years in a poor neighbourhood in Algiers but was later able to study philosophy at the local university. He is mainly known for his novels, such as *L'Etranger (The Stranger)* from 1942 and *La Peste (The Plague)* from 1947, two works that highlight how absurd the world and life are. He won the Nobel Prize in Literature in 1957, using the money to buy a house at Lourmarin. He was introduced to the Luberon by a friend, the poet Réné Char. The mountains, light and colours reminded him of North Africa, where he was born. Camus died in an accident on 4 January 1960, when the car of his publisher Michel Gallimard crashed into a plane tree at Villeblevin, en route from Lourmarin to Paris. Camus was just 46 years old. He was buried in Lourmarin. His humble tombstone reads 'Albert Camus 1913-1960'.

251 GRAVE OF HENRI MATISSE

AT: MONASTÈRE ET CIMETIÈRE DE CIMIEZ
77 voie Romaine
06000 Nice
Alpes-Maritimes

Henri Matisse died on 3 November 1954 in his studio in Hôtel Régina in Nice. After becoming bedbound due to abdominal surgery, the artist needed a wheelchair to get around. He suffered from sleep disorders and depression all his life and yet he was able to create a world of colour, solace and beauty. His tombstone, which is near the cemetery wall, is a simple design, by his son Jean. His wife Amélie Parayre died four years later and was laid to rest with him.

252 **GRAVE OF GRACE KELLY**

AT: CATHÉDRALE DE MONACO

4 rue Colonel Bellando de Castro
98000 Monaco
+377 99 99 14 00
visitmonaco.com/fr/lieu/monuments/94/cathedrale-de-monaco

Grace Kelly (1928-1982) was an American actress who worked with several great film directors during her short film career. She owes her fame to Alfred Hitchcock, who cast the icy blonde lead actress in three consecutive suspense thrillers: *Dial M for Murder* (1954), *Rear Window* (1954) and *To Catch a Thief* (1955). The latter, which also starred Cary Grant, was largely shot in Cannes, Nice and Monaco. While heading the American delegation at the Cannes Film Festival in 1955, Grace Kelly was introduced to Prince Rainier of Monaco. They got married and she retired from acting at age 26. As Princess of Monaco, Grace mainly focussed on charity work, children's rights and the arts. On 13 September 1982, she had a stroke while driving. She was driving back from France to Monaco with her daughter Stéphanie, on a steep, winding road very similar to the one in *To Catch a Thief*. Grace lost control of the car and drove off the road and down the mountainside into a ravine. She died the following night. Her daughter suffered a hairline fracture of the cervical vertebrae and a concussion. Princess Grace was buried in the family vault in Monaco's cathedral. Rainier, who never remarried, was buried alongside her in 2005.

253 **CIMETIÈRE DE FORCALQUIER**

Avenue Fontauris
04300 Forcalquier
Alpes-de-Haute-Provence
tourisme-alpes-haute-provence.com

There are no celebrities in this cemetery. It's the cemetery itself that is unique. In fact, it is so unique that it is now a listed monument. In the 19th century, it was moved from uptown, next to Forcalquier's cathedral, to a new neighbourhood. In the early 20th century, one of the municipal gardeners had the luminous idea to plant yew trees in the cemetery and divided it into three terraces. These are separated from one another by neatly pruned yew hedges, that are hundreds of metres long and up to three metres tall, forming a veritable labyrinth with gates and corridors. Quite unique.

254 GRAVE OF HENRI CARTIER-BRESSON AND MARTINE FRANCK

AT: CIMETIÈRE DE MONTJUSTIN

04110 Montjustin Alpes-de-Haute-Provence

Two photographers in the same cemetery. The Frenchman Henri Cartier-Bresson is the most famous one. He was the master of candid photography and 'the decisive moment', capturing spontaneity. All that counted was the photographer's gaze and pressing the shutter button at the right time. He mainly made black and white images. Together with Robert Capa and David Seymour, he founded Magnum Photos in 1947, a photo agency that chronicled the lives of people. Henri Cartier-Bresson met the Belgian photographer Martine Franck in 1966 and they got married in 1970. Franck created artists' portraits, photographed landscapes, travelled far and wide and had a soft spot for Asia and Buddhism. She joined Magnum in 1983. During the last years of Henri's life, they lived in a house at Montjustin. Cartier-Bresson died in 2004 aged 95. Martine Franck died in 2012 in Paris, after becoming bedridden due to bone cancer. They are buried alongside each other, with lavender growing on both their graves.

255 GRAVE OF LE CORBUSIER

AT: CIMETIÈRE DE ROQUEBRUNE-CAP-MARTIN

2708 Prom. de la 1ère Division Française Libre 06190 Roquebrune-Cap-Martin Alpes-Maritimes

The French-Swiss modernist architect Le Corbusier loved the French Riviera. He built his 'Cabanon' at Roquebrune-Cap-Martin in 1952, the name he came up with for his mini chateau, where he spent summers with his wife Yvonne, until her death in 1957. Le Corbusier frequently returned to this Cabanon and liked to swim in the Mediterranean although his doctor advised against it. He died of a heart attack while swimming in 1965. His body washed up on the beach soon after. Le Corbusier was 77 years old. He is buried next to his wife under a tombstone of his own design: simple, in concrete, with a few primary colours. Le Corbusier is buried in Carré J, number 3. The view from the hilltop cemetery of Roquebrune is simply amazing.

256 GRAVE OF JEAN-MICHEL FOLON

AT: CIMETIÈRE DE MONACO
Avenue Pasteur
98000 Monaco
+377 93 15 22 77

In 1983, the Belgian artist Jean-Michel Folon moved to Monaco. He created slightly melancholic drawings, animation films and posters, as well as stained-glass windows and sculptures in his large studio. He died of leukaemia in 2005 and was buried in the Principality's cemetery. You may wonder why his tombstone features the letters 'Maria'. In 1996, Folon had created a marble bas-relief for the grave of Maria Cernuschi Ghiringhelli, a prominent Italian art collector. In 1970, Folon had exhibited his work in the Milan gallery of her husband Gino Ghiringhelli. Moreover, Folon's had married their daughter Paola Ghiringhelli, his second wife. The tombstone features birds holding the letters of the word Maria in their beaks. Ultimately, the family chose to use this bas-relief for Folon's own grave.

257 MEMORIAL TO CAMILLE CLAUDEL

AT: CIMETIÈRE DE MONTFAVET
Chemin du Cimetière
84140 Avignon
Vaucluse
+33 (0)4 90 32 27 23
tombes-sepultures.com/crbst_534.html

Camille Claudel. 1864-1943. A brilliant, trailblazing sculptress, who lived a tragic life. After her tumultuous love affair with Auguste Rodin, working alongside him as his assistant, she slowly went mad. In 1913, her mother and her brother, the writer-diplomat Paul Claudel, had her interned in the asylum at Montfavet. She remained confined there until 1943, although her physicians regularly contacted the family requesting that she might return home. In all likelihood, she died of starvation during the war, like the other patients. Nobody was available to make arrangements for her funeral, not even her brother, who refused to bury her in the family vault. Her remains ended up being interred in an unmarked grave in this cemetery. In 2008, 65 years after Camille's death, her second cousin Reine-Marie Paris had this simple memorial erected for the artist, whose work has been rediscovered in recent decades and who is finally being given the space and the honour that she deserves.

258 GRAVE OF JEAN MARAIS

AT: VIEUX CIMETIÈRE DE VALLAURIS
Allée du Souvenir Français
06220 Vallauris Golfe-Juan
Alpes-Maritimes
vallaurisgolfejuan-tourisme.fr

An extremely bizarre and imaginative funerary monument. Jean Marais was a famous actor, who is mainly known for two films that he made: *La belle et la bête (The Beauty and the Beast)* from 1946, in which he played the roles of the prince and the beast, and *Orphée (Orpheus)* from 1949, in which he had the title role. Jean Cocteau, Marais's much older life partner, directed both films. After Cocteau's death in 1963, Marais continued to make films, including the popular *Fantômas* series with Louis de Funès. Marais plays the role of the elusive gangster Fantômas, wearing various disguises. The actor died aged 84 in Cannes. He designed his own tombstone for the cemetery of Vallauris: the grave is flanked by two lion's heads, that are loosely based on the mask that he wore in *La belle et la bête*. An impressive sphinx sits atop the monument, with horns on its head and a mermaid's tail. Nobody knows what the symbolism behind this creature is. In 2016, vandals damaged the grave, breaking off one of the lion's heads and taking it with them.

259 LES ALYSCAMPS

Avenue des Alyscamps
13200 Arles
Bouches-du-Rhône
+33 (0)4 90 18 41 20
patrimoine.ville-arles.fr

The cemetery of Les Alyscamps, Provençal for 'Elysian Fields', is situated just outside the city centre of Arles: a tree-lined avenue, flanked by a long row of tombstones and sarcophagi from the Roman era on either side. Both lugubrious and poetic/romantic at the same time. The cemetery was used well into the late Middle Ages. Vincent van Gogh and Paul Gauguin liked to walk here and made several paintings of Les Alyscamps. The Église Saint-Honorat, which was never completed, stands at the top of the avenue and hosts contemporary art exhibitions during the summer months.

Eye-catching
FOUNTAINS

260 **FONTAINE PICASSO**
Place Pablo Picasso
66400 Céret
Pyrénées-Orientales

After attending a corrida in Céret on 20 September 1953, Pablo Picasso was received by the local communists in the Grand Café. In memory of this meeting, the artist drew a 'sardane', a local dance that is performed in a circle, with a large peace dove above it. He made the drawing for his comrades at the newspaper *Le Travailleur Catalan*. It found its way into the collection of the Musée d'Art Moderne in Céret. In 2013, Juliette and Jacques Damville designed a colourful fountain for the city, incorporating Picasso's drawing, which is executed in ceramics. The fountain is still in Place Pablo Picasso, near the Porte d'Espagne in Céret.

261 **FONTAINE DES NEUF JETS**
Place des Neuf Jets
66400 Céret
Pyrénées-Orientales

The *Fontaine des Neuf Jets* is an iconic fountain in Céret. It has undergone many changes over the years, a reflection of the region's strategic importance, which often changed hands over the centuries. The fountain was built in 1313 under the rule of King Sanç I of Majorca. In the 15th century, King Ferdinand II of Aragon had a lion, the symbol of Castile, placed on top of the fountain. At the time, the lion faced Spain. After the Roussillon was annexed by France, the plinth was inscribed with the following inscription: *'Venite Ceretens, leo factus est gallus'*: 'Come, inhabitants of Ceret, the lion has become a rooster'. The Catalan lion was thus 'replaced' with the French rooster. The lion's head, meanwhile, looked towards France. After a recent restoration, the lion's head has been turned again and he now gazes at Spain once again...

262 **L'EAU DES FONTAINES D'AIX-EN-PROVENCE**

INFO: OFFICE DE TOURISME
300 avenue Giuseppe Verdi
13605 Aix-en-Provence
Bouches-du-Rhône
+33 (0)4 42 16 11 61
aixenprovence tourism.com

Impossible to miss: the imposing *Fontaine de la Rotonde* is one of the eye-catchers at the top of Cours Mirabeau in Aix-en-Provence: rising to a height of 12 metres with a basin that measures 32 metres across. This truly is an homage to the water, which has always been important to this city. Aix-en-Provence was already well-known in Roman times for its beneficial thermal baths. The three Graces that sit atop the fountain at Aix symbolise values of the modern age: they represent agriculture, justice and the fine arts. Starting from the monumental fountain, you can take a 'water walk' through the city and see a total of eleven fountains, including an elegant obelisk with four dolphins and a simple, mossy boulder in Cours Mirabeau.

263 **FONTAINE DU PARC LONGCHAMP**

AT: PALAIS LONGCHAMP
Place Henri Dunant
13004 Marseille
Bouches-du-Rhône

Another imposing fountain, right in front of the Palais de Longchamp – with the Musée des Beaux-Arts in one wing and the Musée de l'Histoire Naturelle in the other – with some gigantic allegorical figures. Strictly speaking, the palace camouflages a water tower: it marks the end of an 80-kilometre aqueduct that has been supplying the city of Marseille with drinking water from the Durance River since the 19th century. The semi-nude woman in the centre symbolises the river. She is flanked by figures symbolising a vineyard and agriculture. They appear to be standing on a cart pulled by four Camargue bulls. The fountain – with its waterfall and basin – is an ode to fertility, which is entirely reliant on water.

264 LA FONTAINE PAGODE

5 place Couverte
30140 Anduze
Gard

A peculiar 'Oriental' fountain, in the heart of the small town of Anduze. It was built in 1649 by Monsieur Latour, one of the city's consuls, who had visited the Far East as a silk merchant and was impressed by its architecture. A silk merchant in Anduze? There used to be lots of silk factories in the Cévennes at one time. The fountain was built to his design, in the shape of a pagoda with a roof made of colourful glazed ceramic tiles. Quite unique.

265 FONTAINE DES TROIS GRÂCES

Place de la Comédie
34000 Montpellier
Hérault

This monumental fountain featuring the three Graces stands in Place de la Comédie, Montpellier's historic main square, right in front of the Opera. They stand back-to-back on a mossy boulder, on which 'angels' sit. According to legend, the three Graces were the daughters of the Greek god Zeus, symbolising beauty, joy and happiness. The fountain was designed by Étienne Dantoine, but his sculpture immediately caused a controversy. He had left for Carrara in the early 1770s to choose a block of marble from the famous Italian marble quarry, returning with a completely finished sculpture group. Rumour had it that Italian stonemasons sculpted the statues. The city council refused to pay him as a result. In the end, Dantoine was paid a lifetime annuity. In 1797, the fountain was erected in its current location. But what you see here today is no longer the original fountain. In 1989, the original statues, which were damaged by pollution and acid rain, were moved to the lobby of the opera and replaced with resin copies.

266 JARDINS DE LA FONTAINE

26 quai de
la Fontaine
30000 Nîmes
Gard
+33 (0)4 66 76 70 01
nimes.fr

The Jardins de la Fontaine are an impressive city park in Nîmes. The gardens were laid out between 1745 and 1755 and are one of the oldest public parks in France. The extensive water features are remarkable: low-lying, semi-underground water basins surrounded by monumental staircases, balustrades and statues of ancient gods. And fountains! The spring was already known to locals before the Romans arrived. They built a Temple for Diana, an imposing ruin that is still worth visiting, and the so-called Tour Magne, part of the Gallo-Roman fortress on the hill behind the park. The Jardins de la Fontaine are a great place to rest and find some shade on hot days. Bear in mind that it can sometimes get very hot in Nîmes, which is situated in a valley.

265 FONTAINE DES TROIS GRÂCES

COLOURS, FRAGRANCES, FLAVOURS *and the story behind them*

267 **MUSÉE DU PASTEL**
AT: CHÂTEAU MUSÉE
DU PASTEL DE MAGRIN
81220 Magrin
Tarn
+33 (0)5 63 70 63 82
pastel-chateau-musee.com

A yellow flower that is used to produce blue dye? Dyer's woad or dyer's pastel (the blue gold of Occitanie) has been known for its medicinal properties since ancient times, but these days it is cultivated for use in the cosmetics industry and for the many shades of blue dye that can be extracted from it. It is mainly harvested in the Lauragais, an area southeast of Toulouse. Funnily enough, the flowers of the pastel plant are yellow, not blue. Spheres of blue dye, or cocagnes, are obtained after a complicated production process. Several woad merchants made a fortune between the 14th and 16th centuries. At the time, the 'Pays de Cocagne' ('country of abundance') referred to the triangle between Albi, Toulouse and Carcassonne, the heartland of woad cultivation and trade. Once people began to import colourfast indigo from Asia from the 16th century onwards, the prices collapsed. In the beautifully situated castle of Magrin, the woad production process is explained with a huge replica of a pastel mill and a drying attic. The exhibit also focusses on the 'pastel princes', who were able to build palaces thanks to the fortunes that they amassed.

268 MUSÉE INTERNATIONAL DE LA PARFUMERIE MIP

2 boulevard du Jeu de Ballon
06130 Grasse
Alpes-Maritimes
+33 (0)4 97 05 58 00

LES JARDINS DU MIP
979 chemin des Gourettes
06370 Mouans-Sartoux
Alpes-Maritimes
+33 (0)4 92 98 92 69
museesdegrasse.com

The Musée International de la Parfumerie MIP is the only museum in the world to showcase the history of perfume in such a complete and compact way: from ancient times to the modern-day perfume industry. Perfume as a means of seduction, as part of a purification ritual and as a status symbol. The mystery of a fragrance, that is the result of magic, chemistry and marketing. First you walk among the plants that are used to produce fragrances – jasmine, marjoram, lavender… – and then there are hundreds of jugs, bottles, pumps and flasks on display in addition to Marie-Antoinette's travel case from 1791 and the 20th-century 'perfume organ' – a vast array of ingredients used to compose a scent – of Jean Carles. At Mouans-Sartoux you can visit the MIP's lovely garden with your museum ticket: two hectares where all the flowers are grown that you need to make perfume.

269 MUSÉE ARTEMISIA

AT: COUVENT DES CORDELIERS
04300 Forcalquier
Alpes-de-Haute-Provence
+33 (0)4 92 72 50 68
artemisia-museum.fr

A journey in scent. The Artemisia Museum is a project of L'Université Européenne des Saveurs & des Senteurs (UESS), a centre that is dedicated to research into aromatic and cosmetic plants. The museum, which is located in a stunning 13th-century convent, has a trail that will interest adults and children alike, teaching them everything there is to know about plants, herbs, colours, scents and their applications. They regularly organise workshops for herbalists and perfumers. The convent also has a lovely, colourful and peaceful garden.

270 ÔKHRA – ÉCOMUSÉE DE L'OCRE

570 route d'Apt
84220 Roussillon
Vaucluse
+33 (0)4 90 05 66 69
okhra.com

Say Roussillon and most people will think of the colour ochre. Here you can walk through the old 'ochre mines', where this pigment was excavated, and visit an old factory, where it was washed and processed. L'Usine Mathieu used to produce 1000 tons of ochre a year but closed in 1963. After years of remaining vacant, the factory reopened to the public in 1994. All the machines have been restored so that you can witness the entire production process: from the excavation of the mineral to the transport of the pigment. The historical relevance and cultural significance of the colour ochre are also highlighted in the exhibit.

271 BASTIDE AUX VIOLETTES

Chemin de la Ferrage
06140 Tourrettes-sur-Loup
Alpes-Maritimes
+33 (0)4 93 59 06 97
tourrettessurloup.com

The region around Grasse is full of surprises. And it has everything to do with perfume. They have been growing violets in Tourettes-sur-Loup, a quiet and charming town, since 1880. Not because they are beautiful, but because they are used to produce perfumes and are edible. The violets flower between October and March, after which they are picked. Some are sent to Grasse to be used in perfumes, the remainder is used to produce sweets: you need 7600 flowers for one kilo of confectionery. Find out more in the small Bastide aux Violettes museum, where you can also visit the violet greenhouses. A fun discovery.

272 LA CITRONNERAIE

69 corniche Tardieu
06500 Menton
Alpes-Maritimes
+33 (0)6 80 26 52 24
lacitronneraie.fr

Call to book:
+33 (0)4 92 10 33 66
menton.fr

Menton is the lemon capital of France, as evidenced by La Citronneraie. This paradise garden is situated 120 metres above sea level, on the south-eastern flank of the Annonciade. The first mentions of a hillside garden date from the 16th century. After World War II, the garden was completely upgraded. Now they mainly grow lemon and olive trees here, as well as grapefruits, mandarins, satsumas and kumquats. The garden enjoys a subtropical climate, ensuring the hundreds of exotic plants that are grown here thrive. Its owner François Mazet, a former Formula I driver, is called Monsieur Citron by the locals. He supplies products to some of the greatest chefs in France. Book your visit with the Service du Patrimoine de la Ville de Menton.

273 MUSÉE ESCOFFIER DE L'ART CULINAIRE

3 rue Auguste Escoffier
06270 Villeneuve-Loubet
Alpes-Maritimes
+33 (0)4 93 20 80 51
en.musee-escoffier.com

Auguste Escoffier (1846-1935) revolutionised French cuisine. Which also explains why he is the only chef to have his own museum, in his native Villeneuve-Loubet. His *Le Guide culinaire* (1903) – a 500-page cookbook – is still considered the chef's equivalent of the Bible. In addition to several recipes of his own creation (including Crêpes Suzette, Pêche Melba and Tournedos Rossini), Escoffier got rid of heavy dishes and sauces, replacing them with lighter fare that was easier to digest. *'Toujours faites simple'* was his motto. Escoffier was only interested in preserving the original taste of the ingredient used – he was ahead of his time in that sense – and also served dishes one after the other instead of serving everything at the same time. Moreover, he reorganised kitchens: work had to be done efficiently and hygienically, everyone was assigned a specific task in the industrial kitchen. Escoffier 'directed' some of the world's greatest hotel restaurants, including the Ritz, the Savoy and the Carlton. Interestingly enough, Escoffier never disposed of leftovers, choosing to incorporate them into new recipes instead. The Musée Escoffier, which opened in 1966, is home to an authentic kitchen, menus and the famous chef's library. And you get to taste his iconic Pêche Melba at the end of your visit.

274 MUSÉE DE LA LAVANDE LUBERON

276 route de Gordes
84220 Coustellet/
Cabrières-d'Avignon
Vaucluse
+33 (0)4 90 76 91 23
museedelalavande.com

In this museum you can learn everything there is to know about lavender, the shrub that colours Provence purple in so many places and the plant that is inextricably linked with Provence. In the beautiful natural stone Mas (the Provençal word for a country house), all the steps of the process, starting with the harvesting of the lavender to the distillation, are shown in an interactive exhibition with large touch screens. The exhibit also delves deeper into the history of lavender and its fragrance, the perfume, and the plant's beneficial effects and cosmetic applications. The Musée de la Lavande also organises workshops. Here lavender is cultivated in an environmentally friendly way at Le Château du Bois, which is owned by the Lincelé family, the museum's founders. Their lavender products are sold in the museum shop under the name Le Château du Bois.

275 BALADES DANS LES LAVANDES

INFO: OFFICE DE TOURISME
Avenue de
la Promenade
84390 Sault
Vaucluse
+33 (0)4 90 64 01 21
ventouxprovence.fr

There's nothing quite like setting out on your own, to explore a region. And there are plenty of opportunities for this in the north of the Vaucluse, where you can walk or cycle through the purple lavender fields. Near Sault and Ferrassières – which is in the Drôme – you can take hikes of 5 and 3 kilometres respectively on signposted trails, with information panels along the way. Or you can take a 33-kilometre bike ride from Sault to Ferrassières and back. Use the handy brochure in French, English and Dutch as your guide. A walk or a bike ride for all seasons.

276 SALIN D'AIGUES-MORTES

Route du Grau du Roi
30220 Aigues-Mortes
Gard
+33 (0)4 66 73 40 24
visitesalinsde camargue.com

An endless plain with pink salt lakes near the centuries-old walled town of Aigues-Mortes. A remarkable sight, to say the least. The salt lakes, with their unique animal population, including hundreds of flamingos, can be visited in various ways: on foot, with your own bike or a rented bicycle, or by tourist train. The plain covers an area of almost 10.000 hectares – the size of Paris. Salt has been extracted here since ancient times. It was so precious at the time that Roman civil servants were paid in salt, receiving a *salarium*, which explains why we still use the word salary today. Every year, they harvest approximately 200.000 tons of salt at Aigues-Mortes. Salt is still indispensable today. While we know it as a flavour enhancer, it is also used to preserve food and has all kinds of industrial applications. Just think of the salt that is used to grit roads in winter. The salt that is extracted from the shallow salt pans is stored, forming impressive hills that you can climb during your visit. The history of the salt pans is explained in the small museum, where you can buy all the products – including the famous Fleur de Sel – in the museum shop.

Legendary FILM LOCATIONS

277 FALAISES SOUBEYRANES

Sur un arbre perché (1971)
D141 between Cassis and La Ciotat
Route des Crêtes
13260 Cassis
Bouches-du-Rhône

If you have a fear of heights, then this (film) location is not the place for you. In 1971, the exterior scenes for *Sur un arbre perché (Perched on a tree)* were shot here on the highest cliff in France, the 'falaises'. This comedy starring Louis de Funès, his son Olivier and Geraldine Chaplin, is based on a simple premise: Louis de Funès picks up two hitchhikers, misses a bend, causing his car – a Chevrolet Impala SS convertible – to crash into a ravine. By some miracle, the car ends up perched on a parasol pine that is growing on the rocks. The passengers have no choice but to remain very still in the precariously balanced car. The film was very difficult to shoot: an artificial tree was installed on the rocks, stuntmen and mountaineers were hired, and everything was filmed from a helicopter. The close-ups in the car were filmed in Paris, with the real actors on a set. All the movements had to be perfectly synchronised. There are various dizzying viewpoints along the Route des Crêtes that will literally take your breath away, including the Falaises Soubeyranes, Cap Canaille and the Falaises de Cassis. Watch your step…

278 BASSIN DE CUCURON

A Good Year (2006)
Place de l'Étang
84160 Cucuron
Vaucluse

Cucuron is a somewhat sleepy village that has largely managed to retain its charm amid the many tourist attractions in the Luberon. The *bassin de l'étang* in the town centre, a water basin lined with tall plane trees and surrounded by cafe terraces, is a nice place to sit. It also proved a perfect location for a number of exterior scenes of Ridley Scott's film *A Good Year* (2006) starring Russell Crowe (Max) and Marion Cotillard (Fanny). The film is based on Peter Mayle's novel of the same name. The *bassin* of Cucuron is the setting for Max and Fanny's first encounter. There are worse places for a first 'date'. So romantic!

279 BEAUSOLEIL

To Catch a Thief (1955)
1009 D53 –
Avenue des Anciens Combattants d'Afrique du Nord
06240 Beausoleil
Alpes-Maritimes
the.hitchcock.zone

"Have you ever seen any place in the world more beautiful?" says Frances 'Francie' Stevens (Grace Kelly) to John Robie (Cary Grant) after parking her car, a light blue Alpine Sports Roadster, in the hills above Monaco. This marks the start of the famous picnic scene in Hitchcock's *To Catch a Thief* (1955), which was filmed in a bend in the road in Beausoleil, where you can still park your car today. Grace Kelly has just managed to shake off a police car that is pursuing them, displaying some admirable driving skills. The police is hot on the trail of John Robie, a famous thief, aka The Cat. The dialogues between Kelly and Grant are filled with double entendres and sexual innuendo. At the time, Grace Kelly could not have guessed that she would retire from acting one year later to become Princess Grace of Monaco. The irony is that Grace died after an accident on a similar road in 1982. In *To Catch a Thief*, she is one of the most beautiful women in the world who is making every effort to seduce Cary Grant (who was 26 years older!). The glamorous film with its sunny locations proved a huge boost for tourism on the French Riviera.

280 CASINO DE MONTE-CARLO

GoldenEye (1995)
Place du Casino
98000 Monaco

The Casino in Monte-Carlo is probably one of the most glamorous film locations that come to mind. In *GoldenEye* (1995), the first James Bond spy flick that was not based on a book by Ian Fleming, Pierce Brosnan – his first time as James Bond – meets the gorgeous but very dangerous Georgian fighter pilot Xenia Onatopp, interpreted by the Dutch actress Famke Janssen. First, he beats her at the gambling table during a game of Baccarat. Then they meet again at the bar. You can visit the casino. Remember to bring ID and wear proper attire. (No shorts, no sports shoes, no flip flops). Tie and jacket mandatory!

281 SAINT-TROPEZ

Et Dieu... créa la femme (1956)
83990 Saint-Tropez
Var

Et Dieu... créa la femme, the scandalous film from 1956 that launched Brigitte Bardot's career as a sex symbol, was shot in Saint-Tropez. Director Roger Vadim could not have surmised that this would also turn the small coastal and fishing town into a popular tourist destination overnight. Nothing would ever be the same again. But despite all the upscale shops and gaudy yachts that are moored in its marina, Saint-Tropez was largely able to retain its old city centre. As a result, you can still visit many of the film locations today. The house of Juliette Hardy (Brigitte Bardot) is located in La Ponche, a neighbourhood to the north of the old city centre, where some of the beach scenes were also shot. The promenade along which Juliette walks provocatively is the Môle Jean Réveille. The newsagents' where she worked can be found at 2 rue du Cepoun San Martin. And de Bar des Amis, where Bardot dances so sensually in the cellar, is situated on Quai Frédéric Mistral although it has since become a pizzeria. Other beach scenes were filmed on the sandy beach of Pampelonne in Ramatuelle, just outside Saint-Tropez, where Le Club 55 is now located.

282 UZÈS

***Cyrano de Bergérac* (1990)**
Place aux Herbes
30700 Uzès
Gard

This spacious, elegant and irregularly shaped square in the centre of Uzès, with its simple houses, has been here since the Middle Ages. Because it has been so beautifully preserved, Place aux Herbes has been used as a film set on several occasions. The most famous film to have been shot here is *Cyrano de Bergerac* (1990) by Jean-Paul Rappeneau, starring Gérard Depardieu. The film makes extensive use of the vaulted galleries that run underneath the houses in the square. Here Roxane meets Cyrano at the baker Ragueneau and here Christian presents the love letters to Roxane, that Cyrano writes on his behalf. The prestigious cloak and dagger film won several French and international film awards, including the Oscar and BAFTA for Best Costume Design, almost all the Césars and the prize for best actor in a leading role at the Cannes Film Festival.

283 VAUGINES

***Jean de Florette + Manon des Sources* (1986)**
AT: L'ÉGLISE SAINT-PIERRE ET SAINT-BARTHÉLÉMY
Rue Haute
84160 Vaugines
Vaucluse

The simple, Romanesque church of l'Église Saint-Pierre et Saint-Barthélémy, with its beautiful forecourt, is situated just outside the village centre, in the shadow of the monumental plane trees. It feels as if you have travelled back in time. The square provided the perfect backdrop for a number of scenes from the successful films *Jean de Florette* and *Manon des Sources* (both from 1986), after the novels by Marcel Pagnol. Director Claude Berri filmed in the Luberon (Mirabeau, Ansouis and the surrounding hills) because the original locations around Marseille had changed too much over the years. The church and nearby cemetery in Vaugines were used as a setting for Manon's wedding and the site where Le Papet (Yves Montand) is shocked to learn that Jean de Florette, whose death he caused, was actually his son.

284 VILLEFRANCHE

***Never Say Never Again* (1983)**
06230 Villefranche-sur-Mer
Alpes-Maritimes

Never Say Never Again (1983) was the last spy film in which the actor Sean Connery starred as James Bond. The film was based on Ian Fleming's 1961 novel *Thunderball*, which had been previously adapted under that name in 1965. Connery played the role of Bond for the seventh and last time, although he had sworn that he would never play that role again after *Diamonds are Forever* (1971). Hence the title *Never Say Never Again*. Connery was 52 years old when the film was made. The storyline centres on an aging Bond who is out of shape and who is reactivated by M. The seaside resort of Villefranche-sur-Mer plays an important role as a location. The modernist villa that Bond is brought to early on in the film is located above the city on Avenue de l'Olivier: it is easy to recognise because of its dark red walls. When Bond is taken to Largo's base of operations in Palmyra, North Africa, the indoor scenes were shot in the majestic Villa Ephrussi de Rothschild at Saint-Jean-Cap-Ferrat, just outside Villefranche. The wild vehicle chase, with Bond on his motorbike, was filmed on and around Quai de la Corderie in Villefranche.

Local
TRADITIONS

285 PÉTANQUE IN LE MUSÉE CIOTADEN

1 quai Ganteaume
13600 La Ciotat
Bouches-du-Rhône
+33 (0)4 42 71 40 99
museeciotaden.org

La Ciotat is famous for having the oldest cinema in the world and the film of the railway station that was made by the Lumière brothers. But it is also the birthplace of pétanque, or *jeu de boules*. This ball game has a very long history but is played differently depending on where you are. Originally the players ran a few steps before throwing the wooden or iron ball (a little like lawn bowls). In 1907, a former champion called Jules Lenoir was so afflicted by rheumatism that he developed a variant of the game. He drew a circle in which the player stood stationary, while throwing his boule to the *cochonnet* (the small target ball). In Provençal, the game was soon called *'pieds tanqués'* or feet planted (on the ground). And that's how the pétanque game was born. In 1910, La Ciotat hosted the first official pétanque tournament. The Musée Ciotaden has all the details.

286 LE PEUPLIER DE CUCURON

Place de l'Église
84160 Cucuron
Vaucluse

A strange tradition that has been maintained for over three centuries in Cucuron. Every year, on the first Saturday after 21 May, a huge poplar tree is tied to the church's façade. The poplar is felled the same day and carried to the village by a group of men, with a child in traditional costume sitting on the tree trunk. The tree must be taller than the church's bell tower. You may wonder how this quirky tradition originated? In October 1720, Cucuron was hard hit by the plague, which spread from Marseille and killed one thousand people in just one month. Apparently, a religious procession put an end to the epidemic, after which the local population vowed to the patron saint of the village that they would organise this procession every year and plant a tree next to the church.

287 **MAISON DE LA BOULE**

287 MAISON DE LA BOULE

4 place des 13 Cantons
13002 Marseille
Bouches-du-Rhône
+33 (0)4 88 44 39 44
laboulebleue.fr

While pétanque or (jeu de) boules may have been invented in 1907, Félix Rofritsch was already producing special 'boules' in Marseille as early as 1904. Rofritsch came from Alsace. After serving in the navy, he was not interested in returning to German occupied territory, which is why he settled in Marseille. La Boule Bleue is still in business 100 years later although nowadays the boules they produce here are no longer made from wood, with rivets. Instead you can now buy bronze or stainless-steel boules. In 2015, they opened the Maison de la Boule in Le Panier, a neighbourhood in the old city centre. This tiny museum explains the history of this ball game, from ancient times to the present day. It has a collection of boules through the ages, in addition to posters and other memorabilia. There is also a petanque court, where you can try your hand and see how good you are at this quintessentially French pastime.

288 MANUFACTURE NATIONALE DE LA SAVONNERIE, ATELIER DE LODÈVE

1 impasse des Liciers
34700 Lodève
Hérault
+33 (0)4 67 88 86 44
www.mobiliernational.culture.gouv.fr

The only branch of the famous Manufacture Nationale de la Savonnerie, the national carpet manufactury in Paris, is located in Lodève. Here a team of 18 specialised tradespeople weave the rugs for the Elysée (the official residence of the French president), national monuments, official buildings and French embassies around the world. It takes approximately four to seven years to weave a rug by hand, a diligent task that is often performed in silence. The weaving mill owes its name, 'La Savonnerie', to the old soap factory in Paris, where King Louis XIII established the manufactury in 1627. The workshop at Lodève was founded in 1964 and was originally set up to facilitate the integration of French women of North African origin who had left Algeria after it became independent. While they produce copies of 17th and 19th-century rugs here, the two workshops now mainly weave contemporary designs, based on the works of such artists as Pierre Soulages and Pierre Alechinsky. Guided tours only, booking compulsory.

French CHANSONS

289 **LA MIETTE – JACQUES PRÉVERT**
7 rue de l'Allée
06570 Saint-Paul-de-Vence
Alpes-Maritimes
saint-pauldevence.com

A little house with a big history. During World War II, the French writer, poet and filmmaker Jacques Prévert moved to Saint-Paul-de-Vence, which was in unoccupied territory. Prévert was able to continue making films in the Studios de la Victorine in nearby Nice. He met Pablo Picasso in Saint-Paul and also befriended Paul Roux, the owner of the auberge Colombe d'Or. Prévert produced collages for the walls of the now famous hotel-restaurant. From 1945, Prévert and his wife Jeanine rented a narrow corner house in the village, which they called La Miette, or the crumb. It is here that Prévert penned his world-famous love song *Les feuilles mortes*. The melancholic song, which was set to music by Joseph Kosma, was used in the film *Les Portes de la Nuit* (1946), for which Prévert wrote the script. Unfortunately, the film was a flop and the song soon forgotten. It was only when Yves Montand recorded his own version of *Les feuilles mortes* in 1949 that it became an international success. The English translation, *Autumn Leaves*, has since been interpreted by Frank Sinatra, Nat King Cole and, more recently, Iggy Pop, Grace Jones and Eric Clapton. Miles Davis, Oscar Peterson and Diana Krall recorded instrumental versions of the song, turning it into a jazz standard. With more than 600 different versions recorded to date, it is safe to say that *Les feuilles mortes* is the most famous French love song ever. La Miette is included in a Prévert trail through Saint-Paul and can be rented through AirBnb as a holiday cottage.

290 **ESPACE GEORGES BRASSENS**

67 boulevard
Camille Blanc
34200 Sète
Hérault
+33 (0)4 99 04 76 26
espace-brassens.fr

The non-conformist troubadour Georges Brassens was born in 1921 in the old city centre of Sète. During your visit to the Espace Brassens, you will learn more about the life and ideas of this singer-poet through his songs, various personal items, photos, concert films, interviews and song lyrics. Brassens discusses his childhood in Sète and his parents in the free audio guide. He had an atheist French father and a Catholic Italian mother. Themes include his anarchism, the women that influenced his life and the importance of eternal friendship – his chanson *Les copains d'abord* is famous – as well as his successes in the French-speaking world and beyond. Brassens died in 1981. He is buried in the cemetery across the street.

291 **MAISON NOUGARO**

AT: PÉNICHE SANCTANOX
Ponts Jumeaux
31200 Toulouse
Haute-Garonne
+33 (0)9 73 67 89 04
maison-nougaro.fr

Maison Nougaro is not a traditional museum. The tiny museum, which is dedicated to the singer Claude Nougaro (1929-2004), who is very popular in Toulouse, is located on a barge at anchor between the Garonne River and the Canal du Midi. Nougaro's songs include several references to these two waterways. The rebellious youth and artistic success of this chansonnier, who was born and raised in Toulouse, is beautifully portrayed with photos, manuscripts of song lyrics, drawings, records and CDs, books about him and even his upright piano.

292 **THÉÂTRE DE L'ALCAZAR**

58 cours Belsunce
13001 Marseille
Bouches-du-Rhône
+33 (0)4 91 55 90 00
madeinmarseille.net

Unfortunately, all that attests to the presence of L'Alcazar, a legendary concert hall in Marseille, is the flamboyant entrance with a wrought iron marquise or canopy in Cours Belsunce in the city centre. The hall was renovated in 2004 and is now home to a public library. Originally, L'Alcazar was a cafe-concert and music hall. The oriental-style building became a cinema and later a theatre and concert hall. Several famous French musicians made their debut here, including Yves Montand, Dalida, Maurice Chevalier and Fernandel. Charles Aznavour, Henri Salvador and Jacques Brel also performed here. Marseille audiences had quite a reputation for being tough and harsh. A young Serge Gainsbourg was booed here in 1959.

293 MAISON NATALE DE CHARLES TRENET

13 avenue Charles Trenet
11100 Narbonne
Aude
+33 (0)4 68 58 19 13
narbonne.fr

The birth house of the legendary French singer, the father of modern chanson, who wrote and performed *La mer, Je chante, Y a d'la joie, Boum* and *Route nationale 7*. Many of his compositions – including *Beyond the Sea*, the English version of *La mer* – went on to become world-famous and were interpreted by Rod Stewart, Bobby Darin, George Benson and Robbie Williams. *Boum* was used on the soundtrack of the James Bond flick *Skyfall* (2021) and in *A Good Year* (2006). *Je chante* was also included on the soundtrack of the latter. Charles Trenet was born in 1913 in Narbonne. He inherited his talent for music from his mother, who played the piano and encouraged him to listen to jazz standards by George Gershwin. After his parents divorced, Trenet followed his mother to Berlin, where he met Kurt Weill and Fritz Lang, among others. By the end of the 1930s, Trenet achieved his first successes with his upbeat, cheerful songs. Their jazzy rhythms and slightly surrealistic imagery were considered an innovation in French chanson. Throughout his long career – he died in 2001 at the ripe old age of 87 after a glorious comeback –, his birth house always was a place of inspiration, just like the trains that thundered past on the opposite side of the street. Trenet continued to visit the house until 1997. The museum, which opened in 2000, shows the house as left by Trenet. The songwriter's quotes on the mirrors and windows – English translation provided – paint a picture of an eternal optimist with a dark side. The displays feature personal belongings, photos, record sleeves and his mother's piano. You can also watch his films and listen to his songs during your visit.

293 **MAISON NATALE DE CHARLES TRENET**

Extraordinary ISLANDS

294 CHÂTEAU D'IF

AT: ÎLE D'IF
13000 Marseille
Bouches-du-Rhône
+33 (0)6 03 06 25 26
chateau-if.fr

Le Château d'If is an imposing fortress on the tiny island of If, offshore from Marseille. The castle was built between 1527 and 1529 to defend the port of Marseille although it was never used for this purpose. Instead, it was a prison for more than 400 years, which is also how it became famous. The writer Alexandre Dumas chose to lock up Edmond Dantès, the hero of his novel *The Count of Monte-Cristo* (1844), in the prison of Château d'If after he was falsely accused of treason. The count managed to escape, found a hidden treasure on the island of Monte-Cristo and exacted his revenge. Although this is a fictional story, you can nonetheless see the dungeon where Dantès spent fourteen years of his life in captivity. Fans of adventure novels: there is a ferry service from Marseille to If.

295 JAZZ À PORQUEROLLES

AT: ÎLE DE PORQUEROLLES
83400 Hyères
Var
+33 (0)6 31 79 81 90
jazzaporquerolles.org

Since 2002, the island of Porquerolles and Fort Sainte-Agatha have provided the stunning backdrop for an annual jazz festival. One of its founding fathers and a returning guest is the American saxophone player Archie Shepp. But there is more! In addition to the main concert programme, the island is transformed into a gigantic jazz stage for one week, with free concerts everywhere, often by young and talented musicians. A brass band has even been known to emerge from the water. Fun times!

296 VILLA CARMIGNAC

AT: ÎLE DE PORQUEROLLES
La Courtade
83400 Hyères
Var
+33 (0)4 65 65 25 50
fondation carmignac.com

Villa Carmignac is a museum, arts centre and sculpture garden on the island of Porquerolles off the coast of Hyères. The Villa is overseen by the Fondation Carmignac, which supports investigative photo journalists with prizes and exhibitions since 2009, among others at the Villa Carmignac. The Villa, which opened in 2018, also has a collection of 300 artworks. Highlights include works by Andy Warhol, Jean-Michel Basquiat, Gerhard Richter and Roy Lichtenstein. The presentation is both unique and surprising: visitors are required to take off their shoes for the visit, part of the museum is underground, and light falls in through the glass water ceiling. "Freedom is Fondation Carmignac's guiding principle", says Édouard Carmignac, who created the Fondation. "Over the last twenty years, the collection has been put together in a pioneering spirit, disregarding borders and taboos." Check it out and prepare to be surprised on this extraordinary island.

297 CIMETIÈRE MUSULMAN ÎLE SAINTE MARGUERITE

AT: ÎLE SAINTE-MARGUERITE
Chemin de la Batterie
06150 Cannes
Alpes-Maritimes

You can find this strange place on the idyllic island of Sainte-Marguerite, offshore from ritzy Cannes. Follow the trails on this forested island and you will run into the Cimetière musulman: a Muslim cemetery, with its distinctive tombstones, which are laid out in circles on the ground. These are the graves of 200 – some sources even say there are as many as 600 – Algerian men, women and children. They all belonged to the entourage of Emir Abdelkader, who offered resistance against the French colonial army for many years. The Algerians were sent to prison in the fortress on Sainte-Marguerite in 1842. Life here was harsh: too many prisoners were locked up together in small cells and the drinking water was polluted. The dead were buried here, far from the mainland.

ANCHOIS ROQUE

SHOPS

Our favourite
(ART) BOOKSHOPS

298 **LIBRAIRIE LES ARCENAULX**
25 cours d'Estienne d'Orves
13001 Marseille
Bouches-du-Rhône
+33 (0)4 91 59 80 37
les-arcenaulx.com

An exceptional bookshop in a monumental building, i.e., Marseille's former arsenal, a 16th-century weapons store and shipyard for galleys. The shop occupies several rooms of this amazing old building, with wooden beams and stone walls. While it's a good place to stock up on literature, books about food and tourist guides, Les Arcenaulx is mainly known for its selection of books on the history of Marseille and Provence. It also sells prints as well as historic and current maps. The shop's other name is Librairie Jeanne Laffitte – Laffitte is a publisher with a keen eye for old and rare publications, which she gives a new lease on life. She also lobbied tirelessly to ban cars from Cours d'Estienne d'Orves so it would become a pedestrian area. There is an excellent restaurant next to the bookshop. Check the 'literary' menus.

299 **LIBRAIRIE MAUPETIT**
142 La Canebière
13001 Marseille
Bouches-du-Rhône
+33 (0)4 91 36 50 50
www.maupetit libraire.fr

Librairie Maupetit was founded in 1919, making it Marseille's oldest bookshop. Situated along boulevard La Canébière, the cheerful red shop windows beckon from afar. It remained in the hands of the Maupetit family, which specialised in university books, until 1998, when it was acquired by Actes Sud. Maupetit is a spacious bookshop with an excellent range of books. The exhibition space on the first floor attests to Maupetit's desire to participate in Marseille's cultural scene as much as possible and attract a diverse crowd.

La gouache
PEINTURE
LETTRE-LIVRE
Monet
Lettres de G. Clemenceau
Monet
Sénèque
Diderot
Sénèque
Lettre à Lucilius
Sénèque
Lettre à Lucilius
LE LIVRE QU'IL VOUS FAUT POUR RÉUSSIR VOS
LE LIVRE QU'IL VOUS FAUT POUR DESSINER VOS PORTRAITS
Selwyn Leamy
AQUARELLE
DESSIN MODÈLE
JEFF KOONS

300 LIBRAIRIE ACTES SUD AU MÉJAN

47 rue du Dr Fanton
13200 Arles
Bouches-du-Rhône
+33 (0)4 90 49 56 77
www.librairie actessud.com

This spacious and excellent bookshop is located in the city centre of Arles. Actes Sud is a chain of eight bookshops (five in Paris, three in the South of France). Originally a publishing house, it was founded in 1978 by Hubert Nyssen and his wife Christine Le Bœuf in Paradou, a small town close to Les Baux. In 1983, they moved to Place Nina Berberova in Arles. Actes Sud was an outlier in more ways than one: it was the first French publishing house ever to be established outside of Paris. What's more, it specialised in translations of foreign literature, unique formats and exceptional editions. This approach is reflected in its flagship in Arles, in 'Le Méjan': a pleasant, well-kept and well-organised shop with plain wood bookshelves. They carry books on a wide range of subjects, including literature, foreign affairs, history, politics and art, in addition to all the Actes Sud publications, of course. On top of that, Le Méjan is also a cultural centre with a cinema, a hammam, a concert hall and a restaurant.

301 LIBRAIRIE GALERIE LAURE MATARASSO

46 boulevard Risso
06300 Nice
Alpes-Maritimes
+33 (0)4 93 87 74 55
laure-matarasso.com

An art bookshop and publishing house with a rich history. Jacques Matarasso founded this bookshop in 1941 in Nice. In addition to selling old and new books, he decided to also buy and sell original graphic art. Soon his bookshop became a popular meeting place for artists and writers and the place to be for exhibitions and book signings by, among others, Marc Chagall, Albert Marquet, Pablo Picasso, Fernando Arrabal, and Michel Butor. In 1993, Laure Matarasso followed in her father's footsteps, but the vision remained unchanged. In 2017, the shop relocated to 46 boulevard Risso, close to Nice's Musée d'Art Moderne et d'Art Contemporain (MAMAC). This smallish bookshop specialises in artist's books, oeuvre catalogues, monographs, original prints and bibliophile and special editions. There's always an exhibition on.

302 LE TEMPS DE LIRE

Place du Four
81140 Puycelsi
Tarn
+33 (0)6 74 80 72 72

What a pleasant surprise it was to stumble across this charming and cosy little bookshop and its carefully curated range of books in Puycelsi, one of the most beautiful villages of France. Local history, art and a nice selection of English books. And all this loveliness in the middle of nowhere.

303 SCARLETT

14 rue Henri Seillon
83990 Saint-Tropez
Var
+33 (0)4 94 97 72 50
scarlett.fr

A stylish, minimalist bookshop with a glossy white interior, design furniture and art objects: this is Saint-Tropez, after all. A small space (50 square metres) with a good selection of international publications on art, photography, design and fashion. A lot of large format and exclusive books. There's also a table with recent fiction and non-fiction.

302 LE TEMPS DE LIRE

304 LIBRAIRIE LA BASSE FONTAINE

2 place Antony Mars
06140 Vence
Alpes-Maritimes
+33 (0)4 93 58 30 82
bassefontaine.com

The perfect spot to snap up antiquarian books, bibliophile editions and prints. La Basse Fontaine is situated on the fringe of the old centre of Vence, next to the fountain that Raoul Dufy painted so many times. The shop opened in 1988 and has been selling rare art books ever since, as well as artist's books in which graphic design is paired with poetry or prose. You can also find some gorgeous exhibition posters here. They mainly focus on artists who have lived and worked in Vence for a short or longer time, such as Matisse, Chagall, Dufy, Dubuffet, Soutine … Recently the bookshop expanded, adding an exhibition space for books and prints. A truly wonderful place.

304 LIBRAIRIE LA BASSE FONTAINE

305 **LIBRAIRIE LE HAUT QUARTIER**

8 rue des Orfèvres
34120 Pézenas
Hérault
+33 (0)4 67 98 27 41

A small, cosy bookshop on the corner of a shopping street in the old, car-free town centre of Pézenas, which was founded in the 1960s by Albert Camus's Algerian publisher. The shop moved to its current location in 2011 and is now run by Fabrice Andrivon. The books are displayed in plain wooden bookcases. Fiction, for the most part, including a children and young adults section, Unsurprisingly, Le Haut Quartier is an active participant in the Festival du livre de jeunesse (an annual children's book festival). There's a table with some chairs, where you can take some time to browse in more detail.

306 **OMBRES BLANCHES**

50 rue Léon Gambetta
31000 Toulouse
Haute-Garonne
+33 (0)5 34 45 53 33
ombres-blanches.fr

Ombres Blanches is Toulouse's largest bookshop and is located near Place du Capitole. The shop occupies several historic dwellings and has a number of beautiful rooms with tall windows. This university bookshop stocks a wide range of foreign literature in addition to books on history, psychology, travel, food and comics. There are chairs in most of the rooms so you can take your time to browse the books. Ombres Blanches has a longstanding tradition of interviews and panel discussions with writers. All of these talks are recorded and made available as podcasts. There's also a cafeteria.

307 **LE PASSEUR DE L'ISLE**

7 place de la Liberté
84800 L'Isle-sur-la-Sorgue
Vaucluse
+33 (0)4 90 20 85 84

Although L'Isle-sur-la-Sorgue can get quite touristy in summer, you'll be happy to know that it is also home to a surprising bookshop. The books are displayed on the ground floor; on the first floor, there is a shop with the most beautiful fabrics from around the world. So what do these two have in common, you might wonder? The answer: a taste for the exotic. The books and the fabrics are an invitation to roam around the world, whether you prefer a real-life adventure or choose to do so from the comfort of your own sofa.

Alluring
MUSEUM SHOPS

308 **MUSÉE BONNARD**
16 boulevard Sadi Carnot
06110 Le Cannet
Alpes-Maritimes
+33 (0)4 93 94 06 06
museebonnard.fr

Before checking out the shop, you should obviously visit the lovely Musée Bonnard first, which is dedicated to the lush garden scenes of the post-impressionist painter and the dozens of intriguing nudes of his partner Marthe while she bathed. The museum's shop is modest but good. Besides a series of publications – large and small, general and specialised – about Pierre Bonnard and his contemporaries, it also sells scarves and other souvenirs with colourful Bonnard-style patterns. Elegant, delicate and tasteful, striking just the right note.

308 MUSÉE BONNARD

309 PARFUMERIE FRAGONARD

20 boulevard Fragonard
06130 Grasse
+33 (0)4 93 36 44 65
Alpes-Maritimes
fragonard.com/en/factories/historic-factory

Ah, Grasse, the perfume capital of the world. If you're looking to buy a scented gift, head to the large, elegant and deliciously fragrant perfume shop of Fragonard. While you're there, you can also learn more about the perfume production process and distilling, filtering and bottling – a nice added bonus. Parfumerie Fragonard was founded shortly after WWI by the Parisian notary Eugène Fuchs. He took over two existing perfume shops, installed his factory in a former tannery and that is how Parfumerie Fragonard was established in 1926. It was named after Jean-Honoré Fragonard (1732-1806), a painter from Grasse who was known for his refined depictions of frivolous scenes.

310 LE MUSÉE DU SAVON DE MARSEILLE

26 Quai de Rive Neuve
13007 Marseille
Bouches-du-Rhône
+33 (0)4 96 12 00 91
savon-de-marseille-licorne.com

Marseille and soap: the two have been inextricably linked for centuries. Legend has it that that the crusaders brought back cube-shaped soap bars from the Middle East, which were then copied in Marseille, using local ingredients. The typical soap cubes from Marseille were particularly convenient for people who washed their clothes by hand in a river or a wash tub. But they also used this soap to wash their hair and body. As all kinds of liquid soaps in bottles became available, the popularity of Marseille soap rapidly declined. But lo and behold, the soap is all the rage again. A natural product – olive oil is one of the main ingredients –, it is also very environment-friendly because it produces almost no waste. Le Musée du Savon de Marseille shows how this soap is made. It's like immersing yourself in a sensory bath, and you also get to make your own soap. You can bag soap in every possible colour with all kinds of fragrances in the museum's large, two-storey shop.

311 LA LIBRAIRIE-BOUTIQUE DU MUCEM

7 promenade
Robert Laffont
(1 esplanade du J4)
13002 Marseille
Bouches-du-Rhône
+33 (0)4 84 35 14 95
mucem.org

La librairie-boutique du Mucem is more than a bookshop; it's a museum shop with an architectural flourish. The tables and bookshelves look as if they are standing in a forest of concrete trees or giant mushrooms – these are, of course, the columns that support the museum building above it. The ambience in this bright, sun-drenched shop is quite special, as a result. La librairie-boutique du Mucem is a general bookshop, with an emphasis on art, human sciences and tourism. Besides books, the shop also sells a nice selection of fine Mediterranean objects, like jewellery, textiles, tableware...

312 BOUTIQUE CAP MODERNE

AT: GARE SNCF
ROQUEBRUNE-CAP-MARTIN
Avenue de la Gare /
Avenue Le Corbusier
06190 Roquebrune-Cap-Martin
Alpes-Maritimes
+33 (0)4 92 15 01 41
capmoderne.monuments-nationaux.fr

The former hangar of Roquebrune-Cap-Martin train station is the starting point of a hike that winds its way to Eileen Gray's Villa E-1027 and Le Corbusier's Cabanon. In this hangar you'll also find a spacious shop, where you can buy publications on the Irish architect and designer Eileen Gray and the French-Swiss modernist Le Corbusier, in addition to reference works on architecture in general and modernism in particular. Please bear in mind that the shop is only open before and after tours.

311 **LA LIBRAIRIE-BOUTIQUE DU MUCEM**

Nice shops for
LOCAL PRODUCTS

313 LA MAISON DES MÉTIERS D'ART DE PÉZENAS

6 place Gambetta
34120 Pézenas
Hérault
+33 (0)4 67 98 16 12
ateliersdart.com

A number of local artists and artisans have joined forces setting up a market in the 17th-century consular residence in the centre of Pézenas. In this magnificent historic setting you can snap up locally-made jewellery, clothing, glass objects, mosaic and textile designs, ceramics, sculptures and more. These are either one-of-a-kind pieces or limited editions. Thanks to its rich history and its exceptionally well-preserved heritage, Pézenas attracts many artists and designers, who set up their studios and workshops in the historic buildings of the charming town centre. Definitely worth visiting.

314 L'OCCITANE EN PROVENCE

Autoroute A51 – Chemin de Saint-Maurice
ZI Saint-Maurice
04100 Manosque
Alpes-de-Haute-Provence
+33 (0)4 92 70 19 50
fr.loccitane.com

Today L'Occitane en Provence is a world-renowned cosmetics brand. But the company has very humble beginnings: in 1976, a 23-year-old student by the name of Olivier Baussan began distilling oil from Provençal plants and herbs – rosemary, lavender and olives – selling it at the local market. He founded the brand L'Occitane in 1977 together with the chemist Yves Millou. And the rest is history as they say. In Manosque, L'Occitane's home base, you can tour the factory where all the products are manufactured according to the principles of aromatherapy as well as the laboratories, production workshops and packing lines. There's a Mediterranean garden and boutique where you can sample and buy the products, with a bit of design history thrown in for free thanks to the fun exhibition with packaging from recent years.

315 TERRE DE PASTEL

629 rue Max Planck
Place d'Assézat
(shop only)
31670 Toulouse
Haute-Garonne
+33 (0)800 940 167
terredepastel.com

In the small shop next to Hôtel d'Assézat in Toulouse, you can buy all sorts of products made using woad: fabrics, ceramics, pastels and also honey. The woad plant is cultivated intensively in the triangle between Toulouse, Albi and Carcassonne. It is used to produce honey and every possible shade of blue dye you can think of. Recently, the cosmetics industry also rediscovered woad. Between the 14th and the 16th century, Toulouse became a very wealthy city thanks to the production and trade of woad as you can tell by the house of woad trader Pierre d'Assézat (next to this shop). There is also a museum outside the city, in Rue Max Planck, where you can find out more about the history of woad.

316 ANCHOIS ROQUE

17 route d'Argelès
66190 Collioure
Pyrénées-Orientales
+33 (0)4 68 82 04 99
anchois-roque.fr

Collioure has a centuries-old anchovy fishing tradition. Anchois Roque, a local business, was established in 1870. Today, the descendants of founder Alphonse Roque still run this popular family business. On the first floor, above the shop with all kinds of anchovy specialities, you can visit the workplace where the small fish are salted and processed.

Charming

ART VILLAGES

317 MONTOLIEU
BOOKSHOPS AND ART GALLERIES
39 rue de la Mairie
11170 Montolieu
Aude
+33 (0)4 68 24 80 04
montolieu-livre.fr
collectionceresfranco.com

Montolieu is one of France's six *'cités du livre'* (book villages). The village north of Carcassonne has an abundance of bookshops – eighteen in all! –, bookbinders, collectors and craftsmen all working with books in one way or another. Visit the Musée des Arts et Métiers du Livre: a small museum about the history of books and book printing, bookbinding and calligraphy. While you're there you might as well check out La Coopérative, where you can see the remarkable art collection of Cérès Franco (b. 1926). She has been showing her support to unknown artists since the 1960s, buying their art. The collection, which is housed in the old warehouse of the local wine cooperative, is slightly left-field albeit thought-provoking. Twenty artists also have their studios in the village.

318 BIOT
GLASS
INFO: OFFICE DE TOURISME
4 chemin neuf
06410 Biot
Alpes-Maritimes
+33 (0)4 93 65 78 00
biot-tourisme.com
ECOMUSÉE DU VERRE
AT: LA VERRERIE DE BIOT
Chemin des Combes
06410 Biot
Alpes-Maritimes
+33 (0)4 93 65 03 00
verreriebiot.com

Biot already had a longstanding tradition of ceramics and pottery. Since 1956, the picturesque hillside village has become France's glassblowing capital, however. The village's famous blown glass is the result of a manufacturing error: the ceramist Éloi Monod (1918-2007) turned the 'air bubbles' that stayed in the glass into his aesthetic trademark. Nowadays, this bubbled glass has become the main attraction of Biot: you can see glassblowers at work or visit specialised galleries in the town. The Ecomusée du Verre, just outside the village, is also worth visiting: they give tours and you can see the huge ovens that are used for the production process. They even offer internships, during which you can learn how to blow glass yourself.

319 SAINT-JEAN-DE-FOS

POTTERY STUDIOS

34150 Saint-Jean-de-Fos
Hérault
potiersdestjeandefos.com

The medieval town of Saint-Jean-de-Fos, along the road between Saint-Guilhem-le-Désert and Gignac, owes its fame to its pottery and ceramics. Every year, in early August, they organise a two-day pottery festival here. First organised thirty years ago, the annual Marché des Potiers takes over the entire town. Don't expect to see the usual vases and earthenware bowls, though. Fifty ceramists showcase their very diverse creations, from traditional earthenware to contemporary ceramics and everything in between, in the town's streets and squares. A great opportunity to see and buy utensils, decorative objects, sculptures and jewellery, as well as porcelain and raku ware, made according to a centuries-old Japanese firing process. Saint-Jean is home to twenty pottery studios, making it the place to go for ceramics year-round. In 2011, the Argileum, a museum dedicated to the history of ceramics and its techniques, opened its doors here.

320 SAINT-PAUL-DE-VENCE

ART GALLERIES

Rue Grande and surrounding streets
06570 Saint-Paul-de-Vence
Alpes-Maritimes
saint-pauldevence.com/en/fiches/galeries

Saint-Paul-de-Vence is a tourist hotspot and home to La Fondation Maeght, France's first private contemporary art institution which was founded in 1964. Soon many other art galleries found their way to this beautiful town. Today there are over thirty art galleries in Vence; the majority are located on Rue Grande, which resembles an open-air gallery. The range – which can be overwhelming at times – is diverse and of varying quality but there definitely is something for every taste and budget. Of course, it isn't all Chagall, César, Jeff Koons and Niki de Saint Phalle but if you're prepared to browse and explore, you'll be pleasantly surprised.

The best places for POTTERY *and* CERAMICS

321 ARGILEUM
6 avenue du Monument
34150 Saint-Jean-de-Fos
Hérault
+33 (0)4 67 56 41 96
argileum.fr

Handmade pottery is all the rage right now. Argileum, which opened in 2011 in Saint-Jean-de-Fos – the go-to place for all things pottery –, is a good little museum with friendly staff. Here you can visit an authentic 19th-century pottery studio and learn all there is to know about the history of earthenware and ceramics, different techniques, and the lives of the craftsmen. That said, this interactive museum takes a refreshingly informal approach, which will also appeal to children, with films and touchscreens. You can also learn how to create your own pottery here and attend workshops – starting from age 5 and up. Obviously, there's also a museum shop with a very nice and good range of choices. Walk into the village centre to explore the other studios in the town.

322 LA CÉRAMIQUE D'UZÈS
1 rue Port-Royal
30700 Uzès
Gard
+33 (0)6 23 93 41 60
laceramiqueduzes.com

You can find La céramique d'Uzès in one of the narrow, winding streets in the historic city centre of Uzès. The artist who runs this minimalistic shop specialises in delicate and almost translucent porcelain. You'll find all sorts of items here, from elegant teapots and painted vases and bowls to engraved cups and porcelain lamp shades. A surprising and elegant selection. The actual studio is a couple of hundred metres from the shop.

323 POTERIE LA BERGERIE

67 Grand'Rue
06140 Tourrettes-sur-Loup
Alpes-Maritimes
+33 (0)4 93 59 35 17
vigroux.com

Yes, there are dozens of potteries in this area, but this one is especially charming. All of the earthenware – dishes, bowls, cups, egg cups, oil dispensers, and so on – is fired on site and then painted by hand. The master potter can usually be found at work in his studio. The Poterie La Bergerie is unique in that it's built against a majestic rock, which serves as the pottery's back wall. Peculiar and quirky. The entire village of Tourrettes-sur-Loup is perched on a rock spur by the way. Be sure to visit the viewpoint at the far end of the village.

324 LES CÉRAMIQUES DE LUSSAN

AT: MAS DE FAN
Route de Saint-Ambroix
30580 Lussan
Gard
+33 (0)6 41 69 31 46
ceramique-de-lussan.fr

This is where the region's most famous guinea hen, the 'Pintade de Lussan', is bred. We're not talking about the actual bird, mind, but its stylised ceramic counterpart. The 'pintade' was originally created by Heidi Caillard, who was born in 1932 in Basel, Switzerland. After graduating from the École de Céramique in Lausannne she moved to the Uzès area in 1968 and set up her own pottery studio. She originally started producing these hens, inspired by the guinea fowl that lived in her garden. It took a lot of time and work before she settled on the pintade's distinctive, stylised shape.

Amazing

ART GALLERIES

325 **GALERIE CATHERINE ISSERT**

2 route des Serres
06570 Saint-Paul-de-Vence
Alpes-Maritimes
+33 (0)4 93 32 96 92
galerie-issert.com

Galerie Catherine Issert stands out among the many galleries in Saint-Paul-de-Vence in a good way. Issert founded the gallery in 1975, representing exciting contemporary established as well as emerging artists from France and abroad. She mainly specialises in sculpture and paintings, which she shows in her simple, nice and spacious gallery at the entrance to the village. Artists who have already exhibited here include John M. Armleder, Ben (Vautier), Tatiana Wolska, Claude Viallat, Bernard Pagès and Anne Pesce.

325 GALERIE CATHERINE ISSERT

326 **FONDATION LINDA ET GUY PIETERS**

AT: PLACE DES LICES
28 boulevard Vasserot
83990 Saint-Tropez
Var
+33 (0)6 70 50 72 27
fondationlgp.com

The Belgian gallerists and art collectors Linda and Guy Pieters opened their own Fondation in July 2018 in a beautifully renovated three-storey building in Place des Lices in the heart of Saint-Tropez. They see it as the crowning achievement of their thirty-year career, showcasing the work of the many artists with whom they have a long-standing working relationship. The conceptual artist Christo, famous for his ephemeral wrapped installations, and his *Mastaba* in London's Hyde Park, was the subject of the opening exhibition. Subsequent shows featured work by Arman, Jan Fabre, Jean-Michel Folon, Robert Combas, Gilbert & George, and Ben (Vautier).

327 **LA STATION**

Halle sud du 109
89 route de Turin
06300 Nice
Alpes-Maritimes
+33 (0)4 93 56 99 57
lastation.org

La Station is a nomadic art initiative, holding the middle between a gallery and an art centre. It originally occupied a former petrol station, hence the name. La Station has since moved to another quirky, industrial location: a former cold-storage warehouse, owned by the city of Nice, close to the marshalling yard of Nice-Saint-Roch station. The 1000-square-metre space is used for exhibitions of the work of emerging artists but is also home to twelve studios. They regularly organise open studios here in addition to artist-in-residence programmes, so artists can create and show their work there on a long-term basis. Famous artists whose work has been exhibited here include Laure Prouvost, Heimo Zobernig, Monster Chetwynd and Brice Dellsperger.

328 GALERIE EVA VAUTIER

2 rue Vernier
06100 Nice
Alpes-Maritimes
+33 (0)9 80 31 76 63
eva-vautier.com

Eva Vautier founded her gallery in 2011 in the Quartier Libération, a lively nightlife district to the north of Nice-Ville railway station, which was undergoing a transformation when she decided to settle here. Besides solo shows – she represents, among others, her father, the artist Ben (Vautier) – Eva also presents retrospectives of the Fluxus movement and the Supports/Surfaces art collective. The gallery regularly hosts 'duo' exhibitions, with one artist inviting another. Eva Vautier also produces art books, editions and multiples, as well as engravings and lithographs, all of which are for sale in the gallery.

329 LATUVU ART CONTEMPORAIN

48 rue de
l'Ancien Puits
11100 Bages
Aude
+33 (0)4 68 48 96 22
latuvu.fr

Bages is a beautiful and tranquil little village, consisting of a steep street lined with houses, just a short distance from Narbonne and overlooking the Étang de Sigean. Not exactly the place where you'd expect to find an art gallery. And yet. A couple of years ago, Belgian artists Sabine Friederichs and Herman Vansynghel decided this was the place where they wanted to present their curated selection of French, Italian, Dutch and Belgian artists. They show their work in temporary exhibitions at the Latuvu gallery (an alternative spelling for 'L'as-tu vu?', meaning 'did you see it?'). Once a year the couple also invites an artist in residence to create new work on location, inspired by the surroundings. Definitely worth the detour.

CAFÉ DE LA PLACE

FOOD & DRINKS

NOSTALGIC
restaurants

330 **L'ÉCOLE DES FILLES**
380 avenue Amiral de Grasse
06620 Le Bar-sur-Loup
Alpes-Maritimes
+33 (0)4 93 09 40 20
lecoledesfilles.wixsite.com/ecole

A lovely restaurant, in a former girls' school, from 1929, in Le Bar-sur-Loup. It was here that Célestin Freinet taught his first pupils and gradually developed his pedagogy around the idea of the free expression of children. In 2000, the school was converted into the aptly named 'L'École des Filles' restaurant. You can still visit two classrooms and see the small wooden desks with the porcelain inkwells. The walls are covered with old classroom photos. The former playground has now become a terrace, where you can eat lunch or dinner under the large linden tree. The interior, a classroom of the old secondary school, is just as cosy with its ochre-coloured walls and wooden beamed ceiling. They serve Provençal cuisine and only use seasonal products.

331 **LE BIBENT**
5 place du Capitole
31000 Toulouse
Haute-Garonne
+33 (0)6 48 71 73 65
lebibent.com

The interior of this cafe-restaurant in Toulouse – which dates from between 1900 and 1910 – is both baroque and belle époque. A visual overload but in a good way, and an absolute eye-catcher. The pacifist politician and journalist Jean Jaurès wrote his articles here. Perhaps he was working at Le Bibent in 1914 when three Serbian students, all members of the Black Hand, plotted the attack on the Austrian Archduke Franz Ferdinand here. He was assassinated on 28 June in Sarajevo. Jaurès himself was assassinated just one month later by a young nationalist on 31 July.

332 BRASSERIE LE NAPOLÉON

332 BRASSERIE LE NAPOLÉON

46 boulevard
Victor Hugo
30000 Nîmes
Gard
+33 (0)6 86 20 07 56

A rococo interior with large mirrors, gilded garlands, lavishly decorated ceilings and red plush chairs. This is the Brasserie Le Napoléon in Nîmes, which was founded in 1813 and which is a monument in every sense of the word. The brasserie, which is situated near La Maison Carré and the Carré d'Art, closed for two years for an extensive renovation. Since then, the Second Empire interior has been restored in all its former glory. The flatware and tableware have been adapted to match the backdrop. The restaurant serves superb, regional cuisine and what's more, there's often a pianist playing in the background.

333 LES 1000 COLONNES

2 place aux Herbes
83300 Draguignan
Var
+33 (0)4 94 68 52 58

Les Milles Colonnes in Draguignan is the third oldest brasserie in France and has been in business since 1760. The current interior, with the wood panelling, mirrors and slender columns, dates from 1839. You can also sit outside on the terrace in Place aux Herbes and listen to the fountain splashing merrily in the background. Les 1000 Colonnes opens early in the morning for coffee, drinks later in the day and serves typical French brasserie-style fare for lunch and dinner, including escargots, foie gras and *steak haché*. There are regular concerts in the square.

334 LE CLUB 55

43 boulevard Patch
83350 Ramatuelle
Var
+33 (0)4 94 55 55 55
club55.fr

The place to go if you want to see and be seen. Club 55 – which was established in 1955 – is a bar and lunch restaurant on the sandy beach of Ramatuelle on the east side of the peninsula of Saint-Tropez. A lot of celebrities drop in, but the owner firmly sticks to this motto: 'The customer is not king here ... because he is a friend'. Le Club 55 is quite near to the location where the infamous beach scene in Roger Vadim's *Et Dieu... créa la femme* (1956) was shot. The film, which stars Brigitte Bardot, was deemed quite scandalous at the time.

MUSEUM

restaurants

335 CHÂTEAU LA COSTE
2750 Route de la Cride
13610 Le Puy-Sainte-Réparade
Bouches-du-Rhône
+33 (0)4 42 61 89 98
chateau-la-coste.com

After visiting the outstanding sculpture park at Château La Coste, you can sit down to lunch or dinner in the vineyard. On sunny days, the summery La Terrasse Provençale is just the place you had in mind. A spacious pergola, where you can enjoy salads, cold soups, a cheese or charcuterie platter or a nice piece of cake and wash it down with a glass of one of the excellent wines they produce here. It can get busy at times and they do not accept bookings. Alternatively, you can also eat in the more minimalistic setting of the pavilion designed by the Japanese architect Tadao Ando, for which you must call to reserve a table. If you're up for a more elegant and lavish dining experience, Villa La Coste is your best option.

336 LE CAFÉ CAUMONT
3 rue Joseph Cabassol
13100 Aix-en-Provence
Bouches-du-Rhône
+33 (0)4 42 20 70 01
caumont-centredart.com

If you're looking for a stylish place to dine after visiting one of the many excellent exhibitions here, then Le Café Caumont in Aix-en-Provence is just the place to go. Step inside and you may be forgiven for thinking that you travelled back in time to the 18th century. But you can also sit outside on the terrace in the lovely garden. Café Caumont is open throughout the day and freely accessible – no need to pay the admission charge for the arts centre. Order a coffee or a more copious lunch. They regularly programme jazz concerts, too.

337 LE CHARITÉ CAFÉ

2 rue de la Charité
13002 Marseille
Bouches-du-Rhône
+33 (0)4 91 91 08 41
vieille-charite-marseille.com

Le Panier, a hillside neighbourhood of Marseille, is always a great place for a walk. Marseille's oldest neighbourhood has long been home to the city's fishermen, with tiny houses lining the narrow, steep streets. Since then, many artists and designers have made it their home. This picturesque neighbourhood, with its many terraces, has plenty of places where you can eat or drink something. One of the quietest spots is tucked away behind the tall walls of La Vieille Charité, a former almshouse, which has since been converted into several museums and cultural institutions. Find the tranquil courtyard terrace, which is a lovely place to sit. Order a simple lunch – a salad or a sandwich – or a drink. The courtyard is freely accessible.

338 LA COMMANDERIE DE PEYRASSOL

RN7
83340 Flassans-sur-Issole
Var
+33 (0)4 94 69 71 02
peyrassol.com

After visiting the marvelous sculpture park and vineyard at La Commanderie de Peyrassol you can enjoy an aperitif (and the sunset) at Le Bistrot de Lou. Book beforehand to be assured of a table. You can also have lunch or dinner on the terrace of Chez Jeannette among the vines, where they serve Provençal-style cuisine. The Commanderie also has guest rooms if you want to make your experience even more enjoyable.

339 BRASSERIE DES ARTS

148 rue François Desnoyer
34200 Sète
Hérault
+33 (0)4 99 02 36 92
www.brasseriedesarts-sete.fr

The cafe-restaurant of the Musée Paul Valéry in Sète. An idyllic place, in a nice garden and some small water features, away from the tourists and the busy city centre. This hillside restaurant overlooks the Mediterranean and the fishermen's cemetery from the flanks of the Mont Saint-Clair to which Paul Valéry dedicated a long poem. They serve coffee and lunch or dinner. The restaurant is primarily known for its fish dishes. Sète is a fishing port, after all.

340 LE MÔLE LA TABLE & LA CUISINE

7 promenade Robert Laffont (1 esplanade du J4)
13002 Marseille
Bouches-du-Rhône
+33 (0)4 91 19 17 81
mucem.org/en/your-visit/bookshop-restaurants-shops/le-mole-passedat

There are two restaurants, that offer breathtaking views of the surroundings, on the roof of Mucem – the Musée des Civilisations de l'Europe et de la Méditerranée. From your rooftop vantage point, you can see the Mediterranean, the port of Marseille and the Cathédrale de la Major. Take your pick. Le Môle La Table, serves a *prix fixe* menu, that changes daily, and can seat 80 guests. Le Môle La Cuisine resembles a large canteen and can seat up to 130 guests. You can also have a drink on the outdoor terrace on the top floor, where food stands often serve quick and tasty bites.

Restaurants
WORTH THE DETOUR

341 L'ESPERLUETTE
28 boulevard Latourette
04300 Forcalquier
Alpes-de-Haute-Provence
+33 (0)4 92 72 53 57

The excellent L'Esperluette is tucked away on Boulevard Latourette in Forcalquier. Just walk through the iron gate and you will spot the restaurant, which is off the main boulevard. The menu at L'Esperluette – the French word for ampersand – changes daily. But it's also a wine bar, meaning you can order a glass of wine and relax on the simple but stylish terrace. The wooden terrace with its colourful chairs and tables is a hidden oasis, with a nice view over the town's trees and roofs. The restaurant itself is situated in a cave: minimalist and colourful. Definitely recommended, also for a light lunch.

342 LA PETITE MAISON
12 boulevard de la Promenade
11220 Lagrasse
Aude
+33 (0)4 68 91 34 09

This tiny cafe-restaurant is situated on the fringe of the medieval village of Lagrasse with its beautiful abbey and bridge. The interior is a nice jumble of styles. Outside they have set up a large terrace with chairs, sofas and benches. An excellent place to unwind, sample a local beer or wine and have a quiche and a salad. They also have other items on the menu, including homemade fish & chips (surprising) as well as the traditional salads. Don't forget to stop in at the neighbours: the vinaigrerie Cyril Codina stocks a stellar selection of olive oil, vinegar and wine in this state-of-the-art shop.

343 MATCHA

18 Montée du Château vieux
84160 Cucuron
Vaucluse
+33 (0)4 86 78 55 96
matcha-restaurant.fr

Matcha is a tiny, nice restaurant in an equally tiny and nice village in the Luberon, called Cucuron. The owners have set up five large tables on the pavement outside. There is not that much space to sit in the three rooms inside. You must book, especially in summer, if you want to be sure of a table. The food is delicious: Provençal-style cuisine with an exotic twist. They only use seasonal products, which they source from local farmers and growers from Cucuron, Ansouis and Lourmarin, which are all listed on the restaurant's website.

344 LE MUR D'ABEILLES

Le Village
04120 Rougon
Alpes-de-Haute-Provence
+33 (0)4 92 83 76 33

What a discovery. If you're driving through the Gorges du Verdon, then do stop in the tiny village of Rougon. Drop your car off in the car park outside this picturesque village, walk past the town hall, look for the sign for the 'Crêperie' and follow your nose as the fragrance of sweet and savoury crepes wafts toward you. Le Mur d'Abeilles is nothing more than a small stone house with tables and chairs on the grass behind it. But the view over the hills and the canyon of the Verdon is breathtaking and simply unbeatable. What's more, their savoury crepes are too good to miss out on.

344 VIEW FROM LE MUR D'ABEILLES

Cafes
WITH A HISTORY

345 **LES DEUX GARÇONS**
53 cours Mirabeau
13100 Aix-en-Provence
Bouches-du-Rhône
+33 (0)4 42 26 00 51
les2garcons.fr

The doors of this brasserie – a listed monument – along the elegant boulevard Cours Mirabeau swung open for the very first time in 1792. In 1840, two *garçons* (or waiters), Messrs Guidoni and Guérini, took over the cafe, which is named after them. This place has always held a great attraction: Paul Cézanne and his good friend Émile Zola were frequent visitors. Later Pablo Picasso, Marcel Pagnol, Edith Piaf and Albert Camus could often be found here. Unfortunately, the cafe burned down in November 2019. It is currently being rebuilt and consolidated at a leisurely pace.

346 **CAFÉ DE FRANCE**
14 place de la Liberté
84800 L'Isle-sur-la-Sorgue
Vaucluse
+33 (0)9 62 25 76 28
cafedefrance-cafe.business.site

In 1979, the French photographer Willy Ronis took a black and white photo of the Café de France, a town institution in L'Isle-sur-la-Sorgue. It's early morning and the cafe owner is just walking out of her establishment while some men sit and enjoy a drink and a chat at two tables outside the cafe. One of the men obviously stopped to pick up a baguette at the baker en route to the cafe. That is what Ronis excelled at: capturing daily life in a snapshot, with his fabulous eye. A lot has changed since then: tourists have found their way to the town and the street has been repaved, which explains the larger terrace. Fortunately, the cafe's old interior has been preserved.

347 CAFÉ LA NUIT – VAN GOGH

11 place du Forum
13200 Arles
+33 (0)4 90 96 44 56
Bouches-du-Rhône

Van Gogh was hell-bent on painting a picture at night. Night scenes fascinated him because darkness makes colours look completely different. He had visited the Café du Forum (as it was named at the time) with his friend Eugène Boch before painting it on 16 September 1888 or thereabouts. Vincent resolved to paint without black and highlight the glow of the gas lantern. In his painting, *Café Terrace at Night*, the cafe's façade and awning are bright yellow while the starry sky is blue and the pavers are a vivid pink and violet. "The question of painting night scenes or effects, on the spot and actually at night, interests me enormously", he wrote in a letter to his brother. The cafe with the yellow awning is still there but is now called 'Café La Nuit – Van Gogh'. Depending on the source and the time of your visit, it may feel heavily geared towards tourists, to put it mildly. But then again, when will you ever get the opportunity to take a seat in a famous painting?

348 AU PÈRE LOUIS

45 rue des Tourneurs
31000 Toulouse
Haute-Garonne
+33 (0)5 61 21 33 45

Au Père Louis is not a cafe. It's a monument. It is probably also Toulouse's oldest cafe, given that it was established in 1889. You may be forgiven for thinking you have travelled back in time to the 19th century when you set foot in the dark interior with its large wine barrels, which are used as tables. The silence – no music here – is only broken by the voice of the cafe owner or the conversations of the patrons. High up on the wall you can see various views of old Toulouse, as painted in 1942 by Paul Almérie. It is said that he gave them to the *patron* in lieu of payment to settle his tab. Try their quinquina, the house aperitif, which is served in small glasses. Quinquina is made from the bark of the kina tree and was both a fashionable aperitif and a medicinal remedy at one time. It is still distilled especially for Le Père Louis.

349 CAFÉ DE LA PLACE

**Place du Général de Gaulle
06570 Saint-Paul-de-Vence
Alpes-Maritimes
+33 (0)4 93 32 80 03**

Café de la Place is a legendary cafe just outside the city walls of Saint-Paul-de-Vence. Actors such as Yves Montand, Bernard Blier and Lino Ventura often dropped in, for drinks and a game of *jeu de boules*. The cafe – which is located opposite that other mythical place, the hotel and restaurant La Colombe d'Or – has managed to retain its charm. It can get quite busy at times, to the detriment of the quality of service. You can still find a place to sit under the trees and observe the boules players.

Bars

IN THE MIDDLE OF NOWHERE

350 **LE TIFE TAFE**
5 place Notre Dame
30140 Anduze
Gard
+33 (0)4 66 61 93 70
tife-tafe.fr

While the nearby fountain gurgles away merrily, you can relax and unwind in this quaint little square. Le Tife Tafe is a cafe-restaurant with a terrace on a raised stone platform in the centre of car-free Place Notre Dame. It serves a wide range of mainly French and Belgian beers. Do sample the local craft beers: blonde, white, amber or brown ale. There are a number of cafes and restaurants around the square, as well as a wine shop. They sometimes organise concerts or a party together.

351 **LES 3 SOLEILS**
Place de Verdun
04500 Allemagne-en-Provence
Alpes-de-Haute-Provence
+33 (0)4 86 74 08 58

Yes, there is a village in France that is called Allemagne or Germany in French. While it has no affiliation with the European country, its etymology probably refers to the Alemanni, a Germanic tribe that lived on the Upper Rhine River in the early centuries of our era. Les 3 Soleils is a nice place to stop when you're travelling from the Luberon to the Verdon by car, or vice-versa. It's an ordinary, convivial and very French cafe, with an unassuming menu, in a quiet square, off the *route départementale* D952. If you have a little time to spare, visit the castle on the other side of the road.

352 GRAND CAFÉ JOUCLA

2 avenue Alexandre Piquet
34260 Camplong
Herault
+33 (0)9 66 02 56 08

Grand Café Joucla is a former miners' cafe from 1898. The miners would stop in to relax, play a game of cards or lotto, to smoke (which they were not allowed to do in the coalmine) and have a drink. The ambience has not changed much since then: a large taproom, a striking all-marble beer tap, tables with white marble tops, a cast iron stove and a beautiful tiled floor. The coalmine of Camplong, which originally supplied the fuel for the local glass industry, was one of the last mines in the region to close down, in 1967. The cafe is still there, however. The industrial heritage of the coalmining industry is still very much a feature of the landscape in Camplong, Graissessac, La Tour-sur-Orb and the surrounding area.

353 LE PETIT CAFÉ

12 rue de Sainte-Cécile
84580 Oppède-le-Vieux
Vaucluse
+33 (0)4 90 76 74 01
lepetitcafe.fr

Oppède-le-Vieux is a beautiful, small hillside village, on the flanks of the Montagne du Luberon, between Cavaillon and Ménerbes. The village was largely abandoned for quite some time but recently things changed. Le Petit Café has a terrace – which is lit with colourful lamps at night – under a magnificent acacia tree in one of the many small squares of Oppède. You can also dine here and even spend the night in one of the three rooms if you want. Le Petit Café was used as a set in François Ozon's film *The Swimming Pool* (2003). The protagonist sits on the cafe's terrace in one of the scenes. Charlotte Rampling plays the role of Sarah Morton, a British crime writer who is suffering from a severe case of writer's block. She is staying in a chic villa with a pool in nearby Lacoste in hopes of finding inspiration. And then one night things appear to go terribly wrong…

A bar WITH A VIEW

354 **LES FLOTS BLEUS**
AT: PLAGE DE SAINT-CLAIR
Boulevard de la Baleine
83980 Le Lavandou
Var

A cafe on the tiny quiet beach of Saint-Clair. Enjoy a drink with your feet in the sand. From the terrace, you have a splendid view of the Mediterranean, which has been immortalised so often in paintings. Nearby you'll find a sign with a reproduction of the colourful drawing of the beach and the parasol pines that Paul Signac made here in 1897.

355 **BISTROT DU PORT**
Place Georges Grammont
83990 Saint-Tropez
Var
+33 (0)4 94 97 03 12

A cafe terrace with a view of the marina and old Saint-Tropez with its iconic bell tower. A panorama painted by many an artist – from Paul Signac to Albert Marquet. You can see their works in the lovely Musée de l'Annonciade at the other end of the square. Le Bistrot du Port also serves breakfast early in the morning. A bit expensive, but a fun place to go.

356 **LA SARDINE**
26 quai Frédéric Mistral
83990 Saint-Tropez
Var
+33 (0)6 77 45 68 75
la-sardine.fr

A pleasant cafe-restaurant with an excellent terrace, away from the crowds and the bling factor of Saint-Tropez. You can stop in for a drink or order one of their excellent fish dishes. If luck is on your side, you may find a table near the water so you can enjoy the view of the expansive bay of Saint-Tropez while you eat. In the evening, the magnificent sunset is thrown in for free. Possibly the most romantic place in town. It's easy to see why painters like Signac, Manguin and Camoin chose to pitch their easel in this charming place. In 1937, Pierre Bonnard painted an almost abstract, blinding sunset over the bay of Saint-Tropez, which you can see at the Musée Toulouse-Lautrec in Albi.

357 BALCO DEL MAR / LA VOILE

9 route de Port-Vendres
66190 Collioure
Pyrénées-Orientales
+33 (0)6 34 89 01 95
lavoilecollioure.com

An idyllic location with amazing views of the harbour of Collioure and the distinctive tower of the Église Notre-Dame des Anges, that Matisse and Derain painted so many times. The terrace of Balco del Mar is a balcony on the water, among the rocks. The restaurant above it, by the same owners, has an even more spectacular panoramic view. La Voile resembles a ship, while white, sail-like awnings provide protection against the wind and the sun. Walk up Rue Jean Bart and follow the seaside path to the bar and restaurant.

357 BALCO DEL MAR / LA VOILE

358 **LA GUINGUETTE DE SAINT-CYPRIEN**
AT: JARDIN RAYMOND VI
31300 Toulouse
Haute-Garonne

Behind Les Abattoirs in Toulouse, you'll find a kiosk with a simple terrace, where you can get something to eat and drink. It's not actually a cafe, but a quiet place with a nice view of the River Garonne and the city centre of Toulouse. On the opposite bank you can see the buildings of le Bazacle, the hydroelectric power station that was built here in 1888 and which is still in operation. You can visit it if you have the time.

359 PUYCELSI ROC CAFÉ

Le Bourg
81140 Puycelsi
Tarn
+33 (0)5 63 33 13 67
puycelsi-roc-cafe.fr

This cafe-restaurant in a hairpin bend along the road feels like it's at the end of the world. Order a glass of the excellent local Gaillac wine, find a seat on the terrace, lean back and enjoy the breathtaking view over the hills and vineyards. The cafe's name refers to the tall rock on which the picturesque walled city of Puycelsi is built. The Roc Café serves food and drinks, as well as local produce and wines that are difficult to find outside France.

360 LE CIEL DE NÎMES

16 place de la
Maison Carrée
30017 Nîmes
Gard
+33 (0)4 66 36 71 70
cieldenimes.fr

A salon de thé and restaurant on the top floor of the Carré d'Art in Nîmes. The terrace offers excellent views of the city centre and La Maison Carrée, the Roman temple on the other side of the street, high above the crowds and the busy streets. A nice place for a quiet coffee early in the morning. The elegant waiters provide exemplary service.

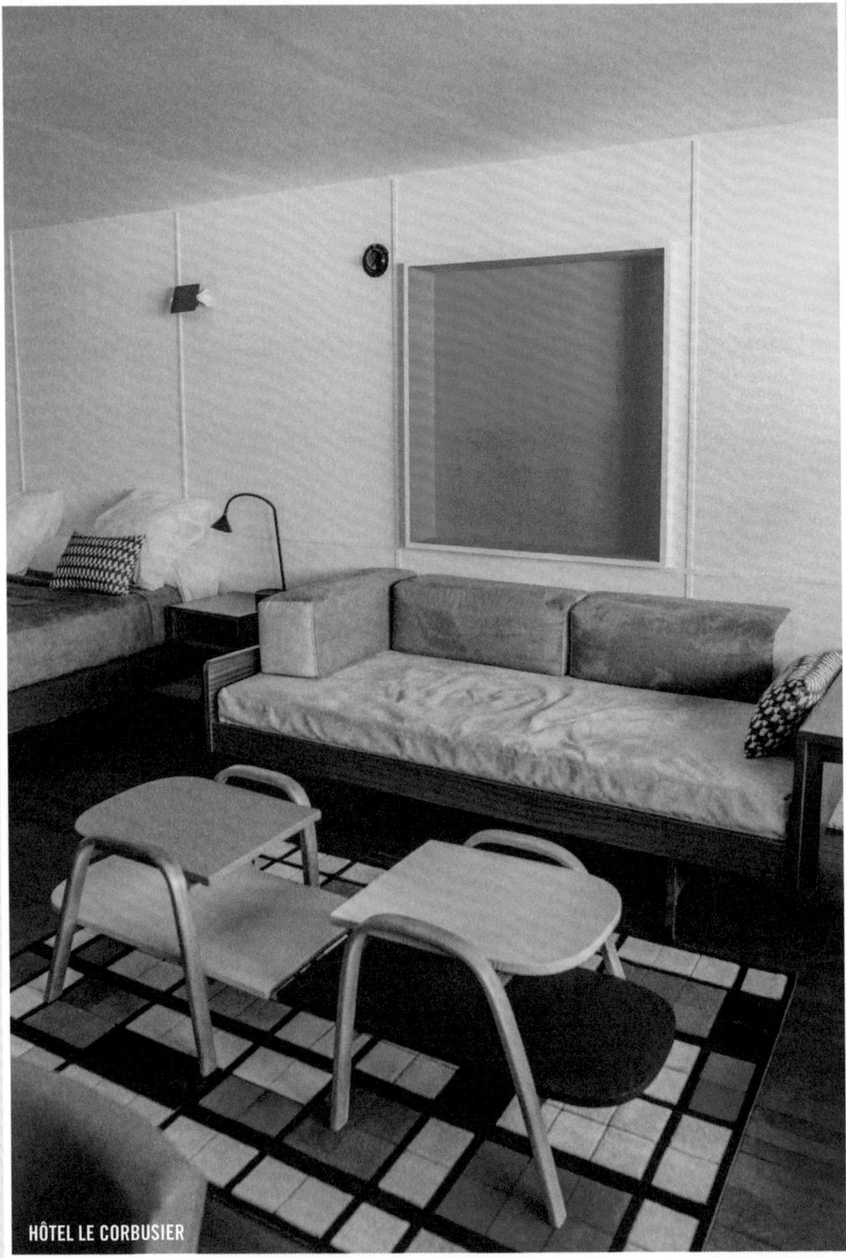
HÔTEL LE CORBUSIER

STAYS

LEGENDARY
hotels

361 LE NEGRESCO

37 promenade des Anglais
06000 Nice
Alpes-Maritimes
+33 (0)4 93 16 64 00
hotel-negresco-nice.com

Hotel Le Negresco on the Promenade des Anglais is one of the more iconic buildings in Nice, with its pink domed roofs. The monumental neoclassical building was designed by the Dutch-French architect Édouard-Jean Niermans and was completed on 4 January 1913. Seven 'crowned heads' attended the hotel's festive opening party. Its owner, the Romanian Henri Negresco, had grand designs, as you can tell. The hotel, which has 100 rooms and 25 suites, never fails to astonish visitors with its fabulous elliptical lobby and staggering glass and steel dome with a gorgeous cascading chandelier with 16.800 crystals. Since then, the hotel is run by the Augier family, which has amassed quite an art collection over the years. The most striking acquisition is the statue of Miles Davis by Niki de Saint Phalle on the champagne terrace next to the Promenade. Other works include a Nana by de Saint Phalle, a portrait of Louis Armstrong by Raymond Moretti and works by Vasarely as well as old masters, including a portrait of Louis XIV by the artist Hyacinthe Rigaud. The hotel even has its own art workshop, hiring restorers every year. Like a real museum, but with more glamour.

362 CARLTON HOTEL

58 boulevard de
la Croisette
06414 Cannes
Alpes-Maritimes
+33 (0)4 93 06 40 06
carlton-cannes.com

Nice has its Negresco and Cannes its Carlton Hotel. A landmark, albeit that the Carlton is enormous: the hotel has 343 rooms, including 39 suites. The Carlton, which was built between 1909 and 1913 for the Swiss hotelier Henri Ruhl, derives its mythical status from the fact that it is the place to be seen during the annual Cannes Film Festival: film stars, directors and producers all like to stay here and it is also a convenient place for interviews. Alfred Hitchcock featured the hotel and its private beach in a number of scenes in *To Catch a Thief* (1955) starring Grace Kelly and Cary Grant. The scene near the floating platform in the water was also shot here. The Hotel Carlton also served as a location for *There's a Girl in My Soup* starring Peter Sellers and Goldie Hawn. In 1983, Elton John's video clip for *I'm Still Standing* was filmed in and around the hotel. The Carlton is currently closed for renovation and expansion. It is scheduled to reopen in 2023.

363 PALAIS DE LA MÉDITERRANÉE

13 promenade des
Anglais
06000 Nice
Alpes-Maritimes
+33 (0)4 93 27 12 34
hyatt.com/en-US/hotel/france

Palatial in every sense of the word. This magnificent hotel was bankrolled by the American financier Frank Jay Gould and built in 1928 after a design by Dalmas Architects. Art deco splendour in an ocean liner that run aground on the Promenade of Nice. The enormous Palais, with its 187 rooms, a casino and a theatre, was supposed to attract and retain the loyalty of summer tourists as they found their way to the French Riviera after World War I. Unfortunately, the original art deco interior was stripped during the 1990 renovation. The reinforced concrete façades and the ornamental sea horses and female figures by Antoine Sartorio were saved from demolition thankfully and have been preserved intact.

364 **HOTEL DU CAP-EDEN-ROC**

167-165 boulevard
John F. Kennedy
06160 Antibes
Alpes-Maritimes
+33 (0)4 93 61 39 01
oetkercollection.com/hotels

Luxurious and mysterious. Fabulously located in splendid isolation at the southern tip of the Cap d'Antibes. The Hotel du Cap-Eden-Roc is a timeless legend on the French Riviera. The rooms are situated in one of the three locations of the hotel: the Villa Soleil dates from 1869 and was originally built for writers who were looking for inspiration. In 1887, a young Italian named Antoine Sella acquired the property, which reopened two years later as the Grand Hôtel du Cap. Celebrity guests include Marlene Dietrich, Orson Welles, Winston Churchill, Charles de Gaulle, and Elizabeth Taylor who was accompanied by Richard Burton. Hotel du Cap-Eden-Roc was also immortalised as Hôtel des Étrangers in *Tender is the Night*, a novel by the American writer F. Scott Fitzgerald. He discovered the hotel through two young American expats, called Gerald and Sara Murphy, who had rented the hotel for the summer in 1923. This was fairly unusual because most people spent winter on the French Riviera. Pablo Picasso and Gertrude Stein followed in their wake, with the Fitzgeralds, Ernest Hemingway, John Dos Passos and Dorothy Parker arriving the year after. Fitzgerald took his inspiration from Gerald and Sara Murphy for the main characters of Dick and Nicole Diver in *Tender is the Night*, which was only published in 1934.

INTERC

ENTAL

365 L'ORANGERAIE

15 rue de
Partouneaux
06500 Menton
Alpes-Maritimes
+33 (0)4 87 75 00 58

Book to visit Palaces
de Menton:
+33 (0)4 89 81 52 70
mileade.com
menton.fr/Les-Palaces-de-Menton.html

L'Orangeraie is one of several legendary hotels to be built in Menton at the end of the 19th century. Originally named Grand Hôtel de Venise, the hotel has largely managed to retain its old-world charm, including the fan-shaped glass and iron canopy over its entrance. You can also take a guided tour of L'Orangeraie's elegant gardens. Reservation is compulsory. After the tour, you can take a fascinating walk through Menton, where dozens of monumental hotels were built between 1860 and 1914 for Europe's nobility and upper class, who liked to spend the winter months here. They often spent six months at a time here to recover from all sorts of pulmonary diseases. Today, you can still see 21 of these spectacular buildings, four of which still are hotels, including the imposing Royal Westminster. While the others have largely been preserved, they have since been renovated and turned into residences with spacious flats. An association called 'Le Cercle des Palaces Retrouvés' is working hard to promote these sumptuous former hotels: with the publication of the beautifully illustrated book *Menton, une ville de palaces* (2019) and a tour that takes you past the Grand Hôtel Orient, the Winter Palace and the Hôtel Imperial. Prepare to have your mind blown: Menton has the highest concentration of palatial mansions in the world.

Hotels
FILLED WITH ART

366 HÔTEL DES TEMPLIERS

12 quai de
l'Amirauté
66190 Collioure
Pyrénées-Orientales
+33 (0)4 68 98 31 10
hotel-templiers.com

The walls of the Hostellerie des Templiers hotel and restaurant are covered with hundreds of original oil paintings, watercolours and drawings, most of which are landscapes and scenes that are related in some way to Collioure and the surrounding region. The current owner's grandfather welcomed many famous painters and sculptors here over the years, including Matisse, Picasso and Dufy, who settled their bills with a work of art. Unfortunately, these masterpieces are no longer there, but what remains is first-rate in any event.

367 LA BASTIDE ROSE

99 chemin des
Croupières
84250 Le Thor
Vaucluse
+33 (0)4 90 02 14 33
bastiderose.com

A treasury of art and memorabilia. Tucked away in an orchard along the meandering River Sorgue, La Bastide Rose is located on an island near a former paddle-wheel mill. Its owner, Poppy Salinger, is the widow of Pierre Salinger, who served as the White House press secretary under US President John F. Kennedy. Pierre Salinger died in 2004 in Le Thor, but his legacy is remembered in a tiny museum at La Bastide Rose. Each room in this boutique hotel mixes antiques with modern comfort and eclectic art. Sculptures dot the garden landscape. Each summer, La Bastide Rose hosts a sculpture exhibition.

368 LA COLOMBE D'OR

Place du Général
de Gaulle
06570 Saint-Paul-
de-Vence
Alpes-Maritimes
+33 (0)4 93 32 80 02
la-colombe-dor.com

A hotel and restaurant with humble beginnings. In 1920, local farmer Paul Roux opened a cafe at the entrance of Saint-Paul-de-Vence. The hotel-restaurant soon became the place to be. In the 1920s, it was the favourite restaurant of the American writer F. Scott Fitzgerald and his wife Zelda. It was also here that Zelda threw herself down a flight of stairs one infamous night in 1925, in a fit after Scott flirted with the dancer Isadora Duncan. During World War II, many artists fled to the unoccupied France, which is how they ended up on the French Riviera and in Saint-Paul. They stayed in the rustic inn, which had a few rooms at the time, and paid in kind. This explains why works by Matisse, Picasso and Léger are haphazardly displayed on the walls of the guest rooms and in the dining rooms. The romance of the French actors Yves Montand and Simone Signoret began at La Colombe d'Or. They married two years later, in 1951, in Saint-Paul-de-Vence. The owner Paul Roux and the writer Jacques Prévert were their witnesses. La Colombe d'Or was the natural choice for their wedding reception. Roux continued to add to this art collection over the years: outside a monumental mobile by Alexander Calder stands at one end of the swimming pool and Miró, Braque and Chagall also donated works in exchange for a room. The most recent addition is a ceramic work by the Irish artist Sean Scully. The Roux family still owns the hotel.

369 LE WINDSOR

11 rue Dalpozzo
06000 Nice
Alpes-Maritimes
+33 (0)4 93 88 59 35
hotelwindsornice.com

To all appearances, Hotel Le WindsoR is just another nice 19th-century building. But once you walk through its doors, plenty of artistic surprises await, starting with what is probably the most excellent art lift on the entire French Riviera. Each room was designed by a different artist. The more traditional rooms feature pastel-coloured frescos of the Mediterranean landscape and coastline while others – the *chambres d'artistes* – were decorated from top to bottom by artists including Ben (Vautier), Glen Baxter, Claudio Parmiggiani, Claude Viallat and Lawrence Weiner. Finally, the tribute rooms are designed around a work or an artist: Jean Le Gac pays homage to Matisse in the eponymous room, and the hotel also has homages to Robert Indiana, Jan van Eyck, Martial Raysse and Niki de Saint Phalle. Every year, the hotel invites an artist to redo one of the 57 rooms. The Redolfi family, which has owned the hotel for more than 70 years, also hosts an annual art exhibition in the lobby.

370 LA CASCADE

635 chemin de
la Cascade
06620 Courmes
Alpes-Maritimes
+33 (0)4 93 09 65 85
cascade06.fr

La Cascade, a former sheepfold, is located far from the maddening crowds of Grasse and Nice, in the lesser-frequented but nonetheless impressive canyon of the Gorges du Loup. The perfect place to unwind and enjoy the art in the guest rooms and breakfast room, in close proximity to nature and near a waterfall. All the work in this bed and breakfast is by one artist: Augustin Hanicotte (1870-1957), the grandfather of one of the very nice owners, is a lesser-known artist. Born in Béthune, near Lille, he lived and worked in Volendam in the Netherlands for several years, where he also got married. He moved to Collioure around 1915, founding a drawing academy for children. His colourful, simple work – portraits, still-lifes and rural scenes – attests to his great passion for ordinary people as they went about their business.

371 GRAND HÔTEL NORD-PINUS

14 place du Forum
13200 Arles
Bouches-du-Rhône
+33 (0)4 90 93 44 44
nord-pinus.com

This mansion was converted into a hotel 150 years ago. Since then, plenty of celebrities have spent the night at Nord-Pinus. Besides Fritz Lang, Pablo Picasso, Simone Signoret and Yves Montand, Winston Churchill, Ernest Hemingway and Charlotte Rampling, the bullfighters were also put up here for the Feria, an annual event in Arles that takes place around Easter and in September. You'll find lots of large posters for the Feria in Arles and other similar events on the walls of this minimalist chic hotel. Many of them were designed by famous artists. The hotel also displays works by photographers like Peter Lindbergh and Peter Beard. Nord-Pinus is situated in a lively square in central Arles, behind the statue of the writer Frédéric Mistral, who defended and promoted Provençal, the language of Provence.

372 HÔTEL DES BEAUX ARTS

1 place du Pont Neuf
31000 Toulouse
Haute-Garonne
+33 (0)5 34 45 42 42
hoteldesbeauxarts.com

The Hôtel des Beaux Arts in Toulouse is a hotel like no other. It is situated around the corner from the city's art academy and is jam-packed with art, from the lobby right up to the bathroom in your guest room. The hotel has mainly relied on local, contemporary artists to decorate the rooms. Head to the lobby for an overview, although the array is dazzling and a bit overwhelming. Each room has its own identity. A sleek modern room provides the perfect backdrop for the photographer Patrick Bouillaud's sensual black and white photos, but there are several completely different rooms in the hotel with the painter Marie Bec's sophisticated portraits, the colourful street art of Reso and the magical realism of Montpellier-based graffiti artist Maye. Here and there, the art verges on kitsch but all in all it is an original art hotel. The excellent restaurant Brasserie Les Beaux-Arts is just around the corner.

Hotels with
AN ARTISTIC PAST

373 LA BASTIDE DU BOSQUET

14 chemin des Sables
06160 Antibes
Alpes-Maritimes
+33 (0)6 51 76 72 73
lebosquet06.com

The French writer Guy de Maupassant (1850-1893), the master of the short story, was born in Paris, lived in Paris but spent the last few years of his short life – he died of syphilis aged 42 – at the Côte d'Azur. He rented the Villa Le Bosquet in Antibes from Christmas 1885 until the end of 1886. Today you can still spend the night in this beautiful mansion with its pink façade and pale green shutters. The charming bed and breakfast is still run by the family from whom the writer rented the house more than 100 years ago. The then owner Maurice Muterse noted in a letter that De Maupassant would pace up and down his room for inspiration after which the words just seem to flow from his pen: "The manuscript, which he wrote in one go, was clean. Nothing had been crossed out. And that is how he sent it to the publisher." It was at Villa Le Bosquet that De Maupassant wrote his novel *Mont-Oriol*, which was published in 1887. But the writer, who was a bit of a sports fanatic, also valued the fact that he could moor his sailboat *La Louisette* nearby, in the port at La Salis. In 1886, he bought a larger yacht, which he named *Bel-Ami*, after his famous novel.

375 HÔTEL CHALET DE L'ISÈRE

374 HÔTEL SPLENDID

4-6 rue Félix Faure
06400 Cannes
Alpes-Maritimes
+33 (0)4 97 06 22 22
splendid-hotel-cannes.com

The writer Guy de Maupassant was a restless soul, never staying in the same place for long. After Antibes he moved on to Cannes. He first rented a flat in the Villa Continentale in 1888-1889: the building is still there, at number 6 of what has since been renamed Rue Guy de Maupassant. Here he wrote his novel *Fort comme la Mort*. He spent the first three months of 1890 at the Hôtel Splendid, an even more upscale hotel on the Croisette. While he enjoyed the sea view, he hated the princes and duchesses, finding that their presence 'marred' the resort's famous seafront. Many of them travelled to Cannes for health reasons. The sea air and warm, dry climate were deemed beneficial for patients suffering tuberculosis. De Maupassant's health declined rapidly: the syphilis aggravated his nerve root pain and worsened his depression.

375 HÔTEL CHALET DE L'ISÈRE

42 avenue de Grasse
06400 Cannes
Alpes-Maritimes
+33 (0)4 93 38 50 80
hotel-chalet-isere-cannes.com

Guy de Maupassant's last stop on the French Riviera was at the Hôtel Châlet de l'Isère in Cannes. He checked in in November 1891. He enjoyed the peace and quiet and the sunny garden. The hotel had no neighbours. From his window he could see the sea, the peaks of the Esterel mountains and the lighthouse. Since then, this neighbourhood has been built up, but the Chalet is still a family-owned bed and breakfast. A plaque on the façade commemorates De Maupassant. He wrote a number of wonderful short stories here including *Le champ d'oliviers*, which takes place on the French Riviera, but the end was near: the syphilis attacked his spinal cord, the writer became increasingly confused, began to suffer from hallucinations and was in excruciating pain. After he attempted to shoot himself, he was taken to Paris in a strait-jacket and committed to an asylum where he would die one-and-a-half years later, aged 42.

376 HÔTEL BYBLOS

20 avenue Paul Signac
83990 Saint-Tropez
Var
+33 (0)4 94 56 68 00
byblos.com

When the young actress Jane Birkin (21) was cast in *La Piscine* in August 1968 – starring Romy Schneider – her jealous beau, Serge Gainsbourg, followed her to Saint-Tropez where he booked a suite at the luxurious Hôtel Byblos. Gainsbourg was jealous because Birkin would be playing opposite handsome Alain Delon, a notorious womaniser. The romantic, psychological thriller was shot in a villa in Ramatuelle, near Saint-Tropez. Gainsbourg regularly hired a limo to drive him to the set. His annoying behaviour caused a rift with Delon, who later would refuse a role in Gainsbourg's film project *Blackout*.

377 WELCOME HÔTEL

3 quai de l'Amiral Courbet
06230 Villefranche-sur-Mer
Alpes-Maritimes
+33 (0)4 93 76 27 62
welcomehotel.com

The Welcome Hotel was established in the 18th century, but artists only started to flock to it in the 20th century. The polymath Jean Cocteau was a returning guest, from 1923 until his death in 1963. His favourite room was number 22, where he stayed while renovating the chapel on the other side of the street. The room has since been redecorated in an homage to the artist. Besides Cocteau, Kiki de Montparnasse, the legendary muse of many an artist, regularly stayed at the hotel, as well as the equally legendary dancer Isadora Duncan. She died on the evening of 14 September 1927 on Nice's Promenade des Anglais in a horrific car accident. Her long red silk scarf became entangled in the hub caps of the open car in which she was a passenger. The dancer was dragged out of the car and into the road…

378 HÔTEL OASIS

23 rue Gounod
06000 Nice
Alpes-Maritimes
+33 (0)4 93 88 12 29
hotelniceoasis.com

The Russian writer Anton Chekhov, who is mainly known for his short stories and plays, regularly travelled to Nice from 1891 onwards. He suffered from tuberculosis, which is why he had to spend the winter in a more temperate climate. After a while, he realised that he preferred Nice over Yalta. He originally stayed at the Hôtel Beau Rivage, at 107 quai des Etats-Unis, where a plaque commemorates his stay. His longest stay was from the autumn of 1897 until the spring of 1898, but he returned in 1900-1901. He rented a room at the Pension Russe, or Hôtel Oasis as it is now called. Here too, a plaque commemorates his stay. "I have a fairly large room, with south-facing windows, wall to wall carpeting, and a separate bathroom like Cleopatra", he wrote to his friend and publisher, Alexei Suvorin. But Nice did not inspire the creative surge he was hoping for. On the contrary even, Chekhov noted in his letters that he was lazy: "I do nothing, simply nothing and if I look at myself and the other Russians here, I am forced to admit that Russians need bad weather or they are unable to work or be themselves". Nice is therefore conspicuously absent in his work. It was only during his last stay, in 1900-1901, that he was able to regain his zeal: while pining for his new love, the actress Olga Knipper who remained in Moscow, he rewrote the last two acts of *Three Sisters*, maintaining an intense correspondence with the director and actors of the theatre in Moscow where the play was performed.

379 RÉSIDENCE BEAU RIVAGE

2 boulevard Louis Lumière
83150 Bandol
Var
+33 (0)4 94 29 43 48
beaurivage-bandol.fr

Two famous writers stayed at the Hôtel Beau Rivage in Bandol. In October 1915, the New Zealand writer Katherine Mansfield visited the hotel for the first time. She spent the winter here and returned in 1918 before settling in Menton. Mansfield suffered from fragile health and would later be diagnosed with tuberculosis, an incurable disease in those days. That is why she enjoyed the temperate climate of the French Riviera so much. At Bandol, she wrote her novel *The Aloe* and a number of short stories, including *Je ne parle pas français*. Ten years later, on 17 November 1928, the English writer D.H. Lawrence arrived, with his wife Frieda von Richthofen. Lawrence stayed on until 10 March 1929, writing a collection of poems called *Pansies*, which does not refer to the flowers but is derived from the French *pensées*, meaning thoughts. In his introduction, Lawrence wrote that the poems were thoughts, which came "as much from the heart and the genitals as from the head." Lawrence no longer felt welcome in Britain. His wife was German – a fact that inspired suspicion and hostility so soon after World War I. Moreover, his novel *Lady Chatterley's Lover*, which he completed in 1927, caused quite a controversy in the UK. The sexually explicit novel was banned because it was deemed 'obscene'. Lawrence also painted at Bandol: erotic canvases that were censored in the UK. On 23 September 1929, the Lawrences returned to Bandol, where they stayed at Villa Beau Soleil until 6 February 1930. But Lawrence's health took a sudden turn for the worse. He was hospitalised in a sanatorium in Vence, where he died from tuberculosis on 2 March 1930, aged 44.

380 PALAIS MAETERLINCK HÔTEL

30 boulevard
Maurice Maeterlinck
06300 Nice
Alpes-Maritimes
+30 2810 333223
fhotels.net

In 1930, the Belgian writer Maurice Maeterlinck – who won the 1911 Nobel Prize for Literature – acquired Castel a Mare: a palace of megalomaniacal proportions, which was supposed to become the largest casino in France but which remained unfinished when the funds ran out. It was built on a rocky outcrop, offering an unrivalled sea view. After three years of construction and renovation work, Maeterlinck was finally able to move in at the ripe old age of 71, with his conquest, the actress Renée Dahon, who was 30 years younger and whom he had met during the rehearsals for his play *L'Oiseau bleu* in Nice. Maeterlinck named the palace 'Orlamonde' after one of his poems. His good friend, the Flemish writer Cyriel Buysse, famously described Orlamonde as 'endless rooms, with bronze castle doors, marble and onyx everywhere, and a pack of greyhounds and Pekinese'. By then, Maeterlinck had all but stopped writing, but he received many guests. He died in his dream palace on 6 May 1949. Initially, there were plans to convert Orlamonde into luxury apartments, but a sumptuous five-star hotel has since opened here instead.

381 HÔTEL BELLES RIVES

33 boulevard
Edouard Baudoin
06160 Juan-les-Pins
Alpes-Maritimes
+33 (0)4 93 61 02 79
bellesrives.com

From May till December 1926, F. Scott Fitzgerald and his wife Zelda stayed at Villa Saint-Louis in Juan-les-Pins. This villa has since become the Hôtel Belles Rives. Here Fitzgerald hoped to complete his novel *Tender is the Night* but he found it difficult to concentrate on his writing, which is why he spent time with Ernest Hemingway instead – who lived in Villa Paquita at 6 avenue des Pins Parasols. Fitzgerald advised him on his novel *The Sun Also Rises*. However, the turbulent social life of the Fitzgeralds was increasingly taking its toll, while Zelda's mental illness deteriorated.

Hôtel Belles Rives commemorates the stay of the Fitzgeralds in more than one respect. There are black and white photos of the couple in the lobby alongside a quote taken from a letter by Fitzgerald to Hemingway from 1926: "With our being back in a nice villa on my beloved Riviera (between Nice and Cannes) I'm happier than I've been for years." So Fitzgerald must have been happy there even though he used his marital woes and his wife's fragile mental state as inspiration to write *Tender is the Night*. You can read this novel in one of the leather armchairs in the hotel's historic art deco Fitzgerald Bar. In 2014, it was used as a set for Woody Allen's film *Magic in the Moonlight*, a light-hearted comedy about a magician and spiritualists in the Jazz Age.

ARTFUL
lodging

382 **HÔTEL LE CORBUSIER**
280 boulevard Michelet
13008 Marseille
Bouches-du-Rhône
+33 (0)4 28 31 39 22
hotellecorbusier.com

What an experience this is: spending the night in a landmark design by the groundbreaking architect Le Corbusier, which is on the UNESCO World Heritage list. You can book a room in the hotel on the third floor of La Cité Radieuse (built between 1946 and 1952), which was designed by Le Corbusier. Jean Prouvé and Charlotte Perriand furnished the interiors. It's like travelling back in time to the 1950s. Even though the rooms have since been upgraded with all the mod cons, you cannot ignore the beauty of timeless simplicity, efficiency and charm. Check out the authentic windows, the built-in shelves and cabinets and the concrete balcony. Hotel guests have access to the entire building. The hotel has a wonderful bar and restaurant with a terrace, from which you have a view of the Mediterranean.

383 **HÔTEL BURRHUS**
1 place Montfort
84110 Vaison-la-Romaine
Vaucluse
+33 (0)4 90 36 00 11
burrhus.com

This hotel, which is situated in the heart of Vaison-la-Romaine, looks more like an art gallery. The 35 rooms all have their own identity and have been decorated with design furniture and art. The hotel also invites artists to design their own room and hosts regular exhibitions. Wherever you go, you are surrounded by art books. Once a year, the hotel organises 'Supervues' with 35 artists 'occupying' the rooms.

384 LA ROYANTE

340 impasse de
La Royante
13400 Aubagne
Bouches-du-Rhône
+33 (0)4 96 18 99 76
laroyante.fr

An 18th-century bastide with a 19th-century chapel north of Cassis. The estate is referenced on old maps as 'the bishop's castel' and probably was used as a summer residence by the bishops of Marseille. The kind of place where you can ascend into higher realms ... You can sleep in the sacristy or the chaplain's room. Or perhaps you prefer to relax in the chapel and listen to a Bach cantata. The neo-Gothic chapel was built in 1870 by the then owners, Fortuné and Thomasine Broquier. He was a lawyer in Marseille, she maintained close ties with the Dominican order. For many years, church services were held here and they proved so popular with the locals that the Vatican became worried. On a less religious note: the rooms are decorated with lovely paintings with views of Cassis. The large sofa in the salon originally stood in Le Jas de Bouffan, Paul Cézanne's parental home.

385 ATTRAP'RÊVES

Chemin de la
Ribassière
13190 Allauch
Bouches-du-Rhône
+33 (0)4 91 72 10 89
attrap-reves.com

A poetic and magical experience that stimulates all of your senses. You get to sleep under the stars, in nature, with 360° views of everything around you. At the same time, you're always protected and comfortable because you are sleeping in a transparent artwork with a unique design. Spend the night in your own pod on this 1,5-hectare estate near Marseille. Your bed is in a giant, transparent bubble. The interiors range from 1001 Nights and Glamour to Pure Nature and Zen. You can rest assured that the bubble is securely anchored and that your privacy is respected at all times: the bubbles are positioned sufficiently far enough from each other and the bathroom is an opaque bubble. At night, you can look up at the stars – the hotel has telescopes you can rent and they throw in a map of the night sky for free. In the morning, the squirrels and rabbits hop past your bubble. You can also rent a small wooden hut, high up in the trees. All the accommodations and the breakfast are eco-friendly.

386 VILLA LE RÊVE

261 avenue
Henri Matisse
06140 Vence
Alpes-Maritimes
+33 (0)6 37 74 86 91
villalerevevence.com

Between 1943 and 1949, Henri Matisse lived and worked in this villa in the English colonial style. The painter left his apartment in the Hôtel Régina in Nice because he feared that the city would be bombed. The vegetation and scents even reminded him of his journey to Tahiti. Matisse's stay at Villa Le Rêve proved to be particularly fruitful even though he had undergone bowel surgery in 1941, which made him a semi-invalid for the rest of his life. At Le Rêve, he created his famous *Jazz* collages and his last series of paintings of interiors, in addition to starting work on his design for the nearby Chapelle du Rosaire. Villa Le Rêve is closed to the public but can be rented by groups and artists. What an experience it must be to live and work in a house that once belonged to Henri Matisse.

INDEX

CHÂTEAU LA COSTE

ARTIST INDEX

COLOPHON

EDITING *and* COMPOSING – Eric Rinckhout

TRANSLATION ENGLISH – Sandy Logan

PHOTOGRAPHY – Arnaud Moro

ADDITIONAL PHOTOGRAPHY – Eric Rinckhout (pp. 30, 47, 48, 59, 79, 84, 90, 93, 105, 111, 112, 141, 152, 173, 186, 192, 220, 232, 234, 239, 242, 279, 308, 315, 321, 341) – Sandy Logan (p. 72 below) – Gerd Moyson (p. 174) – Jean-Luc Armand (pp. 99, 100-101)

CREDITS – Architectes Rudy Ricciotti et Roland Carta / Mucem (pp. 120-121, 130-131, 285) – Gruissan Tourisme (pp. 210-211) – Office de Tourisme Val de Durance (pp. 99, 100-101)

GRAPHIC DESIGN – Joke Gossé and Sarah Schrauwen

COVER IMAGE – Musée Fernand Léger (p. 104 #80) – Eric Rinckhout

The addresses in this book have been selected after thorough independent research by the author, in collaboration with Luster Publishing. The selection is solely based on personal evaluation of the business by the author. Nothing in this book was published in exchange for payment or benefits of any kind.

D/2021/12.005/6
ISBN 978 94 6058 2790
NUR 450, 510

www.lusterweb.com – WWW.THE500HIDDENSECRETS.COM
info@lusterweb.com

Printed in Italy by Printer Trento.

MIX
Paper from responsible sources
FSC
www.fsc.org
FSC® C015829